# TREE

## Essays & Pieces

Other works by Deena Metzger

Non-fiction
*Writing For Your Life: A Guide and Companion to the Inner Worlds*

Fiction
*Skin: Shadows/Silence*
*What Dinah Thought*

Poetry
*Dark Milk*
*The Axis Mundi Poems*
*Looking for the Faces of God*
*A Sabbath Among the Ruins*

Plays
*The Book of Hags*
*Not As Sleepwalkers*
*Dreams Against the State*

Forthcoming
*Intimate Nature: The Bond Between Women and Animals (co-editor)*
*The Other Hand (novel)*

# TREE
## Essays & Pieces

Deena Metzger

North Atlantic Books
Berkeley, California

**Tree: Essays and Pieces**

Published by North Atlantic Books
P.O. Box 12327
Berkeley, California 94712

*Tree: Essays and Pieces* is sponsored by the Society for the Study of Native Arts and Sciences, a nonprofit educational corporation whose goals are to develop an educational and crosscultural perspective linking various scientific, social and artistic fields; to nurture a holistic view of the arts, sciences, humanities and healing; and to publish and distribute literature on the relationship of mind, body, and nature.

Library of Congress Cataloging-in-Publication Data

Metzger, Deena.
    Tree : essays and pieces / Deena Metzger. — 1st North
Atlantic Books ed.
        p.    cm.
    Contents: Tree — The woman who slept with men to take the war out of them — Re-vamping the world — Personal disarmament — Healing the planet/healing ourselves — Healing circles.
    ISBN 1-55643-245-3
    I. Title.
PS3563.E864T74    1997
814'.54—dc21                                    96-50153
                                                CIP

Cover Design by Andrea DuFlon
Cover Photo © 1980 by Hella Hammid

# Contents

Foreword   by Barbara Myerhoff                                    vii

Preface                                                           xi

Tree                                                              1

The Woman Who Slept with Men                                      93
    to Take the War Out of Them

Healing Circles                                                   227

Re-vamping the World:                                             235
    On the Return of the Holy Prostitute

Personal Disarmament:                                             241
    Negotiating With the Inner Government

Healing The Planet/Healing Ourselves                              255

Afterword                                                         267

# Foreword
## Barbara Myerhoff

"Dreams Against the State," the title of another of Deena Metzger's works describes her particular vision and her purpose, as a writer, for in all her works she uses her words to battle for freedom, against various life-defying forms of oppression. She attacks the most obdurate structures of society, the inflated sacrosanct pronouncements of Ideology and Culture, the Authorities, and the diffuse conditions—pollution, exploitation, greed, blindness—that oppress and destroy as surely as more concrete foes. Her weapons are allegedly flimsy: desire, possibility, dream, metaphor—but she wields them with fierce determination, a warrior in Eros, asserting interconnection over division, vitality over indifference and deadness. In this work she is like a few other contemporary women writers who are equally obsessed with overcoming divisions. They are a subversive little band with no respect for genre, blending memory and anticipation, intellect and passion, myth and biography, transcending categories of time, convention and propriety, writing for Life, for their lives, for our lives. I am thinking here of Meridel LeSueur, Doris Lessing, Maxine Hong Kingston, and Deena Metzger—shall we call them Poets of Politics, or Politicos of the Imagination; oxymoron is essential to convey the contradiction in their vision. Above all they blend the inner and outer life, and regard the individual as the microcosmic expression of the macrocosm. Thus one cannot be addressed without the other. It is no accident that all are women who carry this perspective of connectedness. It is the Female Principle that they represent, the voice of the Anima. They sing the song of the soul itself.

The two pieces of Deena Metzger's presented here are war stories, agnostic in form, portraying an immense struggle with the highest possible stake—Life, her life. They are ultimately stories of triumph. Or put another way, they are adventure tales, depicting the female equivalent of the Mythic Hero Quest. The woman hero is called irresistibly to this struggle, descending into the under-world, giving herself to forces she does not fully understand, but realizing her cosmic task is self-completion; by making herself whole, she will restore life to the Wasteland. This is the cosmic work of a woman hero—providing bridges, coming to realize that her own well-being and the well-being of the outer world are inseparable. By these books, she completes the hero's task, returning from her voyage, from her trials, bearing the spoils of conquest. This is the message she gives her readers: news that her vision of connection is fulfilled. As we hear it, we become a part of the adventure. We receive the elixir that restores our spirits, the fundamental ancient truth that we are part of each other. This, finally, is Deena Metzger's morality: our consciousness of the web of relations among us becomes conscience. We cannot abuse those whom we see as part of ourselves. Healing becomes wholeness; the divisions that have obtained since Paradisial harmony was forfeited are at least briefly overcome. Like a dream, this message is couched in symbolic language, but it is nonetheless immediate and specific, a literal truth with no "as if." The social condition and the personal condition are inseparable, literally; metanymically not metaphorically.

This is seen most clearly in the woman hero's struggles with the enemy in these two tales. In *Tree*, the enemy is within the woman as well as outside her. She is attacked indirectly, her own body carrying the danger. Cancer is a metaphor for the confusion and chaos of a society that attacks its own citizens but it is also a literal threat that can only combated by a complex, personal response, directed toward herself as well as toward the environment. The enemy must be transformed; the woman must achieve self-knowledge in order to live. She is required to find the most complex posture in relation to her illness; searching herself and the world for its roots, continually judging, choosing, differentiating, wide-awake to every possibility—she must never be blind to anything. She listens acutely to everyone's advice and interpretation, but chooses finally and only for herself. She must learn to receive as fully as she is able to give to those she loves, but realizes this does not allow her to give herself the views of anyone else.

*Tree* has an entirely different tone from *The Woman Who*. It is as specific and grounded as *The Woman Who* is stark and mythic. The hero in *Tree* has a biography, is an alive and familiar contemporary person, living in the moment, with an address, physical features. We watch her applying her hyperalert mind to everything and everyone with a searing and minute clarity. Her friends shout at each other over her body; all have different opinions. She must listen, love them, select, looking outward and inward with exact balance, alone and absolutely responsible. Here we have a vision of morality under the magnifying glass that is provided by the proximity of death. She watches herself engaging in the sorting process, enjoys the workings of her own mind, reflexively interpreting its operations. Her sustained position of human vulnerability and stunning tough-minded courage and resolve are cause for awe. It is a quality of being, carefully, slowly, consciously acquired and maintained.

In *The Woman Who*, the enemy is The General, one who destroys indifferently, without awareness or choice. The Woman sets herself against his deadness. She conquers him by taking him in, absorbing him, using her body to assert the fundamental anatomical truth, that a man and a woman uniting briefly make the two into one. This primordial form of connection is a vanquishment by taming—her body the cauldron that transforms him from the Other into one who is momentarily a part of her, a partner. In a dramatic but quiet moment, the alchemical work is done: he covers her feet against the cold with a rough blanket. The General has developed enough imagination and therefore empathy to feel what she feels. So this is why women have always slept with warriors, even those who have killed their loved ones. Not out of fickleness, envy or attraction to power, not because destructiveness is an aphrodisiac, as some misogynists have suggested. To sleep with the enemy is to make them their own, to assert their commitment to life over death, in final refusal to believe that anyone who understands can continue to destroy.

I wonder how many women think that. When I was a child I had a recurring daydream. I wanted to meet Hitler in person, to tell him what he was doing. I was convinced that my childish innocence and sincerity would at least make him see my humanity and the humanity of those I was pleading for. I would shatter his indifference, and sanity would be restored to the world. If only I could make him see, if I could find the words... I think this urge is not uncommon among women. Perhaps that is why I am so moved by the final image in *The Woman Who*. A band of women raises stones as the one who sleeps with the enemy passes by. Will they stone her? No, she is not a traitor. The stones will be used to make a road. Connections. A wall laid on its side becomes a bridge. The women's work is fulfilled.

As I write these words of praise, I am conscious of my lack of objectivity. I have, after all, been deeply involved with the author for twenty years or more. We have come to regard ours as one of the Great Friendships of our day, two decades of intimacy, delight and passion, our lives and work joined at every juncture. I am even a participant in Tree, engaged in the struggle among friends for Deena's life. How can I consider myself detached? Though I thought I knew everything about the events described here, reading them together in this way gave me a fresh vision of their theme and significance. Looked at together (with a bit of distance, though not objectivity), they strike me as nothing short of inspirational. Perhaps it is possible to learn the Great Lessons from someone else, though I doubt it. Our essential victories ultimately must be only our own; nevertheless the knowledge that someone else has preceded us and returned alive and well to tell the tale is a major consolation. This is an unexpected piece of good news, so that when we face blindness, cruelty, and indifference, in ourselves and others, we may remember that someone has encountered these enemies and conquered them. Then we can aspire to no less than victory for ourselves. By saving ourselves we change and save others, first our loved and closest ones, our community, then strangers, then everything. Read on: there's not a moment to waste.

# Preface to the Second Edition
Deena Metzger

These two books were fifteen years ahead of their time. If only they were outdated now. Unfortunately, cancer is more rampant and the Generals on our planet abound. The questions I raised years ago gather increasing urgency: How can we go to the General without becoming the General? Can love heal violence and war?

Cancer and the General are one and we are equally their victims. To each, we must respond in new ways, if we are to escape from the cycle of destruction. Ultimately, we are defeated when we bombard our bodies with destructive weapons in order to cure them, though, at the present time, we have few other treatments. Ultimately, we are not protected by making war on the Generals — one General only leads to another — though at the present time we claim to have no other strategies. War is a cancer. And cancer makes war on us. And so it goes.

Statistically, medical advances in the last fifteen years have made little, if any difference in the survival rate from cancer. But there is evidence that ancillary methods, holistic approaches, are improving the length and quality of peopleís lives. Similarly, recent wars, international as well as civil, prove that any war is a war against ourselves. Increasingly, there are no winners. The world has become too small, small as our bodies. When we attack one part of it, we attack the whole and we all suffer. And even as we pride ourselves on scientific and technological advances we are increasingly aware that through progress and its demands, we have devastated the environment. But there is also evidence that simpler and more ecological ways of living are also deeply satisfying and restore the soul.

When I wrote *Tree*, I was looking for the threatened life force within myself. Now I look for the similarly threatened life force of the planet. Knowing full well the extent of environmental and socio-political factors in cancer, it is essential to look within ourselves and find those hidden conditions which make us vulnerable to the disease. I began by looking for the silences within — for cancer is silence, erupting and struggling to give voice to the unutterable. Simultaneously I looked for imperialism within, for cancer is a larger political metaphor. Finding these within and without I began to imagine new ways of responding; building, in effect, new worlds governed by new laws.

We have no choice if we wish to survive, but to discover healing and peacemaking as tactical and expedient responses to current conditions. In order to heal, we must search out what is lethal within and toxic without, scrutinizing the psyche, body politic and environment in order to transform our lives accordingly. Illness and the violated planet demand this.

It has come to this. The same actions which will heal us of physical diseases, heal our societies, physically and politically. One action and a multitude of possibilities. Can love heal war? Can love heal our lives? We will have to discover how, for there is no alternative.

*For Greg and Marc*

# TREE

This book records a social drama which had, nevertheless, individual participants. In the text I deliberately avoided specific identification of the people to emphasize the commonality of the experience. However, I wish to provide here in order of mention a list of those people who, each in his/her own way helped to heal me.

Eloise Healey
Robert Cohen
Lee Myerhoff
Alida Sherman
Jane Rosenzweig
Barbara Myerhoff
Karen Klugman
Ariel (Merilyn) Malek
Naomi Newman Pollack
Sheila De Bretteville
Victor Perera
Candace Derra
Marc Metzger
Greg Metzger
Anne Ebersole
Honor Moore
Holly Prado
Susan Brown
Suzanne Lacy
Ruth Hirschman
Louise Bernikow
Ruth Adams
Stephen Gans, M.D.
Bert Sommers
Harold Lieberman
Dyanne Simon
Anais Nin
Edith Sullwold
Dana Chalberg
Susan Bechaud
David Kunzle

Margaret Kunzle
Lucy McDougall
Bradley Smith
John Sullivan
Judy Gortikov
Corey Fischer
Joe Boskin
Susan Yankowitz
Albert Greenberg
Judy Chaikin
Katya Beisanz
Audre Lorde
Meridel LeSueur
Brugh Joy
Gioia Timpanelli
Jaquelyn McCandless
Harold Stone
Ariel Dorfman
Gloria Orenstein
Maia Pollack
Tina Preston
Burke Byrnes
Bella Posy
Arnold Posy
Sharon Stricker
Paula Menger
David Finkel
Susana Torre
Arlene Raven
Connie Katzenstein
Elaine Hilberman

This book is dedicated to the above named people and to those unnamed as well, particularly the women of The Woman's Building and the members of my workshops who gave to me from their full hearts their palpable and usable energy. In addition, I wish to acknowledge Barbara Myerhoff, Jane Rosenzweig, Naomi Pollack, Sheila De Bretteville, and Robert Cohen for their extraordinary devotion and love. For a long time my life was in their hands.

*CHEN*   THE AROUSING   (Shock, Thunder)

above Chen The Arousing Thunder
below Chen The Arousing Thunder

The Judgment:
  Shock brings success.
  Shock comes—oh, oh!
  Laughing words—ha, ha!
  The shock terrifies for a hundred miles,
  And she does not let fall the sacrificial spoon and chalice.

                    from the *I Ching*

TUESDAY, FEBRUARY 1, 1977

Looking for the moon, light falling, falling, light breaking time falling. Moon sway, moon break, ice heart breaking, night cry breaking down, down. Moon fall singing, light falling, break break, moon falling, hold hold, heart holding, break breaking, ice drifting, dark dark, light singing, hold hold, light singing, break break, night singing, hold hold, break break, light light. . . .

Yesterday I returned from New York. My going was part of trying to change my life. Tomorrow I will be . . . Never mind. While leading this workshop, I try to distract myself by doing the exercises I assign: Let the past return as if in a dream . . .

Boardwalk and stars. No matter how often I am asked, I always remember the Boardwalk and stars, the three houses leaped up in flames and the madwoman dropped brown paper bags of boiling water down upon us. Ring around the rosy on the boardwalk. All fall down. The plague. The plague. Old men play chess while their old women wrapped in winter coats lean back onto the beach chairs with folded metal sheets under their chins to reflect the winter sun. I spoke the *mamalushen* then. Why did no one tell me about English? Did they want to keep me from speaking? Fireworks on Tuesday nights. The Baby Parade. Mother saved the metal cup which tarnished so quickly. "They wanted to give me another baby in the hospital, but I screamed, 'No! No! My baby is so beautiful.' " She always tells that story. Parachute jump coming down in a whoosh. There were so many sailors walking up and down. I thought they were creatures from another country. I also wanted to sail away. Dark sand under the Boardwalk. When we were eight, the man scared us just as Stewart kissed me. We ran home. This month Eloise wrote to me: "I didn't know I would still be wanting at my age."

THURSDAY, FEBRUARY 3, 1977

She was not surprised to find herself alone, but wondered how she was to react. She was not surprised . . . *She?*

Yes, *she,* not *I.* Not during this time of crisis.

I am most with myself at this moment, everything extraneous has fallen away, still I must, at times, slip outside myself to see the woman I am. Perhaps I am so confined as to be available for this scrutiny. I am alone. In such times one is always alone. She is alone in a small cell. It seems I am both prisoner and jailer. It seems I watch myself. I have much to learn and some knowledge is only accessible to my own dispassionate eyes. Some different knowledge, of course, comes without words or is not of the mind. The time is urgent, the knowledge essential and . . . perhaps I say "she" on those occasions when I cannot bear her—my—pain.

\*                    \*                    \*

There was literature to be sure of others who had been confined. Prison literature—certainly. But the terror of prison was not only being alone, but being with others. If she were to be completely alone, she thought, for a time, a specified time, that known and agreed to in advance, then, she could survive. In the hole, for example, if there were light. She could not live without the light. When was it they had marched in the cold, zero degrees, for Assata Shakur's freedom? . . . three hundred days in solitary, but that wasn't the worst. Three hundred days without light. Cruel and unusual punishment. No. She couldn't be without the light.

\*                    \*                    \*

I am in the hospital, fully dressed, seated crosslegged on a white bed. I make the room my own, bringing into it the books I love, though I intend to write. I read Nazim Hikmet, "Some Advice to Those Who Will Serve Time in Prison":

> If instead of being hanged by the neck
>   you're thrown inside
>   for not giving up hope
> in the world, in your country, in people, . . .

and Robert Cohen's poems, especially "Things You May Not Have Known":

> I've discovered another incredible thing!
> My friends, any of you who miss your kids
> will especially appreciate this:
> It's a messenger rainbow
> yes, a messenger rainbow . . .

Poems full of joy and life and the determination to struggle. I have a bottle of red wine in my purse. Lee brought me to the hospital; we have been family for each other for twenty years. I read

Robert's poems because they are full of people with stars in their pockets. And fists.

Here is the writing of Adrienne Rich, an anthology of women poets, Eva Forest's *From a Spanish Prison,* and the poems of Neruda. Oh, Robert, a hundred years from now, we'll know how to transform ourselves into energy to fly the three thousand miles between us in five minutes flat. We could make love tonight.

*        *        *

Hundreds of women live alone. Thousands. More than anyone has counted. Millions. How do they manage it? That is what I want to know. Where do they go? Where do they travel? What do they do at night?

So. I am returning to the beginning, but I don't know where it is. Step by step. I thought I had gone back to the beginning five years ago; I thought I had started again. I thought I was learning how to be an honest woman. I thought I was making a new life.

"But this time we have to do it with men," Alida said. Alida. Oh, Alida is also alone. Her meaning is sometimes incomprehensible. She is speaking in her own language, has gone mad, has declared herself a bonafide madwoman. And who will make the effort to understand what Alida is whispering? Now I understand; now I don't. I also must strip all my words, actions, objects, events of their acquired meaning, must throw everything into a pot and cook it down to the basic cellulose and begin again. Not chaos, but no assumptions either. *Beginning Again.*

*        *        *

And why do I think about the Rosenbergs now? Why bring a book by a woman in a Spanish jail? It seems I give myself over, put myself in a stranger's hands. The man with the knife is one I've only met once.

The room is pleasant but institutional. A man I don't know puts a needle into my vein and blood bubbles into it, fills four different test tubes. I watch it, the strength of it coming from my arm, darker always than I imagine. This is what keeps our lives going. I was never able to give blood to Anais. And she fought for ten years.

But why do I think of Ethel? And why do we have secrets and why be concerned with this as I am seated in a purple gown against

the white sheets, enjoying the silence, the view from my window
across the city?

\*                    \*                    \*

I am sitting in a hospital room, crosslegged on a hospital bed,
typing a new book at 11:30 p.m. No, I will not have a sleeping pill.
I can't afford to lose another dream. The moon rose at 9:30 and
appeared in the window like a plump fruit. She did not look like
a woman. Now it glances down at the paper from the roof top.
Hidden as by a veil of purdah. Only the eyes showing. She does
not look like the man in the moon either. "For years you have
wrestled with death," Jane said. Oh, yes, I was brave and I came
close, but I have decided to reverse the journey, to go back the
other way. I am about to wrestle with life and discover what that
means. Having faced the lesser demon, I feel ready to take on the
greater power. Almost everyone is afraid to live. I am not saying,
"I am not afraid," as I am also trying to give up arrogance. But I
am going to try to look fear square in the eyes.

This is a warm-up. Bare prose. A woman alone in a room. It
could be a prison. It could be a cell. It could be the bare room of
a nun. It could be the widow's bedroom or the tiny bedroom of
someone's maiden aunt, the one who never married—you know
who she is. But I don't want to stop in these rooms, only to point
out to you that they exist, that we have always known about them,
have always suspected that they are created especially for us, that
the rooms where men live alone are noisier, are full of newspapers
and brown paper bags and stiff jeans and textures which rub and
crinkle. Women's rooms are quiet. So we do not know what goes
on in them. I have written about silence since 1965. Now I want
to write about noise. But I am not interested in just any noise.
Keening, for example, which always fascinated me, keening and
laments and dirges—I am not interested in these. If I am going to
come out of silence—and I am determined—then it will be with a
big noise. A woman's noise. But not to exclude the man's noise.
But of that later. Alida says this time we must go out in the world
together. But then every one of us must be ready and everybody
must put on party clothes and everyone must change their noses
and collars and transform. And there are dancing lessons to be
had—oh yes—dancing is required.

\*                    \*                    \*

This is a book about the kind of silences which must be broken. Some I know and some I don't know. And it is also a book about the kind of stillness which must be preserved. And the confusion which exists between these. But first I would like to sing a little song, because not knowing how to sing, I have always maintained a silence here. So I think we shall have a little ritual silence-breaking. And I will do what is difficult to do—and you can hum along if you like. Now I assure you that I have never been able to sing "Happy Birthday" and knew only two lullabies to sing to my sons and those I sang poorly. When I sing this song now it is with a flat and shaky voice and without knowing what words will come . . . the song created as quickly as my fingers can record it and the tune itself also improvised, but that is the best kind.

It surprises like lillies of the valley—Barbara's favorite flower— tiny and powerful—or as crickets or salamanders or the centers of raspberries always surprise. This is a book about beginning again . . . so it goes in at least two directions: at once forward to what I do not know, and backward to recover what we've lost without standing still. I am not talking about compromise, but change. You see between any two poles is another country of coexistence which is not neutral and that is the one we are going to try to discover. And we are going to try to be playful about it because one of the silences has been play. We have been afraid to play or certainly I have been afraid to play. Do you think I got here playfully . . . ? Oh, no, until now this journey was undertaken with the utmost gravity in long black robes. But now I want to hitch up my skirts to learn a jig or a lusty dance or to leap across the waterfall.

This book is a beginning, it is a search. I'm looking for—well, I told you, didn't I?—"Life"—and when I find it I will bed down wherever it is and suck it into my body pore by pore. And I will not stop because I am afraid.

\*                    \*                    \*

But first a little song:
If the moon had a belly, what would it eat?
If the stars had elbows, what would they touch?
The leaf is a language the sun can believe
And the rain has something to teach.

Well, it's not much of a song, but it is a song and it is a beginning. And that is what this book is—a beginning. You see I went all the way to age in *The Book of Hags*. There I became an ancient hunch-backed crone going to the last moment when the hag knows she will step over the border without papers or exit visas and only the skin on her back, and even without that.

> Old woman. She has a chin like a scythe, a back like the moon. She eats like the hookworm. She devours.
> When she takes off her clothes, the mirror turns aside. Looking at her hands, she says, "How did I come to these?" Fingers like bones stuck through a grate.
> The bone structure is good. The flesh is sparse. Transparent. Everything is revealed. The light is very bright. She is devoured.
> Devoured by death and madness. A thousand early forms. Old thin woman who has only the bones left, who has eaten herself clean, who has been eaten, who has left her bones in the sun for the birds to pick.
> Her mother said, "You are so thin, your bones are showing." When she undresses at night, the skin peels away in great wide hides.

So now it is time for me to come back and to straighten my back a little, to make a little incision into life with the voice and begin to sing. And a little child shall lead me and a young girl and an adolescent and a young woman and myself who is not young nor old but about to break silence about everything. Break all the taboos. I want to take life by the horns as if it were a young bull, but I won't stab it in the flank nor pass a sword through its throat nor thrust myself over the horns, not that, but I will dance with it, dance with the awkward bull. Dance.

What are you afraid of? When you think about dancing you cross your legs and lean back in the chair as if you were tired, saying, "No, I think I'll sit this one out."

*          *          *

Everyone's asleep except the nurse who does not go home until dawn. Does she think dawn is a sunset? Does she go east thinking it is west watching the sun set up into the sky? As a child, my son Marc looked at the world upside down through his legs and laughed with glee. Perspective.

When I go home I will pick a grapefruit and ask the tree to tell

me what it knows. I will shout into its bark and the neighbor be
damned, the one who cut the branches of the apricot tree so that
no fruit would fall on our side. But it was too late, too late. Fruit
had already fallen and buried itself and the new trees are coming
up, directly from the seed. I had forgotten that was possible. Karen
brought me a knot of fused eucalyptus seeds found by the sea.
And Merilyn brought a feather from the underbelly of a duck. A
feather which has a secret . . . it turns blue when it is held below
the eyes. These are quiet beginnings. When you are depressed go to
the zoo and look at the little animals first, one creature a day,
working up slowly—snakes, chickens, monkeys, golden cats,
pumas, bears, giraffes—then, when you're ready, elephants—and
you're cured.

Well, it's like looking for the life force. It isn't under a stone, you
know, it isn't lying by the side of the road in the pile of leaves
waiting to be blown back onto the lawns, it's got to be dug out,
blown open, wrestled out of the tree trunks, pulled down from the
sun. It's a battle and all the time you're scared because everyone is
screaming, "beware, beware, beware—wooooo, woooo, wooooo,
we're scared of such spirits, sprites and ghosts," and you are, too,
and how do you know you're not going to be burned up as you're
standing there—well, you don't know! But take the fire if you find
it and pour it on your head and pull it up through the hole between
your legs which is made for fire no matter who you are. Did your
mother say, "Don't play with fire?" And did you listen? Shame.

I asked you to tell me what you are afraid of. I'll leave a space—
you fill it in—whisper it—don't be afraid—you can shut the book
again and no one will ever know. Not even——————————you.

*       *       *

Tomorrow I need to tell the doctor that I must go out and sit in
the sun for ten minutes before the biopsy. Well, without that how
does he expect me to get well? "In your robe?" he'll ask. "Well,
what will the neighbors think?" He'll say I'm mad. I am. Madly in
love with the life force. We'll have to give him a name. We'll have
to give her a name. We'll have to give it a name so you won't be
embarrassed and squirm when you read "life force." This is a
story, after all, and it's no fun if it makes you twitch. What shall
we call it? We need one of those funny names which has no gender.
Like Toots.

You know, this may not be the way back. It may occur that I will
have to be more serious, may have to begin at the end, at the other
place where we had come to and may have to re-enter more slowly
and more seriously. It may also be that I will have to frighten you—
well, you're prepared for that, aren't you? For what in this society
at this time is more frightening than life? You know about that—
there's legislation against it. How many bills are written each week
to stamp it out, stamp it out, stamp it out? But I don't want to alarm
you to begin with. I want us to play. Let's sing another song.

*          *          *

Secrets. Barbara is asleep. Jane is asleep. Naomi is asleep. Robert
is asleep. Sheila is asleep. Victor is asleep. Victor has just returned
from the jungle and has not been bitten by snakes, but by other
things. He has watched the whales and the fish prancing and knows
that the leaves will grow back on the mahogany trees which are
almost totally felled and destroyed, though he does not believe that
now. Victor believes in men who, growing old, look like wood and
appear when they are summoned by harmonicas and he believes
in trees even when they are cut down. He believes in whales and
other beasts which can hide in the ocean and so he will be saved.
Victor is sleeping, however. And Robert is dreaming of rainbows
and he has sent one here and I have caught it. Do you think I can
write this alone? I am sending it back. What he calls his unique
messenger service. Candace brought a pillow which she made, as
lumpy as my breast and covered with the colors of the dawn,
pomegranate and sky, and also a purple talisman from the cata-
combs, something rescued from the dead—and do you know what?
Candace is asleep now. Marc is asleep and Greg is asleep and Marc
wanted to hear a sleep story before he left the hospital room and so
I told him about Mr. Wind, but Greg was too tired to listen and so
we will have to send the wind to him to whisper the story into
his ear. He thinks he is too old for such foolishness. But he must
just be too young. I am always writing about my friends because
they have a little of Toots in them. In fact I do not spend time with
anyone who is not a friend of Toots. Why waste my time? There
are millions who are afraid of Toots but just a few who take Toots
to bed. Who are you? Which side are you on?

*          *          *

I'll tell you what I've put on the walls of my room. A flying horse, a pegasus that Anne made and poems by Robert and Deena, by Honor, Neruda, and Holly, two Cuban posters, one of a Vietnamese woman, and the other of two birds who say *a trabajar.* One has lace pantaloons, but we argue about whether it is a she or a he because her colors are brighter—still you know how nature is! There is also a photo that Donna took of a bird of prey—yes we need those, the brave birds to catch Toots while she scurries through the field pretending to be a little furry mouse. Hah!

*          *          *

FRIDAY, FEBRUARY 4, 1977

Morning. Surgery at 12:00. Shots at 10:00 to tire me when I am already tired from the sleeping pills and the nursing staff entering throughout the night. Still, health flows through me, purple and white lights, creativity and mind. When I think of the healing force, I think of light. What stopped the flow in my breasts? Was it not taking the time to write? Did I refuse to understand the work I had to do? There's a large body of work—still I think the writing always came last.

Milk. I wanted to have milk. Was there not enough milk? "Look how hungry the child is," Molly said, "you don't have enough milk."

I want to give up mothering; it creates an inequality between us. I question the quality of my mothering but Barbara remembers the stories I told of Mr. Moon and Mrs. Sun. I gave the boys different milk. It wasn't my mother's milk. It was my own.

It is close to dawn. Almost everyone in the country is asleep. Some are preparing to wake up and some are snoring. Robert is a tuba when he sleeps or even a trombone and so is Greg. They put their souls into breathing. It's an art form. But they are sleeping now, singing in their sleep on different coasts.

*          *          *

SATURDAY, FEBRUARY 5, 1977

I have cancer!

This is indeed a new book. The shock hasn't entered the system yet. No panic. No fear. Work to be done. The plague has hit. This is not the time I wished to spend on myself, I was ready to emerge. Dawn is coming up, very rosy against a blue sky. So, Hikmet, "I didn't know I liked the sky . . ." Dawn doesn't last. I have work to do. This is a workbook. Don't you know you're writing for your life?

*              *              *

SUNDAY, FEBRUARY 6, 1977

Yesterday I had a camera here and was documenting the room and this event which is called disease. Let it be said that the first day I refused to sleep. Awakened after surgery, I was outraged to discover I had dozed before I was wheeled into the operating room. When I woke up, I thought nothing had happened to me. Now they've scheduled a week of tests. And then? I go home. And then? Perhaps I return. But why? They say they must cut off my breast.

Jacquelyn suggested that Anais died because she had completed her work. Have I done mine? Was *Book of Hags* my work? But I still need to write. And haven't I started a book here even on this hospital bed? And haven't I named it *Beginning Again*?

MONDAY, FEBRUARY 7, 1977

I'll tell you how to get up in the morning: Watch for the dawn. You need less sleep than you think. But when you see the dawn through your closed eyelids, don't snap them open as if an army had invaded your room. Wait. Allow the dream to repeat itself. I forgot mine this morning; I think I was too anxious to see the sun. It isn't lost; it isn't in the wastepaper basket; it's somewhere but I can't find it in words, so I think it's lost. That is one of my limitations. A pale dawn. Gray clouds and a lemon yellow sun which spreads, thins, across the sky.

Every now and then I am going to stop this dialogue and whisper something in your ear—the same phrase over and over again—"I want to tell you a secret." There are a thousand secrets to be told, a thousand. And even more. After all, this is about breaking silence which is as important a ritual as breaking bread. So the secret I want to tell you is that I think we ought to bring down the Defense Department. You see, I've said it aloud. Quick, someone yell,

"Treason." Oh come on, you know how to yell it. "Treason" sounds the same as "Fire." It mobilizes everyone to believe she or he is in danger and to stampede over the body of the next person to the nearest exit to get out. Out. Out. You don't want to be in the room with someone who might not be loyal. And what is loyal? And who do you have allegiance to? Several things occur to me— once again for the thousandth time in my life I am not going to have false loyalties. I am going to take a risk and say what has to be said. And the first thing we must get straight between us is that the Defense Department menaces our health.

The external Defense Department and the internal defense department. The ones that arm to the teeth. In the world and in our psyches. Are you afraid? I am afraid. Will a bomb protect you? Is that its purpose? Or is it to take something that belongs to someone else? Does it protect you or something called money? And what does the bomb cost you? Is it that you must not speak? The more bombs stockpiled by the defense departments, the more silence stockpiled as well. Do you disbelieve in bombs? Will anyone listen to you?

And in my own internal defense department, what weapons do I create against what enemy I've established and which voices do I silence? Which inner selves have I imprisoned because they objected to the system I created but which makes me ill? Which parts of my self are too greedy, which selves go hungry, wither and die? Which selves explode, grow helter-skelter out of thwarted urge to be?

Oh, bring down the Defense Department which itself requires a defense department, which also to perpetuate itself requires a defense department, which because of protests and demonstrations at home requires a defense department, which is, in reality, an offense department launching an offensive, not against the theoretical enemy but against anyone here who might protest. In other words, you or me. They're after your ass, my dear.

The Defense Department is in me, but don't think it isn't a menace on the outside as well. Someone, somewhere wants to be free and independent. Our Defense Department launches an offensive. It makes me ill. Someone wants to make an exorbitant profit and it affects my health. Someone puts something in my food which makes me ill. Someone puts something in the air which makes me ill. Someone puts something in the water which makes me ill.

Someone radiates the soil which makes me ill. Someone builds weapons, the research and the manufacture of them alone, before their use, makes me ill. Someone defends these actions. A defense system, but it isn't mine. Someone turns a deaf ear which makes me ill. Someone says, "I will never listen to women." It makes me ill. The system by and of and for these someones has made me ill.

*             *             *

The disease is in the conflict between the authentic inner voices and the external voices against it. The mother-father-terror voices. The be-a-good-wife, the don't-divorce, the don't-quit-your-job, the don't-agitate, the don't-put-your-work-before-your-children voices, the be-a-good-neighbor-cook-housekeeper voices, the stay-with-the-man-you're-with voice, the financial-security voice, the don't-agitate voice, the don't-be-a-radical, don't-be-a-communist, don't-be-a-feminist voices, the don't-take-risks, don't-make-waves, do-fit-in-temper-assimilate-be-quiet voices. . . .
No!

*             *             *

This may become a guerilla manual. A feminist manual about guerilla warfare for those living in a state of seige written by an anonymous woman who has just discovered she has a life sentence. Like the rest of us. Like the rest of us.

*             *             *

When the doctor comes I will have to ask him to check the pathology report or to do the biopsy again. Not only because I believe there is a mistake but because we must challenge authority wherever we find it. And anyway doctors are limited in their training and narrow in perspective, can sometimes cure but can not heal. There is more to know than they know.

*             *             *

Old friends call. We ponder this dilemma. The truth of the matter is I don't know why I'm here, having been cognizant of the lethal aspects of our lives for the last years. How did it happen?

"Cancer is silence," I wrote. But I have not been silent. "Cancer is insolvable conflict, is the illumination of the inner world without the ability to shine in the outer world." But I shone, I shone, determinedly, like the moon which visited me last night androgynous and misshapen and beautiful, astounding the sky and enhancing the dark. For we do not know that there is dark unless there is light. Isn't that true? Nor do we know about the light unless somewhere there is a shadow. Keep your eye on the light. Keep your eye on the light. Pay attention! Every day and every night, a ball of light floats across the sky, like the bouncing ball which teaches us to sing in the darkened movie hall. Keep your eye on the bouncing ball. Sing.

                    *                *                *

WEDNESDAY, FEBRUARY 9, 1977

My old friend, Susan B., comes to see me. After how many years without seeing each other? We met in the park. She was pregnant and tired and I offered to push her son while I pushed Marc. One two three; one two three. You never lose a friend. Friends come back and remain. Love given is never lost. Love received is never lost. I have to learn, we have to learn how to take in as well as to give out. Take a lesson from electric current. "I am learning," she says, "that I will be able to live alone." In an empty house, in a little room, in a cave, in a cell, in a hospital room, there are all these women who are trying desperately to live alone. "But I don't want to live without passion," she says. The question is: How do we get up alone in the morning? And who populates the inner house? There have been so many voices in me and so many voices outside. I have lived in an inner city all my life. At this moment, am I alone if this is written for the robins? What is the meaning of "living my own life?" How do we survive in prison? What memories can we retain? bring back? What authentic voyages can we make?

And what can we recreate?

                    *                *                *

This morning when I spoke in a meditation to the Indian dancer with the fat thighs who has breasts like oranges she said, "Swallow fire!" So I did.

*                    *                    *

I can see what acts against the spirit, how quickly it can be demoralized. But the sun on my face this morning, at this moment, reminds me that there is much we haven't begun to know. I am not alone when I say, "I don't know what questions to ask." I am a woman with feet in two worlds and I dare not slip in either. There is a way to create a harmony between the two worlds and there is a way for one to neutralize the other, or worse for enemy camps to form across the river. Everything in me speaks out to follow the light this time, to follow the light. "It is not," I wrote once, "that our light is inadequate or a fraud but that the evil is powerful." That vision must be changed. When I told Robert that I didn't know how to fight guns with roses, he told me I was not looking at the roses; I was not aware of what other resources I had, lazer beams for example. Light! Light! Light!

And he cautioned me against bringing the armies against myself looking for guilt, for culpability, trying to answer the question: "What did I do wrong?" However, when we take responsibility for our own lives, when we say there is a path to health we have to walk on, then we must know not only how to go forward, but what has brought us to this juncture. Fate is not cause enough. Additives are not cause enough. Challenging the so-called Defense Department as it agresses against other helpless people or defends itself against ourselves is a good start, but it is not enough. There are also our own personal internal defense departments as well. When do they defend us against a real danger and when do they offend and attack our very life force?

*                    *                    *

There are two questions I could ask: Who are the demons who live in the dark tissues and say, "die?" But I am tired of asking that question. I would like to know who are the spirits who live in the flesh and say, "live?"

Wrestling with life. It is more difficult than wrestling with the angels. It requires courage. Even knives. But mostly courage. I want to fight for life with the methods which come from life. This is no different than making a revolution. I am still struggling with the problem of the gun. Of being a warrior. Where are the new weapons, the new agendas, the new strategy and the new strategists? Show yourselves.

When we are afraid we fall back on the old methods. We've seen that in the schools, at home: at the last straw—swat. Yet the Eskimo asks with astonishment, "Is it possible that a large adult would hit a small child?"

*     *     *

Suzanne L. offers to bring me a green candle and meditates for me in the morning between 7:00 and 7:30. Sometimes I dismiss such actions as mere gestures of affection and sometimes I comprehend how this energy can be harnassed and transmitted. How much we don't know. How much we don't know. Talk to a Victorian about radio waves, tell him you can make sounds jump through the sky. "Humbug," he'll say. I was looking for someone else you should consult. I was going to say, "Talk to an aborigine child," but you see they already know. It is that we have forgotten, that we have forgotten that we have forgotten.

The trick is to believe that I am not making this up. A primer. A survival catalogue. Not a book of religion, but of knowledge. Learning to think from the right brain. Now there's a task.

*     *     *

It is later in the day. Or it is tomorrow. I was up and down on a merry-go-round. But this time there isn't any ring to catch.

Sometimes the phone rings and I am completely alone. As soon as I answer the phone, the cell closes, the walls of the body close over me and I don't know how to get out—there is this long cord that reaches another human being and still does not reach, it is so far, so far from our own fate and pain to another. I manage to find the songs in me, the spirit, the courage, but I don't know how to find the red devil rage and to let it out against the walls. When Alida calls, she says, "You've done all your work. You can't write a book without living it. You've lived it after the fact instead of before. Now lay back. You've done what you can. Let your friends work on your body. All the love you gave comes back to you."

"Pluck it out!"

\*     \*     \*

It feels essential to record this. As the calls come in. My astonishment. That a woman in prison can receive such communication through the walls. I keep lists obsessively. Then turn away embarrassed. Why do you want to remember this? Is it important to remember who called? I am afraid I will forget. My memory is poor. I am afraid I will forget a single drop of blood, a single moment given from another life.

My spirit surprises me. How did I come to this? I wonder. Who are you? How do you manage to light the candles tonight, pour a glass of wine, eat a meal, wolf a meal rather, when something is shouting in you, "No! No! No!" It is the same silent shout which you couldn't release when Anais died the very day after you discovered you might have cancer and you sat on a mat in an empty dance studio with the music turned on high and the phonograph voice singing singing singing and you trying to shout trying to scream at the top of your lungs No! No! No!

I want to take a survey. They say, one out of 17 women gets breast cancer. Or is it one out of 15? 12? 10? I'll tell you a secret—I met a woman who said one in 4! How many men have made love to a woman with one breast? With none? Maybe I should have both removed for the symmetry of it. I know a lot of men who wouldn't mind making love to a young boy. It's the asymmetry that bothers me. Secrets. When do you tell that you won't take off your gown?

\*     \*     \*

I think the secret is breaking the rules. I should have sneaked out today when the nurse said, "You can't walk in the sun. You're hospital property. You can't go out without an attendant." Why, you can't even leave the floor without a companion. What if something should happen? We can't risk it because of the insurance." Listen, my friends, I know a jailer when I meet one. This one is called *Money*. Have you heard that before? Well, then what are you going to do?

\*     \*     \*

She answers the phone. She talks to the nurse Irma with an "I" from Brooklyn, who babies her, says "Stop working, play with clay, call occupational therapy." She doesn't light the candles from conviction. She lights them out of character. It makes a difference. Someone walks into the room and is surprised. Is it only in this society that a woman wonders if she will be loved without a breast? What does the beautiful Vietnamese woman in the poster think as she takes the raft down the river, sacks of rice covering the bodies which she must transport, armies hidden in sacks of rice? Does she wonder if she will be loved after the napalm hits? Have we grown yet to such loving that we can embrace the scars made by our enemies on those we love?

A story. I wrote it a while ago, when I had more faith.

> And it is written that the women put on deer skins and false beards and hid in the forest for three days until the skins softened and the beards were full of briars.

> And the men were left alone.

> And they returned to the village and no one recognized them. And one woman took wool and wound in her beard and braided it until it came down through her legs on both sides of her body and it hung about her ankles.

> And she chose the strongest man in the village and lay down upon him when he slept, and the bearded woman tied them together with her own hair and the wool of her braids before he could awaken. And they were lashed to each other with their clothes between them as a sail is tied about a mast, face to face, and she upon him.

> Then he was given a choice, for he desired her, and she desired him, but it was his choice as he was taken by surprise, whether their clothes would be burned out from between them with fire or acid or torn to shreds with nails, or whether they would be dampened and left to rot away, or pulled out as the couple thinned of hunger, or whether the cloth would be eaten by ants or other creatures.

> For what had always been easy to enact was now to be difficult, and their joining was not implied in their simplest desire but was to be struggled for with the full force of their joint energy, stamina, and hope.

> And one year, one man chose fire, and one year, water, and one year, time. Each according to his need and his fortitude and patience. And when they were released from their bind-

ings and finally naked with each other, they saw the scars on their bodies and enjoyed them even more than the places where the flesh remained young and new.

For youth had been given to them, but the scars were made from their own courage, love, and capacity for desire.

*          *          *

I promise to love you no matter what.

I do not want to put you to that test. I confess, I do not trust anyone enough yet. We are all already so deformed and mutilated— what do we have to give with?

I wonder, when will I dance again? For surely I will dance again, belly dance again, do the dance of love again, even if everyone turns aside wondering if I as a deformed woman have the right. Will I continue dancing then? Or will I sit down to cross my legs. Will I dance alone in the dark in a room where the mirrors are also dark?

*          *          *

When I heard the news—when I first heard the news in New York, I danced. Alone in the empty dance studio where I was living, I danced, noticing that I was wearing black, an accident— still, I danced. It was not posturing nor denial, but dancing. I did the life dance. I will not dance with death. I thought the edge I walked was sharp and precarious. I do not mean to be overdramatic, but to look circumstances in the eye.

Alone in an empty gallery she danced. The night she discovered she might have cancer. I am not afraid of dying of cancer, she thought, I am afraid of dying of other things, of brutality, of greed, of America. To be sure I will not die of these, I danced.

*          *          *

I remember the calls of strangers and acquaintances. What does Ruth H. say? "The world is Buchenwald and we do not need to choose to live in it by their terms." But those in the camps lived. Survival at any price. Forced their life in the guard's face like a fist. It was the only weapon they had.

*          *          *

I try to exercise, to remember my body which does not let me
forget it. I hold my right breast so that it will not jar from the
momentum. I realize it may be the last time I hold this breast. I am
tender to it as to a child. I have always loved to rest my hand on
my breast. Next week I may be flat like a boy.

Is it a secret that women hold their breasts in their palms to
comfort themselves or for the sheer pleasure of the soft curves of
the flesh against the hand?

I consider having my breast removed. Sheila says I will look like
an amazon, that we will change the image of amazons. Louise calls
and offers to send me a bow and arrow. I wonder how these decisions are made. Shall I call a couturière? Will Blue Cross pay?
I imagine that I will never make love again. That what has been
more important to me than anything has been taken away. It is
not the loss of pleasure that I lament. I believe in making love as
a way of life, as a metaphor, as a reminder that we must come together, not stay apart. The Buddhists say we must let go of what
we hold most tight. Or whatever we attach to will be taken away.
I thought I had a light touch. In the past, I have been arrogant,
judging others, saying, "this one or that one succumbed. They
wanted power too much," I said. "They wanted beauty too much,"
I said. "They wanted fame too much." And the power or beauty
or fame were taken from them or it made them ill. Or I said, "They
were afraid and chose silence and the silence was more devastating
than their worst fears." I was arrogant, I thought I could avoid all
the pitfalls of desire. Have I wanted love so much that it has been
taken away? What I loved most has made difficult, if not impossible, what was already so urgent and so difficult and impossible:
connection, the sexual mating. Anais who loved beauty was torn
from it in her last year, and Deena who loved coupling thinks she
may be torn from it, and yet we cannot give up what we love best.
We cannot relinquish it! We must love it, and honor it, though it is
torn from us! And we must go on trying to reach it, though it
resists us. For it is not in the loving that we are in error, nor in the
wanting, but simply that we are tested.

And finally, I have nothing to say about cause, or effect, or meaning, for I can find meaning, but no succor, meaning without con-

solation, knowledge without light. There is nothing to be done, no meaning that will restore time, that will give me another chance, and I am left only with the bare dregs . . .

I have nothing to say to the women to whom I hoped I had something to say. I have nothing certain to say about healing, nothing certain to say about madness, nothing certain to say about cancer.

She had only to say what she had always had to say. She said, as she always had: We have no choice but to live our lives— deeply.

Now I know there are no guarantees, it may get us nothing—no time, no insurance, no health, not even happiness—but our lives, we will have our lives.

                    *                    *                    *

When the woman around her went mad, she studied madness; when they got cancer, too many and too young, she studied cancer. She thought her knowledge would protect her so she could put her energy into other things. She thought community would protect all of them, so she put her energy into building that for fifteen years. It had not always been easy to build a network, it unraveled in the hands, it fell apart, was invaded from without, took too much time, had no financial base, seemed impractical and against all current social forms. Still they had managed it. It expanded and contracted, altered from day to day, but essentially survived. It had been hard to learn to rely on anyone but oneself, but they learned that as well. She had always said "As a poet, I believe in metaphor, in what brings us together not what holds us apart." In this way, more than any other, she thought she had done what was necessary and possible on behalf of her life.

And now, oddly, for of anyone she knew she had been the least alone, she felt absolutely alone.

TUESDAY, FEBRUARY 8, 1977

The mood shifts. Today is another day. There is a balance between dark and light. Don't you remember? I told you the moon was necessary to help us see the night. I have spent time looking at things, beginning with miniatures and moving up and out. Unlike Ruth and Anais, who have died, my life may not be closing in upon me now, but opening up.

Ruth waited until August to die. July had been such a black
month. Neither her terror nor struggle was sufficient against death.
She fought better than anyone I'd known. But even the connection
to life is not sufficient. Or it wasn't. Or it came too late.

Today there are other decisions to be made. It appears I have
choices: self healing ("suicide," they say), lumpectomy ("unre-
liable," they say), radical mastectomy (mutilating), modified radical mastectomy ("preferred," they say). Or I may be able to insist
upon making a choice. Perhaps it isn't so difficult to decide what
to do. I could walk up to the surgeon, holding my breast in my
hand, and say, "Here it is, cut it off. Now."

It doesn't make sense, I know, but if I keep him guessing even
for four days—that's all I have—it's a victory of sorts. I didn't sign
a paper saying he could cut according to his discretion. Would
you? Too many have. Let it hereby be known that Deena Metzger
cedes to John Doe, M.D., a total stranger, the right to act according
to his judgment on her behalf. While she is dreaming—anesthetized.
—I refuse.

                    *                    *                    *

I dream I go to the hospital because I have a fatal disease and
need to be killed to avoid the pain. After the doctor gives me the
shot, I will be dead in two hours. Or I have only two hours to live.
As I explain this to Marc and Greg, I realize that I feel well. I turn
to the doctor, "I feel well. Let me go until I get sick. There is no
point in my dying now."

I awaken and fall back to sleep again. I am walking on a beach
beneath high sand cliffs. A man approaches me who resembles Z.,
who has been threatening my life. Only in the dream, he is a priest.
With elation, I tell him about my reprieve. He asks, "But why were
you willing to die in the first place? Why did you conceive of
following those doctor's orders?"

And I answer, "I find it difficult to challenge authority."

Even when my own life is at stake, I acquiesce.

                    *                    *                    *

I am not obedient. I am not cooperative. I will not acquiesce.

I say this is a cell. You say it is a lovely room, that the sun comes in, that the food is good. You say the clink is never like this. You say the lady in the white dress is not a warden. You say that everything is being done for my own good. You say the care is loving. You say that are doing the best they can, that the doctor is kindly, and professional, that he is not responsible. I think I have heard this before.

*   *   *

Bert is helpful. He rebalances me. I have just decided to submit my body to the doctors. The surgeon strops his blade against the apron. Do you want the fat trimmed? Ground? I was ready to give myself over like the other one out of ten.

Without protest. Without rattling the bars. Without asking questions, without asking why.

I demand a Senate investigation. I want to know where the doctors invest their money. I want to know if they own stock in pharmaceuticals, in agribusiness, in pornography, in cattle ranches, in nuclear energy, in genetic research, in uranium mines, in Dow Chemical, in preservatives, in hormones, in additives, in artificial color, in Bank of America, in asbestos factories, in munitions companies, in defoliants, in pesticides, in crop dusters, in the T.V. networks, in the newspaper business. I want to know how they vote on water, air and earth. I want to know what they have already done against my life.

This is the moment we must come together. It may be too late for me to ask these questions for myself—but it is not too late for you. I pass on the charge—you ask them for yourself and your two-breasted sisters.

What are the causes of cancer? Why are surgery, chemotherapy, and radiation the only treatments? Why do we cure by assault? Who are the culprits? Are they the FDA, the AMA, the NIH, the BIA, the CIA, the FBI, all the initials you combine? Everyone who is in the stress industry, the poison industry, the war or the alienation industry, the suppression industry, the fear industry or the death industry . . .

*J'Accuse.*

You fill in the names.

*   *   *

Bert rallies my confidence. The next call pulls me down. Bert says, "I have total confidence in your ability to heal yourself."

I listen to him deep inside of me as his words push away the shadows and fears which Sheila and Barbara brought out of their great love for me. "Listen," Lee says, "the important thing is to live. Is to live. We want you to live."

Barbara says, "Cut." Sheila says, "Cut." Lee says, "Cut." He says, "You'll be as sexy with one breast as two."

That's not the issue now. That's not the issue yet. That's not the only issue. I stay neutral for seconds at a time, pretend to be doing research, gathering information and data. I am taking a poll. There is overwhelming support for surgery in crisis medicine. At best, I have a choice of poisons. Surgery. Chemotherapy. Radiation. There are a thousand ways to keep a body dying slowly. Kill it a little bit at a time, and it dies more slowly. Treating cancer is like strategic bombing.

I am afraid again. I wait for another call. Perhaps my strength will be mustered again. How many for? How many against? "You will have to scream for support, for belief," Bert tells me.

Scream? Didn't I tell you I couldn't scream?

"You will have to surround yourself with those who will support you on a daily basis, who will believe that the psyche can mobilize all the forces of health." When I listen to Bert, I believe him. When the phone rings again, I am afraid to pick it up.

*          *          *

I am beginning to understand what the issue is: Can I utilize medical knowledge without undermining my belief in my own healing powers?

"I believe that you can heal yourself," Victor tells me. Is he a dreamer? He brings me a book on dreaming. At night, I wait for the dreams to come to see if I have one to send him in exchange for the one he promises to send me. Dyanne is writing a book on bartering, but I don't know if this exchange qualifies. One dream for another to help us stay alive. When I talk to Victor I feel strong. I turn my back on the nurse when she comes in and look for the sun in the street. But when I read the book, I'm frightened.

Victor visits me straight from the jungle. He is writing a book about the last survivors of the Lacondon Indians. They are dying out, dying out. Dying of Old World diseases. A population dying which had not been dying before. And the guilty are not punished. Have you noticed that the guilty, the carriers, the human rats with the lice in their fur are not punished? "The Marya ruins, the homes of the gods, were defiled and the guilty *chicleros* were not punished. It was rather the Lacondones who continued to sicken and die, and those who escaped the plagues were not saved by their gods, but rather by Occidental medicines brought by the same *chicleros* who had brought the disease."

Who will come and help me hunt the *chicleros*? But we must hunt them now, now, for if you get sick . . . well, then, will you be able to turn against them, or will you ask them for Chiclets, Medicine and God—in order to live?

          \*          \*          \*

Jane stays neutral. I ask her, "What do you vote?" She doesn't answer directly. "You have to vote," I insist. "All good citizens vote." Jane says she has no agendas for me. "You are better equipped than anyone," she asserts, "to make this decision."

I am beginning to understand this dilemma. To see the battle-ground. There are no absolute victories. I do not fantasize about conquest. I only want to be loyal to Toots, to do what is right, to keep the moon in the sky, to keep the sun in its place, to keep the dreams coming, the dreams coming.

          \*          \*          \*

Sometimes it isn't clear what I am trying to decide. Or why it is so difficult. And how much is at stake. As much as I know I cannot think of this as anything but a battle for my own life, yet that is impossible. Harold sits by me, the second time in less than a week. He will come back once more but I will be unable to talk to him then. Do you know that we have only met once, briefly, in a theatre lobby? Yet here he is a second time by my bedside. Perhaps he is still in his grief, his Edith having died of breast cancer after nine years. How many years do I have? How many years can I gain? At what price?

"Are you afraid of losing your sexuality?" he asks. He offers to ask me all the hard questions. He agrees to answer all the hard questions. I wonder why he is going to such lengths to be kind. It is a new definition of kindness, one with a sharp edge to it. I need to look at things brutally and openly. To cut open my fear with a knife. I cannot do it alone. Odd, I should do a part of it here and now with a stranger. But he is a man and knows what none of my sisters know. And Alida says, this time we can't do it alone. And so there is this unlikely alliance.

What's in it for him? I wonder. Then I learn. "You are important to a lot of women," he says. "You are important in this community. I'm worried about what you're going to do. When you say mastectomy is a political act against women, I worry about all those who will die following your lead."

A man is sitting in my hospital room wondering how my words will affect others. Will they cause them to die? I am crosslegged on the bed. He is in a chair. This is called fighting for our lives. All battles are not fought in the scrub. He thinks I am listening to him; I am also listening to the words I wrote a year ago. They go through my mind like an old song. Maybe I can set them to music.

> For years the women have been dying. One by one. Stricken in their youth or middle-age just as things were beginning. An unknown assassin. Just at the moment when everything was possible. Education. Power. Consciousness. Self. They sickened and died. That is not true. They did not die of their own accord. Something sickened them and they died. They were murdered. Stricken. Poisoned. Assassinated. Suddenly.
>
> The doctors call it cancer. It is. But of what nature? And why now? And why so many?

I write that in the *Book of Hags,* then I asked in my journal, "Why am I so obsessed with cancer? With madness?"

At the Woman's Building, Diane D. said, "I want to talk to you about cancer—because I have it." I do not think she was twenty at the time. Leah, as well, had cancer. There were others. At Valley College a young student was going to the hospital for a biopsy. I knew too many women who had cancer. I began to look for causes. To fight it. To stop it. Again, in *Hags,* I found these words:

> The women are attacked. . . . These women are attacked in their sex. . . . They are fed male hormones. . . . The women are like young boys, but they are past the adolescent prime. Their milk is cut out of them. They have become like the amazons who cut off a breast to shoot an arrow. They have been taught that survival depends upon shooting arrows,

though perhaps it is not for women to shoot arrows. They
have been taught that survival depends upon shooting arrows
. . . and they have a right to live . . . and so they lose their
breasts.

I didn't picture myself here. I didn't know what it would be like
to sit on a bed contemplating becoming a warrior. I haven't thought
of that stance before. Perhaps that is what I have to learn. I do not
want to live in a world where we shoot each other with bows and
arrows. For forty years, I have avoided that action. Now, maybe,
that is what I have to learn.

How can I explain this to Harold? He is afraid I will hold on to
both breasts. He is afraid I will die too soon. He is afraid others will
imitate me. I am not only interested in finding out what to do now?
I want to know how I got here? I want to know who legislated it.
I want you to help me find out. I want to know why surgery is the
only statistical cure. I want to know why I have never been trained
to heal myself.

                    *                *                *

I don't want to forget a single gesture of kindness or the gracious-
ness of friends. I am aware how unusual my treatment is, so I am
more than grateful. But also I remember how long we all worked
for this. Building a community is not easy and there were many
times, exhausted and disillusioned, we wanted to give up. Still,
each in our own way, we persisted over the years. Seven years,
ten years, maybe longer, consciously building this network. Today
I receive the benefits, tomorrow we will mobilize for someone
else. Under the best of circumstances we need each other, but in
these times, this state of seige, it is essential.

I am in good spirits again. Every now and then I remember I am
fighting for my life. I am not only fighting for a breast, that is a
small fight, I am fighting for time, for years, for life. I hope I am
fighting for others as well. Even after the surgery, there will be
battles ahead of me. This skirmish in the hospital room is a minor
encounter. The other engagements with the hidden enemy will be
more serious and prolonged.

I gather evidence about all the possible causes of cancer: diet,
additives, air pollution, stress, exhaustion, sexism, silence, repression, alienation, hostility, all the modern poisons which are festering in my life. I do not know how it is possible to live a healthy

life. Everything for health in this society must be done against the grain. If you want to live, you must go underground, become a guerilla fighter, snatch life out of the fists of those who smash it.

At first glance, I appear a sane woman, calm and self-possessed. But even seeming to manage the grammatical order of words is a lie. Everything I discover is immediately contradicted. No one knows anything; everyone is an authority. Dogmatism abounds. "The best lack all conviction while the worst are full of passionate intensity." My sanest analyses are ridiculed; what seems quite mad to me is inevitably the procedure of choice. I have been glib, saying, "This is an irrational universe." Now I know the meaning of my words. Sometimes I want to stop gathering information, to scream and to strike out. My name is Cassandra. The woman most cursed by the gods.

These days are devoted to tests. Machines zoom over my body like radar scanners looking for the hidden invaders which might have entered my territory. Halloo, where are you? They look in the flesh, I look in the psyche. We've created a division of labor: The doctors think about viruses; I think about politics. Or stress. I know how hard it has been for the woman to survive these last years. Has anyone asked the woman alone how she lives?

How does she earn a living—alone?

How does she raise children—alone?

How does she do political work—alone?

How does she pursue her own work—alone?

How does she run a household—alone?

How does she walk down the dark streets—alone?

How does she know she is human—alone?

I am obsessed. And this is only the beginning. The future opens like a dark maw.

Naomi says, "Artists think they are depicting an external reality when they are creating images for the world to contemplate. They don't realize they are painting their own inner torment."

When Wolf ran his car over bananas to make an art piece, did he realize he was creating his own death image? When David lost the same piece on the freeway and drove over it, did he see any warning there? And Wolf did die in his car. The artist touches the dark forces, but how often does she touch the light? If I write out my own darkness here, do I create it as well? If I only write the light, the book will be a lie.

I became a woman alone. D. was not healthy for me. I wrote, "Physician heal theyself," but I didn't heed my words. Fears smothered me and I was not quick enough to give up the maternal role which was killing us both.

For Anais, Henry was the conduit to the streets, to passion, to anger and grand gestures, to zest. Later she seemed a paragon, perfection itself, a porcelain doll. Perhaps without Henry the rage for life, the great passions went underground, were stifled. For five years, I lived with a finger in the dike. Henry was the torrent. What torrent will come to help me now?

                    *                    *                    *

"Am I dying?" Anais asked me.

"No," I said. It was the wrong answer. I tried to correct it. "But everyone must be ready," I said.

"But I'm not ready," she whispered. Her voice was like a dry leaf. When she closed her eyes, I watched for breathing. Breathe, Anais, breathe," I begged.

"I'm not ready," she said. "There's still so much life in me." I agreed. She was like a young girl. Outside her bedroom window was a half-finished dream tea house. I do not know if she entered it before she died.

Brugh Joy says, "Every disease is an obstruction of the soul." Everything must be re-examined, altered, transformed. What was simply unbearable before is now lethal. What was painful is deadly. But I do not want to devote my life to fighting cancer. I do not want to think about cancer day and night. I think of myself as a builder; I have work to do in addition to preserving my own life. Who is keeping me from my work? In whose interest has this distraction occurred?

The voices beseige me: "You've done your work." "You haven't done your work." "You've done too many different kinds of work." "You haven't focused on your own work." "You work too hard." "You never cease to work." "You don't work hard enough." "You neglect your real work." "You never play, it even spoils your work." "There's nothing more important than your work."

And didn't the inner hag cackle, "Even if you get cancer, you won't make the necessary sacrifices to write." Didn't the bitter inner critic shriek, "Die!"

*              *              *

"Write poems, women," are Honor's words in the poem hanging on the wall. Yes, write poems, women, write women, I continue to say. I do not know if it heals; I do not know if it cures, but I know it gives us our lives.

*              *              *

Dyanne brings me a little sack of *milagros,* a silver eye to ward off the evil eye so like the trinkets I brought Anais. I paste Barbara's letter into my journal. This is not the only book. There is another black book for wailing and howling and dreaming. This book is for talk. Barbara. Barbara. Barbara. I know how she is suffering. She reads my book of howls and sees an image of caution there she hates to recognize as hers. Everything is exaggerated of course. If I am holding up a mirror to anything, it is the mirror in Steeplechase and the funhouse. Barbara writes, "Beware of magic and old religion," avoid the belief that right living or thinking or magical objects can save your life.

I understand what she is saying. And maybe she thinks I'm mad, but things are not as simple as they seem. This disease does not feel like chance alone. And if I'm going to pull some hours from the teeth of death, then I'd better know what feeds him. I am not willing to be a victim and to go like a lamb when someone snaps his fingers and says, "It's time."

This is the moment of danger, I know it. What shall I decide about being responsible for my own life? You know what the problem is: If transformation of my life holds the possibility of health—and it does, it does—then what are the consequences of old habits and blindspots?

Beware of magic. Beware of surgeons. Beware. Beware. Things are not as simple as they seem. I can't find the straight road. Thinking good thoughts alone won't change my life but I'm not sure either of the effects of surgery, of what will happen, for example, when the lymph which fights the cancer is cut out. I am an army sacrificing a battalion in order to save the war—don't you find that magical thinking too? Are the doctors so far from the notion of sacrifice?

I am not sure of my power to heal myself. I do not know if I can find all the sites of the psychic cancers and cut them out. I have cut and cut, spent days, cutting and cutting, I have always lived here as in enemy territory, whittling away.

This is not new to me. Before the woman suspected she had cancer, she was already attempting to change her life. Two months at radical inner surgery and ten years of hard work before that. ''I don't want to get cancer from this,'' I screamed and walked out. Still a thousand poisons remain, a thousand causes I cannot find or name and a thousand unknown pressures, and a thousand conditions I cannot change. I do not seem to have the knives to excise all.

Barbara, you are right. Magic is the search for power, for impossible control. It is as you say, limited, authoritarian and ineffective. I know there is no justice, there are no rewards. We cannot simply pray or chant for health.

Health is something else. The path to it less certain and more precarious and I do not know where I am going. I cannot have it simply by the wanting of it; I cannot have it simply through good deeds. Yet, if I can create harmony where until now there has been war; if I can exhume and revitalize what has been denied and buried—if I can transform what limits me—then . . .

$$*\qquad\qquad *\qquad\qquad *$$

Toots, come play your pipe. This is too hard. My head hurts. Where the lump was excised, my breast hurts. Toots, where are you? If it were night I could see you in the sky, a little light in the dark, like a moth caught in the white shadow a flame casts. I'll tell you a secret: I'm lost. The writer is lost at this moment. The woman is lost at this moment. She announces it to the universe without shame.

Lost, lost, lost. When Hansel and Gretel were lost in the woods they had to deal with the old witch before they found their way again. Okay, Witch, where are you? They also had to deal with their father who had lost them to begin with, but he was an old fool and as lost as they were. Better deal with power, then, and learn something. Where are you, witch?

I wish it weren't so late. I would call friends and ask them to sneak over here to pass the night. Let's play monopoly. Let's get stoned. When the cards say, "Go to jail, go directly to jail, do not pass go, do not collect $200," I'll say, "No." But orders are orders. The card says, go back and begin again, that's how you play the game. You go to jail, you sit in a cell, you are alone, you lose three turns (unless you have money). Do you have money? If you don't, why should I? I go to jail, I'd rather sit it out and wait for you, read a little if they allow me books, watching the light come in, if they allow me light. Eva Forest made a friend of a fly. I have not had to be so alone. I have made a friend of the little bit of light which comes in from the sky.

*          *          *

Barbara stands on one side; Naomi on the other. My dearest friends disagree. I am Solomon's child, divided in two and trying to grow the parts together. There is something I know about healing, there is a path we can choose to help us bypass what makes us ill. We do not need to be like the Lacondonians. Women—we cannot allow ourselves to be wiped out.

This is not the first time my life is threatened. This is not the first time I have been on trial. This is not the first time I have been in the dark. When I was in New York, Marc read my FBI report to me. I had applied under the Freedom of Information Act. Seven pages, all blanked out. What information is being kept from me now?

Our lives are constantly threatened. Cancer and madness. Chemicals, pollutants, radiation. Fascism and war. And now the rise of the solitary erratic assailant. Edith said, "Be compassionate. I believe in the power of love. Meditate upon him compassionately." The police psychiatrist said, "Do not be compassionate, even in your dreams. You can only save yourself with coldness, ice, and hauteur."

Demons invade the room. All the dark forces are here. I call Naomi in the middle of the night because she believes in the light. What light can she shed against these shadows. In San Francisco we protested the Vietnam War by holding bouquets of flowers against the guns. I wish I had gone mad last year, broken into a thousand pieces and reassembled myself in a new shape.

The women who had died of cancer, had all tried madness first and their madness had been plastered up, sealed, glassed

in, submerged. Then they lived a few years and cancer
erupted which could not be submerged, ignored, boxed in,
cut out, irradiated or controlled in any way. It was a fierce
raging growth and it took their lives. I don't want to die. I
don't want to die.

And how long ago did I write that? If I had let the anger out
then? Where is the energy blocked in me? Where is the light ex-
tinguished. Cancer is an inner wall. Did I build it? If not, how can
I break it down? I am afraid that the thoughts of health are not as
strong as the demons of cancer. I am afraid that we are impotent
against the forces which attack the light.

We meditate. Naomi acts as a guide. For a moment, I feel whole.
I see a woman with fire issuing from her breasts. The fire enters
me. For a moment, I am whole. There are two sentences which
struggle in me. I must learn to say them at once, to speak from both
sides of my mouth. "Listen, bring down the defense department."
Heal yourselves. Disarm the enemy, fortify health. They are distinct necessary actions. One path is not enough.

Naomi meditates with me, Barbara holds me, Sheila calls me in
the morning, Jane calls at night. Everyone is here, fighting along
with me. I am coming to know that I am not alone.

*                    *                    *

Things happen too fast to record. The woman who was alone is
not alone. Yet, she is alone. There are dozens of people calling,
the nurses and doctors zoom in and out, the tests are unending.
Yet there are spaces in which she is totally alone. There are things
she must answer for herself.

Why does she feel on trial?

This is a crucial question. It occurs to her that again she is being
tested. She survived rape. She survived political trial. She survived
attempted murder. Now it is cancer. How will she fight it? How
will she survive? What transformation will occur? What use can be
made of this? How will she retain her spirits? How will she remain
strong?

If she feels that there is always a trial to be met, a test of her
energy, strength, spirit, courage and survival, does she create
these trials? It is as if she does not deserve to live, as if she must
earn an afternoon with Toots. Or is the trial her willingness and
ability to choose life? She talks well, but will she act?

Nothing is casual. She scrutinizes each word, each thought, all habits of mind. "I took it in with my mother's milk." What did she take in at that breast? The bitterness? The concentration camps? The devaluation of women? Is it that? The basic human survival hunger fear and the other more terrible fear: Would she have been able to survive in the camps? With dignity? Would she have been able to resist? Would she be one of the *lamed vovs*? She had wanted to take on all the world suffering, thinking it was possible without being harmed. She wanted to feel what everyone in the world was feeling. She did not want to set herself apart. This is not only love, this is hubris. It is a crime and she must set it right.

She sets this down to study it. It must not feel like self-punishment. She understands deeply that she is not being punished for lacking the consciousness to have transformed herself enough to avoid the disease. She understands that the pressures and pains are old and that everyone of us is vulnerable. She is able to accept her own mortality. She is pleased that she is facing this with courage. She would not be without that courage. And she would not be without her good spirits, though yesterday yesterday yesterday she thought they might be gone from her forever and she was not sure that any bird could fly fast enough to bring them back. But she does not want this to be a test of her courage or of her resilience or of her bravery. She wonders if the test she should apply is the one of being able to give up these trials.

*       *       *

Some little truths occur. I have lived my life this week despite the setting. Lived my life in the little room which is not larger than a cell but has been transformed by posters, feathers, books, candles, wine, talismans, fans, articles of love. Each seems to have been chosen with love. And if nothing had entered, if I had been here in among the bare walls, if I had been here alone, I also would have survived. After all, I have been up at dawn each day watching the sun rise. And isn't that a gift? And tomorrow, too. At home, my room faces to the east. I have not been deprived of light.

The gifts have made a difference and the calls and the letters and the gestures; each to be remembered and treasured, each building a little cell of strength within her, a little cell moving her toward life, engaging her in life, implanting life in her so thick and firm nothing can cut it out. She tries compulsively to remember, tells the gestures again and again like rosary beads and in the end she is restored.

Dana comes to play the flute, Debussy streaming through the room like light. Barbara would like to play the flute for me, but instead her task has been to write me that terribly stern letter urging me to give up my overblown belief in my own power to create disease and to cure myself. She says no harm will come to me from amputating my breast. Barbara says she risks losing my friendship forever by offending me, but adds, "I am willing to lose you to life, but I am not willing to lose you to death."

*                    *                    *

In her room, alone, she wants to record everything. She is desperate now to capture experience, for trying to remember everything, even when she knows the sun will rise again and tomorrow will be as full as yesterday and she can rely on the fullness of her life as she can rely on apples. Toots, after all, has not deserted her though he hid under the bed last night and for a time she thought she could not live without her breast, would rather die. Did she think that? She teetered and all the time wanted to write a poem about not teetering, about courage, about loving life despite despite despite.

And now she is tired. And she struggles. Knowing that now she must listen to the body, must let Toots go, must snuggle into the dream, must give up the pleasure of writing it down, holding the day, yesterday, the two most difficult days of her life, must let them fall back into the sea like a wave which has spent itself bringing water to the shore, because now she must learn to sleep when she is tired, rest when she is weary, and in order to do that she must say "no" and "no" and "no" to those who would whisper to her when she wants to talk to herself.

WEDNESDAY, FEBRUARY 9, 1977

I'll tell you how she's dealt with loneliness. She makes alliances with strong and passionate women. She follows them to the perimeters of their courage. So her body is stretched like a tent over the radius of sticks and bones. She moves in the largest circle she

can find. Or irregularly, like a paramecium or an amoeba. Stretching first here and then there. Is this what has brought her to this
predicament? Is she exhausted? Has there been too much energy
for the body to hold?

Some of the gifts are quiet. My student Susan B. brings me a
spider to remind me that nets are broken and woven again, that a
spider never falls, so Susan says, "It always lets itself down."

*     *     *

And David comes weeping and brings two flowers. One from
own garden encased in a funnel of clear plastic and another un-
wrapped but from the park. A daisy and a tulip. The plain and the
voluptuous. He takes down the poster which says, "*a trabajar.*"
He says I work too hard. David's sister Margaret has written me
a letter. My family expands even as it shrinks. David will never
again be my lover. Margaret will always be my sister.

Maria the nurse reads my book, turning the pages gently with
her smooth fingers and painted nails. "I will tell you a secret,"
Maria says. "I have always thought these things when I am with
a man but I have not known how to say it aloud."

*     *     *

We are not deformed and mutilated. We are deformed and
mutilated. How can she say we are deformed and mutilated when
she sees the gifts which are given to her? How can she say that
when she is witness to the extension of love? But she sees the evidence of deformation in her own body not the physical crippling,
but the cancer as evidence of her failure to be whole. There was
an unconscious amputation before the fact of the most vulnerable
parts, or a failure, despite the struggle, to survive. Or, she does not
see it yet. She reaches gently being careful not to raise her arm
too far, too fast, keeps her bandaged breast in a bra, so that the
scar will heal delicately and fast. She is as tender and loving with
that breast as she can be, preserving it from further harm and
distortion. But in a week it will be gone and her right side flat
as a boy's but for a scar. Her father had a scar on his chest where
he burned himself when he was a child. So finally they will come
to resemble each other. She had hoped for a different kind of

mirror. She wants to live as long a life as he has lived. He is over eighty. He does not know his age. She knows full well that she is forty. She had said at forty she would change her life. And she did.

She has always loved her breasts, loved the mound of flesh round as oranges, soft as persimmons, loved the blood every month, the tiny stretch of her ovary in the middle of the month, the tide in her body, the going toward and away from the moon, the sea in her, holding the salt, letting it out. She has loved her body from a distance, counting on its presence as she has counted on the sun. But now she can count on nothing. The sun warms her back at this moment. Is like a belt, a girdle belonging to a dancing girl, a silk sash. She doesn't count on anything to be there another day. These are just words. She says them again and again trying to build a reality from language. Breast cancer. Mastectomy. Reconstruction. Breast cancer.

*               *               *

People send me poems about death. Women say to me, "I am afraid." Friends say, "Reassure me that you won't die." Everyone is locked into her own little cell at night telling herself stories, singing, "hush hush hush" or, as Barbara says, "there there."

I speak with a forked tongue. I say, "there is no cause for this disease. Nothing in my life has been so dire; I have been able to overcome everything, to survive. Nothing has been so terrible, everything has also caused me to grow, to transform. I have had a rich life, the richest life. How can I be ill?"

But another voice in her stands back with pain, examines the events of her life, the surrounding world, and wonders how she has come so far and remained intact until now.

*               *               *

I suffer from overweening ambition and pride. I want to be able to survive anything, anything. And I put myself on trial. And even this is a trial. And I do not know how to quiet down, how to sleep, how to stop the thoughts, how to meditate on a single image: I do not know how to sing "hush hush." When someone says, "there there," I ask where and run, "where?" and run, "where?" and run.

\* \* \*

A secret. When no one is about, I cradle my breast in my palm singing it a little song to give it ease. There is nothing I have encountered in my life which has filled me with such loss.

\* \* \*

"Where's Toots?" she wonders. Oh, Toots is about, but it's not time for her to enter. Toots is always there. But somehow has not gotten the cue to come onstage. Toots is not sleeping but is not in the limelight now. A presence. A shadow on the stage or an empty chair.

Shall I go room to room on this floor, I wonder (for I have been told so many times that I have no right to leave the floor without permission and official escort—and aren't I a grown woman and a warrior in the world?) and ask everyone in the other little hospital cells, "What is attacking you? What are you dying of? What fears come to you at night?"

\* \* \*

She watches Jane's face tremble, the cheeks quiver as the flesh pushes up against the eyes to keep the tears in. Jane is crying for her, has not gone to work, is sitting with her, about to break in two or a dozen pieces. I watch it from a great distance. Knowing someone is crying for me; it seems hundreds of women are crying for me. In fact they are crying for themselves as well. Our lives are intertwined. We share a common fate and these tears keep them safer.

Lucy writes her a letter. "I've been thinking of you so often. I've never known anyone who had so many people actually concerned and caring for her as you." She does not understand—this is true—she does not understand it. It seems such a little thing whatever it was she gave each of them. Is it more than she knows? Did it cost more than she reckoned? She will not believe she is dying of over loving. If that is the case, then let her die.

The isolation she feels now is the loneliness in the midst of a loving crowd, a swarm. She has withdrawn in order to find what she needs to survive. She is busy tending the fires of living, of enjoying the day, making her life here, even in this room. Peonies on her left. A Japanese fan. A typewriter. Messages from the Woman's Building. Chrysanthemums from Marc and Greg. Yellow chairs. Today she paces the cell. Twelve steps square. She has been here six days. Surgery, then tests and more tests, an endless looking for more disease. She was like a caged animal when Bradley came at eight in the morning eating a lemon. Another yellow fruit. Was it the mercury she wondered, the tiny trace of mercury going through her brain for the sake of photographs, which had made her so restless, mercurial, tense, and mad as a hatter? And her life? The banquet table in Alice in Wonderland—everything crowded together at this end—and someone yelling, "No room, no room." Let me out, she had been shrieking inside. Let me out. Let my voice out, let my body out, let the truth out, let the fear out, let the grief out, let everything out. Free all political prisoners.

They had marched just recently in zero degree weather trying to free a woman who was also on trial and kept three hundred days in the dark without sun. And Robert had cried heartily from the top of his lungs, "Free her, free her, free all political prisoners, free Assata Shakur;" but she, finding it difficult to shout, had used the occasion to practice, to let the little voice out in a whisper, "free all" she has whispered in her little voice, below her breath. Everyone thinks she talks loudly, that she holds nothing back, that her books say everything that could be said, that there are no restraints. But she knows what a shout is in her, what a scream is in her, what a bomb of rage and outrage and pain is in her, to be mutiplied by a thousandfold for everyone she knows who is suffering as well, who is afraid now, who is weeping, who is alone in a cell, who is dying of the defense disease and of the diseases of heaven and hell. And she knows if she let that scream out she would be torn apart by the violence of it. A woman can only give birth to an infant; a woman cannot give birth to a scream the size of an elephant or a locomotive or a planet. It would tear her apart. She opens her voice and tries to shout, as Robert, in a dream, finally yelled, "Freedom."

His poem is by her bed, she reaches for it as if it could help her.

In the dream
we were permitted
to utter one word

one word,
just one word . . .

We were silently waiting our turn.
Worse than taking orders at bayonet-point
was our obedience to the rule of
one word
with no soldiers
or fascist generals in sight . . .

As in the dream he submitted under duress and yelled, "Freedom," so she opens her mouth and tries screaming—as she had that
day when Anais died, when she was told she might have cancer,
when she broke up her home all in one day and went to an empty
room to practice screaming, turned the phonograph on high, practiced screaming as she had practiced laughing, artificial, cere-
monial, but desperate acts, trying to control the volume, to let a
little bit of voice out at a time, let it leak, screaming up in her head
around the eyes, a scream like a wire rather than the full-throated,
full-breasted screams which she desired to pull out of her heart.

                    *               *               *

These are contradictions I cannot bridge yet. At the same time
that I am watching Jane cry, I wonder if I will ever cry for anyone
again, as I am unable to cry now, to scream, to rage for myself.
I have reached for comfort, put my head on Sheila's beautiful
breasts, have allowed Barbara to ease me, though Barbara's role
has been more difficult and stern.

I see from a distance how Barbara is suffering, also how severe
Barbara looks, how drawn, as if Barbara has been fighting for my
life. Barbara has been the angel I have been wrestling as I have
tried to find a path to walk and have not known how to go. Barbara has seen a path which is dependable but I am afraid of that
path, afraid it is a trap, afraid it keeps me from another path more
precarious but more authentic, a path that had opened up in my
heart not in the world but which I am committed to nevertheless.
Paradox: I am afraid if I do not walk the new path I will die. I am
afraid the cancer comes from my fear of that path. But Barbara
knows that if I walk only on the new path I will die. I do not have
the strength to walk on that path alone. I am not strong enough,

not enlightened enough, not committed enough, not brave enough.
I am frail after all. I am not only the warrior but also the little
sparrow I used to watch from my bedroom window when I was a
girl. The new path is the route of the heart and the imagination,
the knife of will and love which comes from a different understanding of the universe. I am afraid every time I have avoided that
path I have betrayed myself. I am afraid the cancer is the record of
those betrayals. A stone wall of dead cells. But here is the paradox:
the other familiar path can cure the same cancer it makes. The old
path can help me cut out the cancer it itself created. What am I
to do? Barbara wrestles with me. "Save your life first," she says.
"Then begin again. Then find the other path." I am tormented.
Barbara is tormented. I know I need all my courage to choose and
all my knowledge and power. I gird my loins with iron, I harness
Toots, whip him saying, "if you have ever served me, serve me
now." I watch Jane cry from a distance, watch Barbara suffering
from a distance, hear the tears in Naomi's voice, watch Sheila as
she pours out her affection and loving, and I am reached by these
women and not reached, for there is something like a wall about
my heart and I forget, which is the worst violation of myself, that
I ever suffered for them, cried for them, yearned for them, ached
for them. I look at these healthy creatures as if they are strange
beasts, mutants from another planet, fantasies of a writer's imagination. What are these feelings that possess them?

*       *       *

She receives letters from friends, students, even acquaintances,
saying "Your illness terrifies me. If I thought I had cancer . . ."
But she is not afraid. Her spirits are basically good. In fact, she
is cheerful. She tells that to John. "My spirits astound me. I have
been more undermined by a leaking faucet. By a missed appoint-
ment. By disorder." She wipes everything away. Even the night she
cries, she does not cry hard. She could howl but she does not howl.
It is again so much like the time she was with Robert and tried
to scream. That is an old dream. Twice she has dreamed now that
she opens her mouth to scream and a scream escapes like a great
tree torn out of the earth by the wind, but it is totally silent, totally
silent, totally silent.
These women come to me like professional mourners, weeping

for me, for in this battle I have forgotten how to weep and afraid that I will never weep again. I want Naomi to sing me a song to make me cry, someone to tell me a fairy tale to make me cry, to read me a poem to make me cry. I want to be a little child again, crying for nothing. I want to be the little girl who cried herself to sleep. I do not want to be going to bed as I do, tired but with a kind of cheer, watching the moon scratch its way across the sky and awakening at dawn, each day earlier and then earlier, as if there is not enough time, not enough time. Watching the sun and trying to find a little voice which is quiet in me and without self-pity as I watch the sun break out above the clouds to make a sunrise.

\*　　　　　　\*　　　　　　\*

There is something about my bravery and good spirits, my cheer, all of which is authentic, not created for the occasion, there is something about my energy, my refusal to be wheeled in a chair, the insistence that I wash my own body, my garnering of my strength, that terrifies me. I want to know I will cry for someone else, if I have turned my own tears to stone, if I do not allow them to myself will I allow them to others—will I be able to weep for these women who are weeping for me? I can hear Barbara yelling at me sternly, "This is not the time to worry about others. This is the time to worry only about yourself."

\*　　　　　　\*　　　　　　\*

But there is the dilemma; it is another of the contradictions. She is trying to survive the only way she knows, stepping away from despair and defeat, but somehow in doing it, she is stepping toward another place quite as terrible. She is caught in a stone room and that is the silent space she has been trying to break through. She has to bring down the dikes and yet she can't bring down the dikes. She has to tear down and let the flood occur. She has to know she can live underwater for awhile.

\*　　　　　　\*　　　　　　\*

In the last hour alone at this typewriter, she has brought in Toots like the whirlwind. Instead of the old nag in the stable she has brought in the horses of the universe. Instead of the horse of the field she has harnessed the horse which pulls the sun. She has connected herself to powers which are too strong and she has not even settled for one. But for many. Life, even life, in such intensity is not life. Naturally, she puts up walls against it. She doesn't know how to minimize, quiet, soothe. She does not know the lullabies. She does not know quiet. When she is in doubt, when she is afraid, she screams, "More life, more life." The power grows in her. Victor comes and tells her he is writing about Faust. He always says the right thing without either of them expecting it. Faust is a modest man in his desires compared to what she thinks she must harness to survive this crisis. To survive this world. This is not only the crack between the worlds. This is not only trying to walk two roads at the same time, this is being drawn and quartered by the horses of light and darkness. Somehow she must open her mouth and let something out. But even as she writes, the current builds. There is a way of writing which is spilling and a way which is intensifying. She feels a needle in her heart. She is the caged beast whose temper rises with each step it takes in the shrinking cell. She cannot sit still. The words expand as she imagines them. She is choking, suffocating. These words are of no help. They teach her to understand but understanding is totally irrelevant now. Understanding is an intoxication, a delerium and a distraction. She needs something else.

Perhaps she needs to sing a little song. To let go. To hum a tune. Who will give this little girl who doesn't know how to sing a penny whistle?

*          *          *

THURSDAY, FEBRUARY 10, 1977

I have made a decision. I will sacrifice my breast. Barbara says it's a proper sacrifice, that it will please the gods. This bit of flesh for life. I wish that there were another way. In a few years, I know this procedure will appear crude and barbaric. But now the accumulated evidence reveals I have no choice. There is enough work to be done to be sure I do not fall ill again. There is enough work to be done after the cancer is cut out. I do not have the skill, we do not have the skill yet to fight the cancer on the cellular level, to confront each individual cell and force the disease to recede. That is, I am not certain I have the skill to fight that battle. Now that I've made this decision, I can go home. Next week I will return for surgery and to begin again.

*               *               *

Thousands of women have gone this path. Thousands of women. In the street I cannot tell them apart from the others and in their houses they undress in the dark. Solitary confinement. Secrets. Body shame. Why have so many been singled out?

*               *               *

MONDAY, FEBRUARY 14, 1977

I walk back into another hospital after four days at home carrying a suitcase, posters and typewriter; in a moment I am in a gown. Yesterday I gave a workshop; today I am back in bed. Yesterday I was well; today I am preparing to be down. Visiting hours, 10:00 to 8:00; in the hours which will be worst, I will be alone.

No pills, please. I want to live this night out. No pills, please, no shots, no television, no distraction. No sleep. Tomorrow there will be more than enough sleep. No sleep tonight. Not even to dream. Nothing but silence, but silence, but silence. Tonight I mourn my breast, tomorrow I begin to salvage my life.

*               *               *

I am back in a cell again. Another room. Another hospital. Carefully yellow again. The doctors have discovered that yellow is the color of light and cheer, that it is the color of the sun, and that it is the color of power and doctors are very interested in power and so they paint the rooms yellow. I do not mind. The yellow is deep and intense. Not quite the color of fruit. Not quite the yellow paper Judy sends me. Not quite the yellow wallpaper for mad women and women alone. Mad women. There are always reminders, aren't there? The color we imagine sand to be. The color of sand when it is wet.

*               *               *

For four days, I was home. Free. Took a walk this morning, even ran to the corner. Free. Home Free. When we ran to the base after playing hide 'n seek, we would yell, "Home Free."

There was a way the player who came home could free everyone, but I don't remember that part. And something else forgotten. The jingle which was circled on the back of the one who was "it" while she leaned with her eyes closed—don't cheat, don't peek—on the maple tree, waiting while they made a circle on her back and then when they stuck a thumb in the center, she began to count, "1 2 3 4 5 6 7 8 9 10,   Ready or Not, Here I Come. Anyone Around My Base Is It. 12345678910. Ready or not here I come Anyonearoundmybaseisit."

            \*            \*            \*

Ready or not, ready or not. She wasn't ready; hadn't been ready. It was a crime to put a healthy woman into a cell, into this tiny room, a new room, rather oddly angled, but a cell nevertheless, where she was treated not as "bad" but as a child. Confined. Men she had never met—men—left "orders" for her. And there was an order, a routine, she didn't understand. And an expectation of order. Questions were asked about the order of her life. There was apparently a philosophy that things should occur at certain times in certain ways. Everyone she met in this strange place believed in the reasonableness of the universe. Believed in sequence. "How are your bowels?" they ask. By which they mean—are you regular? How often? How easily?

But I don't ever eat in an orderly fashion, and I don't live in an orderly fashion and I don't sleep in an orderly fashion—how can I? There might be a friend to see or a sunset or an unscheduled meeting. There is never enough time so there must always be time made or stolen. We can have breakfast or not. Or lunch. Or not eat until dinner. Or gorge ourselves at midnight on carrot cake smearing it into our mouths with our fingers, or eat hot burning chiles, drink wine at dawn, eat soup for breakfast, and the bowels, if they are healthy, respond to the rhythm of the day. My life does not begin like the sun does in the morning and end at night. I do not rise every day at the same time. I do not go to bed at a regular time. How can I? There is Toots to be thought of and her penchant for the extraordinary. Toots is not to be restrained by a schedule. Toots sleeps when she can and dances, dances at all other times.

\*            \*            \*

Or weeps. "Wailed," Naomi had said. Wailed, groaned, grieved,
shook her fists at heaven, for the pain of it. Tonight Naomi was
alone, another woman alone, alone alone alone. The same Naomi
who had said, "Men can't bear to be alone. They do not know
how." But we bear it, we bear it. We know how. We have practiced long and hard. A woman alone. But I told Naomi, "It is not
possible to do it alone, to be alone." I am sitting in another hospital
room. Tomorrow I will lose a breast. I gaze at my reflection in
the window. The view is not as good from this window. There will
be neither dawns nor sunsets. A little light falling at an angle into
the room and another great building across a mall. I can see the
little cells across the way. Is everyone asleep? Who has nightmares?
Does everyone have someone she, he can awaken to share a dream?
No, most people awaken from their populated dreams alone. I gaze
at my reflection in the glass. The deep pink cloth falls smoothly
across the little breast. This is the place where two children were
fed. This is the place of love, of food, of comfort. Heads against my
breast. Mouths against her breast. There is something hidden,
lethal, inside my skin which needs to be cut out. I can not see it.
I can not reach it with my fingers, my mind, my hopes. What does
the prisoner want to eat for her last meal? Can I put a child to
suckle here one last time?

\*            \*            \*

I think I ought to wail or rage. But the wailing has all been done.
Perhaps tomorrow there will be new anguish. But something in me
is quiet tonight. I have already wrestled with all the devils I know.
Perhaps there are tears in me; perhaps they will flow tomorrow,
next week, next year. When will I let them out? Tonight I am calm.
I like this new pink gown, the quiet, the yellow walls, the images
of North Vietnamese women building a dike together. My friends
have been doing that. Birthdays cancelled. A state of emergency.
Top priority. They are all here; together or in shifts. Every hour
covered. The community rallied—a call an hour. "What can I do?"
"It's the network," Jane says.

*                    *                    *

With this network, she thinks, we can bring down the defense department.

*                    *                    *

Robert is afraid of my anger, that it will get me in trouble. Be careful, he urges, when you attack the Defense Department. "Oh," I wonder, "Will they want to arrest me too? Are they not satisfied with this subtle torture? What more could they want than this pound of flesh?"

*                    *                    *

I have to take chances somewhere. If somehow I am not to cry tonight, am to meet the enemy tomorrow calmly, even in good spirits? The condemned woman ate a hearty breakfast. ("Don't eat anything after midnight.") Somewhere there must be compensation for this moderation and calm, somewhere this proportion must be balanced. And I know where the crimes are committed. I do not know all the crimes and I have not fathomed my own complicity and my own negligence and my own inadequacy and my own errors and my own acts of violence against myself and all of these exist, nor have I accounted for all the traumas of life which are sustained in the struggle to live honestly. But I do know that in the outside world there is war, gratuitous, vicious, habitual, and cynical, a war against innocents. And you know who is waging it. You know.

*                    *                    *

Sleep comes. Uninvited it becomes another companion. Somehow to get through the night. Somehow to get through the morning. I give myself over to the doctors. They will institute paralysis, I am told. They will pass a tube down into my chest to breathe for me. Every gesture of control taken from me, even to my lungs, my breath; yet now I will sleep. This is my own sleep, without pills, without coercion. My own dreams. Or dreamlessness. My own remembering or forgetting. And tomorrow I will have to reckon with a new body. To learn how something can be cut away and remain. How will I manage? I do not know.

*          *          *

   She is going to tell another secret. You have heard it before. It is early morning. Barbara and Lee are asleep. Naomi is asleep. Sheila is asleep. Jane is asleep. Jane did not want to leave, they pretended that she could stay; they would both sleep in the narrow bed putting the rails up to keep them safe when they turned. Being here is like being a child. The bed like a crib. The orders. The lack of knowledge, of control. They have taken her power. And yet, they expect her to get well. Marc is asleep. Greg is asleep. Greg says he never dreams. Marc tells his dreams as long elaborate sagas. Chases. Hunts. Greg dreams of explosions. He is the one blown up. Robert is asleep. There are other names. But these are the important ones now. Odd that Robert is here, that one can come quickly into the heart and stay there. Some plants grow slowly and some spring immediately from the seed at the first rains. Corey is sleeping in New York. Susan Y. is sleeping in New York. Joe is sleeping in Boston. Alida is sleeping in New York. Candace is sleeping in Los Angeles. She is sleeping in my bed at home. She is Goldilocks and I'm pleased that she is with my two sleeping bears. Victor is sleeping in Santa Cruz. And there are others. There are seven who are most important now. The four women, the one man, the two bears. Even Coyote is sleeping, the poor dog whom I must warn whenever I leave, for otherwise he is bereft and sulky and, fearing loss, shits on the rug. Everyone is afraid of loss.
   Now they are asleep, but she knows in the morning they will be with her. Their thoughts will stream to her in a deep green light. She prepares to go to bed, to open herself to that light. She cannot even see the moon, but she will feel that light come into her. The doctor will assume he was the one who cured her. And why not? He is a fine man. A kind man. And skilled. But the truth is the deep healing comes from somewhere else. The healing does not occur in a moment, with a knife, but minute by minute, day by day, enacted through a green light.

*          *          *

TUESDAY, FEBRUARY 15, 1977

There are only a few hours until surgery. I can feel the anxiety mounting. "Are you ready?" the resident asks. What is ready? What does he mean by that? He means nothing profound. I mean only something profound. I wonder, am I ready? How will I incorporate these changes into my system. "Write something beautiful," Sheila says. She calls me "beautiful" on a daily basis, knowing I need to hear it, to allow myself to affirm something deep inside of me, to find the source of beauty and to know that it does not disappear under surgery.

I do not have a lover. The man I love is in New York; I may never be with him again. The man I loved will turn away, against his will, from my altered body. There is no way I will know if beauty will still reside in me.

While I was with Anais on one of the last days of her life, Rupert approached the bed to gently place a velvet bow in her hair. I dreamed him grieving on the beach after her death, while my old lover said "I'll never miss you in the daily life," then went about talking about his hair.

How flawed we are. How deep the culture is in us. How deep the fears, the self-doubts. We have all been raised in an enemy country. I have said this before. Living in exile without a land of our own.

Write something beautiful. Is this the time to write a story? To let the images take over? To give over. There are lessons in this— giving myself over even to anesthesia, relinquishing even a little power over my life—we have so little, yet somehow the desperate tension to control to control must be given up. Learning to float more than fly. "Surrender and transform simultaneously," Naomi says. But how? How?

*         *         *

A little story (I don't know where this will lead.): Once upon a time, once upon a time, once upon a time . . . A forest. Yes. Of course. A forest. And a stream of water. And thin saplings growing up from the water. Dense growth and dark green foliage that looks like shadow. Shiny hard leaves with razor edges and an underbrush of twigs and decaying leaves. Smells of dark organic growth. Renewal in the guise of decay. This is not home ground. This is not the place from which stories begin. This is the middle of the story. This is where she has come to. You know her. She. She. She.

Once upon a time a wise old woman named Crone lived at the entrance to the forest. Her job was weaving, weaving the roots of the trees into the earth, the branches into night sky. She held the sun in its white orbit with the orange threads she spun from fire. Corn was woven from the silk of her hair and life itself was the thread of her vision which she spun, twined, tied, knotted and cut . . . But the finest thread she spun, was the unraveling of her heart.

Once upon a time a woman found herself plunged into the middle of a story. The same woman who was so used to being in the beginning and assuming she would be there at the end. Setting out joyous and expectant of an adventure and found herself . . .

But there is a break . . . .

*          *          *

WEDNESDAY, FEBRUARY 16, 1977
Anesthesia, surgery. It is a new day. She is tired. And then . . .

*          *          *

THURSDAY, FEBRUARY 17, 1977
It is two days later.

*          *          *

She is wearing a pink gown with gypsy sleeves and shirring over her breast. Singular. On the other side there is a heavy bandage. The truth is she can feel the breast which has been removed. She can feel the flesh, the nipple, the shape and contour of it though it is gone. Gone. She has not looked yet. Today the surgeon will come and change the bandage and she will see that it is gone. But, in the meantime, she can feel the nipple soften and become erect. In the meantime, she is certain she has two breasts. She passes her soft hand over the bandages on her right side. Yes, it is there; she can feel the nipple respond.

They say she ought to remain here seven days. But the doctor has already told her she is one in a thousand. She was off the bed within hours and walking up and down the hall and moving furniture around—making this her house, her space. Something has altered and she is not sure of the process by which it happened. There was in her a great despair, a dark helium balloon of despair which said, "there is no time, there is no time," and she had wrestled with the dark angels and had looked with the finest scanning machine for all the hidden cancers in her soul and there was nothing nothing nothing she was unwilling to cut out—nothing she is unwilling to cut out because she is certain that what is lethal is not lethal for her alone and what life she brings to herself is not for herself alone and she has learned something deep in this experience for which she has no words, or which has already been put into words so many times to Naomi, Barbara, Sheila, Jane, Robert, Marc and Greg that there is no need to repeat them. Perhaps it would have been worthwhile to write them here—there is so much that could be here that is not recorded, yet there is an inkling here of what could be said. It is not details alone, it is an attitude which I wish to capture and pass on. This piece, of course, I do not write only for myself—I do not want to spare even you the dark night of the soul, the moments when the brutes and the shades of brutes emerge to strangle what life they find. But that is not new to you, you have been cowering in the corner afraid of confronting them for years. Okay, I point the finger. You and you and you. How much will you give away, my dears? They have your life, what else do you offer? After they take your tits, what will you bargain with? So I write this because I wish you to know, we are not as fragile as we think, soft as we are. We are not as fragile and even in our little cells even cut off from the light, isolated and pummeled by dark forces we hate and fear, we survive.

I don't see the moon anymore. Nor the sun. The sunrise happens elsewhere. My window looks onto another building, so I have to find the sun elsewhere. I believe in it instead.

*          *          *

FRIDAY, FEBRUARY 18, 1977

I come back to the page as hesitantly as a lover who has been away a long time. It has only been a few days but being deprived, even self-deprived of pencil and paper is like being in jail. There is not much that we need to survive, but what we need, we need. Needs cannot be negotiated.

I am flat as a boy on my right side. There is a horizontal scar running across my chest and on one side I am a boy and on the other I look like a girl. I am not Tieresias. That is not the division I am managing. Edith said once I had to reconcile myself to the man in me. And I dreamed of a young man who flew after he gave up a stone which he had used for ballast. Instead of holding the stone on his heart, he removed it, polished it, and placed it on a pile of glowing stones so much like fire he could watch it while he flew. I watched him fly with awe. I didn't know how to attain such flight. I didn't know how to trust my eyes. Now I will have to learn. This week they are supposed to put on another breast. Underneath the skin will be a young boy as underneath the skin is also a young girl. We have come to a reconciliation, he and I, she and I. A truce.

\*        \*        \*

A dream. While undressing before the mirror, I see my deformed breast sticking up at any angle as if the drainage disc were my breast. It is so ugly. Greg is in the room and I realize he has seen my body. Ashamed, I apologize. The breast is now down to my waist. Jane and Sheila are also present and I apologize to them as well. I can not hide my body even when I throw myself face down upon the bed. But the breast is only pinned on. As I unpin it, I see the nipple hanging on like a tag. And I see I'm flat . . .

As indeed I am.

\*        \*        \*

SATURDAY, FEBRUARY 19, 1977

The room fills up with flowers and music. Albert brings his guitar and Judy reads *Even Cowgirls Get the Blues* while Katya massages my body. "You took the pain and cancer in from Anais, out of your love for her," Katya says solemnly. "It sometimes happens to healers. We know how to take in and don't know how to let out." When I sat with Robert and his heart broke open under my hand the first time we truly met, I was not afraid of taking the pain into my body. I put my hand upon his heart like a poultice sucking the poisons out. But, as with rattlesnake venom, you must be prepared to spit.

\*     \*     \*

SUNDAY, FEBRUARY 20, 1977

Edith says this relates to Anais, something Anais couldn't finish, perhaps, and I am finishing. The risks of friendship. Is our story finished now that I saw my chest and didn't even think of weeping? I don't think this is a postponement of mourning. I think it is a recognition of the invisible. I can feel the nipple and the soft flesh when it is gone. I am told there are photos of leaves taken after they are cut in two where the entire leaf appears nevertheless. A hum of energy. Some things cannot be cut away though they appear to be severed. I do not think the issue is snipping and cutting. I think the issue is the flow again. What we allow to continue to move through us; what we take in; what we are willing to give out. Those of us who live as though we were dikes, dams, fortifications, and those of us who can think of ourselves as water.

\*     \*     \*

This is Anais' birthday. It is forty days since she died. The Tibetans say the soul wanders for forty days and then is reborn. Anais is dead. Or with me. I hear footsteps in the other room. She did not have such a heavy tread.

\*     \*     \*

TUESDAY, FEBRUARY 23, 1977

The woman is home and goes mad. Or tries. Or is wracked by changing moods. Did you think she was a saint?

It is a Wednesday afternoon. It is raining. The drought in Los Angeles has ended and we are in the throes of a premature spring. Judy brought a bouquet of spring flowers including sprigs of peach blossoms and daffodils. "The flowers are going to have to bloom twice," she said. Last year the apricot tree was similarly impatient and flowered like a peacock long before her time. There was no fruit. Tomorrow when the rain stops, I will go out and have a talk with that tree. She can have her blossoms early if she wishes to be intemperate, but this year she must give fruit.

At this moment the mood is good, a moment ago I raged. I sit at home and write, type at a desk for the first time in weeks. I am not in bed. I walk from room to room trying to remember how to live my life.

If you know how, don't tell. I have to find out for myself.

*         *         *

I write a letter. "Dear Audre: You asked me to keep in touch. I did through the ether. I lost a breast. Perhaps it is not so bad to look like an amazon. We are new kinds of warriors. There is no cancer in my lymph. My life sentence is not as short as it might have been. What I wrote in *Book of Hags* still stands. I am a survivor. I write to you briefly and in love. I knew you were with me all that time I was wrestling with the demons. I know you are with me now."

*         *         *

I remember more than I can record. I learn more than I can understand. In the spring, Meridel wrote a warning, "There is something lethal in you, cut it out." I hoped it was symbolic. I could see the lethal stone but I myself was not wise enough to cut it out with my vision. We can see into the flesh, but still we must use the knife. I think of Chile. I was a pacifist until now. Someday we will make the revolution without guns. We must move toward that transformation. But we are not entirely ready yet. Now I understand cutting out the Junta with a surgical knife, with radiation, with whatever weapons, guns are at hand. I do not have as many answers as before. At this moment, Meridel is in Arizona following the birds, that is what I wish to do at her age.

*         *         *

A friend called me on the phone and without knowing said, "Okay, Toots." No one has ever called me that before.

*         *         *

Toots Shore and Anais died within hours of each other. Shore had an obit on page one of the Times and Anais was confined to the back pages. Honor wrote a letter protesting, but Barbara said that when she was left out of a list of "mourners" after Ruth's death she was only affronted for a moment. She realized her grief was not for the newspapers.

She is not very displeased to have missed the memorial for Anais. The moment Anais died in Los Angeles, she fell in the snow-bound streets in New York. She mourns her in her own way. Their relationship was always private. No one, not even Rupert knew what they had together. Especially at the end. Let it be that way. At the memorial, Corita Kent said Anais had come to visit her. I was glad to hear that but I am not ready for that visit. I had wanted to pull the pain out of her but it was too great a task and there was too much distance between us and I didn't push enough and she didn't yield enough and I think in the end we were dis-appointed. Brugh also says I must examine my relationship to her. I called it "mysterious." I am still looking for the cause of this cancer. For what is blocked in me. For what was dammed up. For what did not flow. But I know I must start looking at other things. How I shall spend the day?

\*                    \*                    \*

WEDNESDAY, FEBRUARY 24, 1977

The moods wrack her. From one moment to the next, she doesn't know herself. This morning, everything is fine. I chat with Jane. Chirp, chirp. We are like two little sparrows. I try to meditate, talk with Naomi. Everything is fine. And then it falls apart. Now it is dark. It is so hard to mobilize these spirits and this health. I think it comes easily and then I lose them. This letter comes to you from Hell.

\*                    \*                    \*

I look at the wrinkled stitches under my arm, a poor seam my mother would scorn. "Cripple," I call out, "behold your scar." I put a chiffon blouse over a sweater. I learn to admire disguise.

\*                    \*                    \*

The telephone rings. This is better than prison. I have unlimited visiting hours, unlimited access to the canteen, unlimited telephone privileges.

                    *                    *                    *

When Gioia calls coincidentally from New York and hears the news, she says, "I was once close to death. I've never been the same. It was so many years ago. I feel my life more deeply, yet do not count on it. There is only the daily resurrection," Gioia says.

But resurrection is difficult. And what if there isn't strength for it? And what if the strength is a sham, or runs out? There is no unlimited supply. It is rationed, doled out by a miser, hoarded in basements and warehouses, perhaps it is not an item permitted to the poor like us. I am a fraud. I am no longer strong. Three days in hell between crucifixion and resurrection. Wasn't the crucifixion bad enough? No one discusses the three days in between. Do you think no one knows what it's like? Everyone knows. I know. I am not going to talk about it. It is so awful, if we looked it square in the face, we would go blind.

I would be pleased for blindness. I would be pleased not to be faced with the light. Give me darkness, and silence, put out the lights.

                    *                    *                    *

I would pack a suitcase and fly somewhere, or drive, if I could lift a suitcase. If I could pack. If I had something to wear. If I had somewhere to go. If I could drive. "Dear Mom, I've run away from home. I'll never come back. I'm afraid of the dark."

It is morning, it is always morning, it is always morning again. The days pass. I wonder if I will ever get up. Who will come and put a stick in my ass so I will stand straight?

So, I am the one people think is a miracle. Hah! So this pouting and cranky self is the one who's an inspiration. Am I the one who heals so fast because her spirit is good? Well, I'm a fraud. None of it is true. I haven't healed and I have nothing to say. Surrounded by everyone I love, I turn to Barbara and say, "I am an orphan. I have no family. I am a charity case."

\*                \*                \*

I was not surprised to find myself alone. I pound out my life on these keys. Words tell me I am not alone. Why else would I speak? For whom am I writing this? Letters arrive; I read them five times till the words are clear. I answer the phone, listening hard. Voices tell me I am not alone. The community of women insists I am not alone. What does that mean? I ask. How can I not be alone? I place my hand on my chest, stroke the twisting muscles that belong to a boy, massage the skin which is tender and tight. Bring my arm over my head stretching with pain. Watch the moon through the night, the leaves in the wind.

Screams in the middle of the night—okay, you bastards, you have gotten me down but you can not have my life.

\*                \*                \*

While the woman is mad, Toots is gone. She cannot find her anywhere. She has searched her suitcase three times, but Toots has not turned up. She slowly returns to work. She prepares food. She sits in the sun. But she has lost the thread. "I can't find my life," she screams. How shall she live her life?

This is recovery, this swing of moods. The phone rings, she wants silence. The phone is silent, she dials friends aimlessly. She works too hard. She returns to old habits, plunges into the thick file of letters and articles inscribed in broad red letters, "URGENT, Must be done immediately." She makes new commitments as a voice whispers, what you need now is rest and time, rest and time.

\*                \*                \*

THURSDAY, FEBRUARY 25, 1977

This is a new day. She begins a manifesto. She intends to document caring, to record each act of love or as many as are remembered, to be witness to the healing acts, spontaneous, cooperative and committed, consciousness and unconsciousness. This act of documentation, this book or journal or monograph, written by a woman privileged to receive such acts of love, this book, this record, by a witness who is myself and is also the beneficiary of this attention, is written to remember, decipher, communicate, in her community, that TREE was discovered applied, and found to be an active and effective principle of healing.

Unfortunately, I do not remember everything. And much occurred outside my vision.

Still if I could type with ten hands on five machines and record the minimum of five different sentences which rush through my brain at the same time—because what happened was so, is so extraordinary, is happening now, is continuing to happen—I would not do justice to the event. But, it is necessary that we recognize what occurred. Though it has happened to me, I am not hesitant or shy, not embarrassed to say, "Listen, this is significant."

*          *          *

The mood has changed. But then she does not account anymore for the change in moods. Blesses herself today. For today. Takes her emotional and physical pulse by the hour rather than by the week. How is it now? And now? Yesterday, do you remember, she was quite mad? Totally in the dark and wrestling with the demons. Overwhelmed. Screaming on the telephone to Susan B., "I'm ready to leave, I can't take it. It's too much." And Susan, the old friend, remember? Came by at midnight, afraid to leave her in such a state. But she could come to no harm in that state, she was so wracked and exhausted by tears and screaming and other's needs and demands that she hated the others, hated them all and wanted only silence, silence, silence and emptiness and freedom from everyone she knew. Everyone is gone. Detachment. Okay. That was yesterday.

*          *          *

And today. This fierce energy seizes her. She sits at the typewriter from morning to night and now it is close to midnight. She has a bottle of red wine to calm her down, but nothing calms, nothing quiets. She is alone. I am alone. This room is not unlike a cell. My face is hot. The blood is running in it from my fingers. What if I were in prison and not allowed a typewriter? Think of those who are in prison without paper or pencil. Think of those who have been so long without the sun they cannot feel their cheeks run red.

Jane says, "Don't drink the wine. Write through the night, find your own rhythms." Last night I thought, my book is too full of she saids and he saids, too full of all the others. "Where am I?" I thought. Last night I said, "Quiet, all of you. Shut up. I don't want to hear another thing." Last night I screamed so loud I couldn't hear anyone but myself.

But this morning, I was listening again. And happy. And I have been writing all day.

*              *              *

This evening I changed the title of this piece. In the beginning, it was called *Beginning Again*. But now I am more ambitious; I have changed the focus of the book and named it *TREE*. The family tree. The Tree of Life.

*              *              *

Maybe this is a mood and tomorrow I will be the mad woman screaming and crying and tearing my hair again. And even now, writing, I am afraid because of all the energy flowing in me and knowing that I do not know how to let it out. That is what I did not know in the beginning and that is what I may not yet know how to do. There are doors in me like there are doors in you and they are still shut despite this flood. The hands which did not go white, which did not shut down in New York, go white again, something in me clutches, closes off. It's nerves, I say. I have a right to nerves. But it may be more than that.

*              *              *

Jacquelyn says cancer is blocked energy like Renaud's disease which I had for years is blocked energy. Edith said cancer is too rapid growth without a means for expression, and she is right. It forces a rapid transformation of spirit if it is to be survived. And when I said, "Cancer is silence," they nodded; they knew I was right. How do I remember the river? There is someone I love I call Rio. Is it to remember flowing and tides?

*              *              *

Two days ago I made a tape with Barbara about TREE. And today looking for that tape I found another, a conversation accidentally recorded. And I hear my own voice a year ago, "When we contact that part of ourselves which has a vision, knows something different, makes art or imagination, is revolutionary, everything in the everyday world which is threatened or perplexed will act to stop it. And the ways are devious . . ."

Warnings? Perhaps. But I am not interested in warnings. I am not interested in discovering enemies. I want to know how to conquer them. I do not need to know how to surrender or evade.

                    *                    *                    *

Listen. There are changes I can make. For example, I can learn to conserve strength. When the phone call comes from San Diego requesting information, I say, "I cannot talk to you now." In the morning. I try to meditate. I give myself time. I write. There are things I do not do yet. I do not leave this typewriter to take a walk.

                    *                    *                    *

Sheila asks, "Do you give yourself healing time? meditating time? rest time?" Sheila is concerned, cried today in a public meeting. Allowed the tears to come for the first time. It is three weeks to the day that they have all heard "cancer." I do not wonder anymore if I will cry for them when they need it. I do not wonder if my heart has turned to stone. I heard my own tears, shrieks, finally yesterday but they were not only for myself, but for someone else. A little one, a child. So I know: We cry for each other. I do not believe I will ever develop a hard heart.

                    *                    *                    *

I have taken this night for myself. It is quiet in the house. My sons are out, the phone is off the hook. I listen to my own breath. How much time do I have? Six months? A year? A decade? Twenty? Forty? Forty is the right number. Forty years in the desert. Forty days of flood.

Every minute begins to count. Every typed word looms larger than it ought to. Every error feels like time lost. I do not know if

there is enough time. There is so much which has to be done. And
I am afraid.

It is not that time is rationed but that living is so very hard. To
speak is dangerous. To organize is dangerous. To build community
is dangerous. To condemn the brutes is dangerous. To live against
the legislated will is dangerous.

HISSSSSSSSSSSSS.

What if I can't survive this enemy? What if their power is
greater than our energy now? What if their fear is greater than we
know? What if we do not learn to utilize our strength? What if
words and TREE are not enough? I will not give up TREE. I will
not give up manufacturing words.

I will modulate my voice in order to be safe.

There is only so much we can be asked to modify, compromise,
or sacrifice. There is a point when the sacrifice necessary to exist
is the sacrifice of our own lives and we do not make that sacrifice
and our life is taken. It's another paradox.

Do you understand? I have friends who did not give names under
torture. I have friends who did not succumb when they were
against the wall. Their lives depended upon their stubbornness.
Do you understand? We cannot afford to cure our cancers at the
risk of our own lives.

You understand then, don't you, where we make our stand. For
Toots and TREE. And nothing less.


                          *                    *                   *


I don't think of pain, of wasting away. That is not on my mind
at all. I don't think about how my time may be lessened or limited.
There is so much to be done and I feel so healthy again, though I
never felt ill except for the time after surgery. The wonder that a
perfectly strong and resilient and energetic woman should suddenly be in a hospital, awakening from anaesthesia, unable to
move, to urinate, to walk. I have not thought about pain or that
my days might be numbered. I intend the years my father has.
Yet, I have lost a breast. And it was not taken by accident. The
lab reports said carcinoma, but they said nothing about causes.
The doctors know nothing about causes. They know how to cut and
sew. My mother is a seamstress.

                    *                    *                    *

Watch what you eat. Watch what you breathe. Avoid intolerable
stress and tension. Watch where you live. "A failure of the immun-
ological system," the doctor said. I translate: A sudden vulnerability. A weakness. Why not? I am not a soldier after all. I do not
raise my sons to be soldiers. Though they carry knives. But I do
not.

                    *                    *                    *

She has several questions that she is trying to answer. Where is
she responsible? That is—to take the burden of guilt away—where
and how can she defend herself in the future? What must be
altered? Where does she have power?
How much accident? Bad luck? Today I remember a chain letter
I ignored and the dire warnings in it. You see—how vulnerable
we are.

                    *                    *                    *

Everyone has these fears. My mother asked me to keep a thread
between my teeth whenever she sewed a garment while I was in
it. "I don't want to sew up your brains," my mother always said.
They put a tube between my teeth when they sewed up my breast
so I could breathe.

                    *                    *                    *

FRIDAY, FEBRUARY 26, 1977
In the morning, the sun is shining. The blessed sun returns. I
want to go out and pick the kumquats which have ripened, but the
words call. Barbara says I am not like her father who, dying,
transformed, looked out of his hospital window, saying, "The sun
is shining; I have a cigar. Who could ask for more?" Barbara says
that when I was on edge, I needed other things to give me life.

                    *                    *                    *

"How did I know to take TREE in?" I asked her.

Just as I wonder how she knew, how Sheila knew, Robert, David F., Bert, Naomi, Jane, how the women in her community and in the Woman's Building where I taught—how they knew.

How did we learn about sending and receiving? After all those were not Hallmark cards they sent to heal me. Barbara says there are moments when we see the edge of the world, when we are pushed into a new vision by the sudden casual presence of the angel of death sitting crosslegged on the living room couch. And when we look up, we know he has been sitting there all along, holding a glass of wine like any other guest. And we reach out— we play the game of chess, with a concentration and ferocity we never knew we had.

*          *          *

There is something different here: TREE. It can heal us all. It is something women used to know and are coming to know again. TREE, not limited to women but loved by them, the preferred weapon. "Listen," I say, "this love is revolutionary," "Oh," Barbara says, "it is very old. The shamans knew it. The Navajo still have sings to cure the patient after the doctor has done the mechanical work." Suddenly I remember a curing mask I found in Mexico, two grotesque faces carved on one to be worn by the friend who stood before the sick one, telling obscene jokes and gossip until the disease exploded out of the body through laughter. It has been TREE; it has also been the journal, the out-pouring of words, the meditations, the searches and explorations in the self. It was the last bad energy which Hal found with his hands and plucked out, leaving me shaking as if the earthquake had come to my own heart, and words, words, words, long buried in me, released unwound, pulled out like we are taught to wind a tapeworm about a pencil. And the sun. Always the sun. Things going in and out. Like making love. Not only the healing rays coming into me, but love and words coming out of me. A two-way stream.

*          *          *

It's what we do for each other that heals.

*               *               *

SATURDAY, FEBRUARY 27, 1977

My strength is coming back. Jane and I drive through the desert,
watching the twisted cacti and bare earth as we engage in one of
our long talks. Last year we drove to Mexicali to release an illegal
alien from the jail maintained by immigration authorities. There
is always something which must be done, someone to be saved,
something to be salvaged, someone to be released.

*               *               *

My arms begins to ache. I have less strength than I think or want.
And I'm afraid the humor is gone. This piece was funny and then
I forgot to laugh for awhile. Sadness arrived. I suspected it might.
I predicted that I might go another route. And yesterday it was
madness. Rage. Loss of perspective. Pain. Howling in the night.
And in the early evening? In the morning? Rage. But in the early
evening. She danced. Alone in the house watching her form barely
reflected in the windowpane. Wondering as she was dancing that
she was dancing. Wondering as she was raising her shoulders,
flapping her wings, an exercise the doctor had ordered, a good one
because the shoulders raised as Robert's raise when he dances,
wondering that she was dancing. That she was alone in the house
and dancing. That she would dance again. Even when she was not
alone.

*               *               *

Oh, you know, it is the music she loves. The music of revolution
and Chile, of Peru and Cuba and Venezuela, and she remembers
as the music plays that there was a time she wasn't silent, there
was a time she could yell, there was a time she could open her
mouth and have a shout emerge and she had done it. The shout has
been set to music. She has said it in a foreign language, the tongue
she has promised herself she will learn this summer. What are
the secret words? *Bruja,* do you want to know? Do you know what
happens when such secret words are spoken? All her life told not
to pronounce God's real name—keeping the power from her. But

these words she is not afraid to pronounce. She has shouted them in the company of hundreds and even of thousands and she knows their power. Listen, cock your head, I will whisper it in your ear so it will not frighten you at first—*el pueblo unido jamas sera vencido . . .*

Why do we shift like this? Why do we talk of revolution and of healing, of torture and of cancer, of fascism and disease?

\*                    \*                    \*

The sun floods in through my study window. Hello sun. And the music blasts through my ears. I have never written with music before. Hello Angel Parra, hello Violetta Parra, Hello Isabel Parra. Hello Victor Jara. Gracias A La Vida. Yes. *Gracias a la vida.*

But I am not going to sing you a little song now. No. I am going to tell you that I am singing, listening to music, but I am writing, that the words pour forth like song and I am going to record a conversation recorded for me. A voice from Europe. A message from Ariel. When you hear it you will understand more specifically, what TREE is.

TREE: Under certain conditions and in certain states not yet fully understood, love can be converted into beams of energy which when sent by one human being and received by another, sustain, nurture, protect, heal and cure.

TREE: Transformative and revolutionary love, created in one body and exerted toward another. Despite distance, proximity, danger, obstacles, ignorance, disease or aggression, TREE can keep that body from harm.

\*                    \*                    \*

If Xavier were here, he would say, "Copyright it. Patent it. Someone will steal it from you." Yes. Indeed. Please steal it. It heals. It works. And anyone who handles it is transformed.

\*                    \*                    \*

Did I tell you what the doctor said? He said, "In the history of my practice, no one has healed as quickly and well as you have."

I'm not a young chicken, you know, though I have been flapping
my wings. I'm forty. OK, it's not old. When I look in the mirror
I still see a young girl. Particularly today. Today I looked straight
in the mirror at my chest, taking the bandages off for the first time
to see my body as it is in reality, to see it for myself not only in
the doctor's office or in my mind, but in the mirror, examining
my reflection like an adolescent who watches her breasts begin
to break out of her flat chest. There was a soft fold, a swelling at
the base which is like the beginning of a breast, the first day of
a breast.

She learns the soft swelling is merely water, not milk. The doctor
takes it out with a needle. She is flat as a boy again.

*   *   *

"*Hola*, Deena," Ariel says. "*Te queremos mucho*. We love you.
We need you. We are with you." His voice comes over the telephone and onto a tape recorder which David played for me last
Monday night. I was just home from the hospital and the black
mood was sitting upon me like a dying crow, like my black hair.
And no one knowing. My usual cheer, a mask between myself
and hell. No one knowing, least of all myself. Yet nothing could
get in. I had all my Nike defense systems up, ready to repel any
ballistic missile, any TREE energy, any love force of healing. I was
in a cell locked in a bunker, in a bomb shelter, didn't anyone know?

Can't you let me out? I hear the voice. And I cry. But it is not
strong enough, the cry. I do not hear the voice yet. It is the voice
I need most to hear. I hear it. I don't hear it. It's Ariel.

*   *   *

I love Ariel because I love Ariel. And I love Ariel because I love
Chile. And it is Ariel whom I love because I love joy. And as I
write that, I want to write, as I love freedom and the revolution
and I think of Robert's dream and I think of the women I love
and our struggles and how everything is not so far away anymore.
And everything is coming together and being learned here even
in this poor body.

*   *   *

"You are truly called," Gloria wrote to me today," even in the
flesh." When I answered her, I wrote, "If I am part of some ex-
periment I do not understand, it has come to a good end because
I have learned something very important . . ." I was thinking about
TREE. Learned something important. Relearned. Remembered.
Recovered from ancient sources. Revalued. I was now the recipient,
not the sender and perhaps I could not recognize it fully, give it
its due before, when I was sending.

Four years ago, I considered it arrogant on my part to hope, to
assume, that I, I could—simply by loving—by paying attention—
by wanting—could . . .

across the miles—through buildings, across borders, through
barbed wire—could protect.

Could I—could we? It sounded like a fantasy of Superman,
Batman, Wonder Woman . . .

all the funnies.

Did we? How many have we saved?

*          *          *

You see this has to do with Ariel. And others. In 1973 we (surely
this has happened before), on September 11, 1973, we started, I
started, the sending, the directing of beams of love, focused, specific, intelligent, determined, transformative, revolutionary beams
of love (that is not all we did—that would not be enough). How
many did we save? I said the names over and over again. But I
don't want the credit. (It doesn't always work and there are no
guarantees. Still . . .) I want to set it down with the dispassionate
accuracy of someone who is writing a military report: At ten hundred hours, we set out in formation carrying four rifles, a bazooka,
food, telegraph, etc. . . . .

Every morning. At a hundred different times during the day.
Without stop. We sent. Dispatched. The light. We said the names
over and over again. All the names I knew. I want to tell you a
secret. I don't know how to account for it:

Everyone whose name I spoke is still alive.

*          *          *

So you see, we are on to something. You see Ariel has learned
this in the revolution and Naomi has learned it in the spirit and
Jane has learned it through friendship and I have learned it in my
body and Sheila has learned it through feminism and Barbara has
learned it from Indians, but it is the same force, the same force,
and we are just stumbling upon it again and not knowing how to
act or what to say or when we carry it or when it works. Some of
us know something. More women struggle for it, recognize it
quicker, consider it a possible alternative to a gun. And some of
us totally ignorant of the force we carry. Sometimes we have it
for only a moment. And then everything is ordinary again. And
some of us, sadly, who want it more than others, who struggle
for it, who think they have it, haven't got it yet. Maybe it is the
wanting, the ambition. Maybe it is hubris. Ego. I don't know.

\*                    \*                    \*

There were days when I was the battlefield and my body
wracked with all the different perspectives, but now watching
Naomi listen, I am a quiet meadow where the cows are grazing
and the shadows of clouds which appear in the sky to be different
are actually the shadows of the same rain and water which rises
and falls and combines into white elephants and monsters and
ribbons.

And we are sitting together, in the afternoon just minutes after
Maia, her daughter, informs me it has been two months since we
have seen each other, and we are listening to Ariel and he is saying:

\*                    \*                    \*

"What I have to say really is that we are taking care of you."
I hear him as earlier I didn't hear him. Now I really hear him.
I open my body to his voice. Little by little, it seeps in. I am dis-
armed. "That we are taking care of you just by living, just by being
with you. We are with you very very very near and deep within
you."

\*                    \*                    \*

The words embarrass me. But I put them down like a good student. They penetrate deeply, deeper than x-rays or ultra-sound or even the sun. They have been cleaned somehow. Cleaned in the struggle we have been in together. Cleaned in the revolution. Cleaned in running. Cleaned in fear. Cleaned in our reality, in our struggle. They are down to their bones. The bone of the magician's staff. The bone of the shaman. The bones of those who struggle together. And the flesh cut away so nothing is left but what we share together. Our common shapes.

*          *          *

"Oh gosh, Deena, we really do love you very, very much. *Le queremos mucho mucho.* . . . I was writing some stories which have to do with what we live, with the experience, with the fact that when you are against the wall, you use the wall to fight the enemy and not only to fight the enemy but to find out what you yourself are, to discover your own body, to discover your own soul and your own love and to find a hand which is next to you when you are against the wall, when they are shooting against you against the wall. And what is most important is that I discovered there, you and David very very deep inside me, you were among the people, perhaps the people who most in the world saw the joy and also the difficulties of life in Chile, then at that period. And do you know what I remember now? I remember now the trees, the first day we met, the light coming through the trees when we talked of the revolution. So that is what I can give you. I mean I can give you that and the stories and all our love and we can give you our love and we can just say that—nothing can happen to you at all. Nothing really can happen to you because you are so deep inside us and we love you so much and we need you so much and you are a witness to so much that we did and you helped us to do it just by existing and now that you have trouble, we have trouble, and we can destroy that trouble together, just by living, just by being the way we are, by being better people and loving more and loving each other more. *Nada mas,* Deena." . . . except there were more words, words in the language I am going to learn, which said, *"que vamos a ir juntos, prontos a Chile, al rio mopoche . . ,"* that we are going back—time is going to collapse—there are battles on every front and all of us are going to live to see them won.

*          *          *

That is the message from Ariel. We have had it from others, on the telephones, through feathers, colored rocks and telegrams, flowers and a thousand talismans and good wishes. It is not a commercial greeting card which heals us, but something new and unusual and also something ancient slipping onto the commercial paper, burning through on its way. It's like the blossoms I watch every day appearing in front of my window on the apricot tree. Despite the cold. (I warned you, tree.) They appear at first like little hard knots, stubs on the branches which turn red and then force their way up and out and open into pale, white, fresh blossoms, which fall leaving hard nubs of fruit.

*          *          *

Someday someone will isolate the frequency of love and build a machine to transmit it. Calling it Smith's Healing Rays, they will charge to beam it at our injured parts. And we may forget it was ours all the time. But for now, we call it TREE.

The fabricated TREE will not be as effective as what we can develop within ourselves. For TREE is individual, each person sending that love particular to her/his being and no computer can simulate the variety, tenderness and efficaciousness of the heart. TREE is particular, but it is also collective, not the act of one person, but of several, not exclusively an act of intimacy, but also of community. And TREE is not what we have associated with healing, the sucking into our own healthy bodies of a disease occupying another, but rather the loving saturation of the other body with the healing light originating in the heart.

We are all novices in this endeavor, have just learned the possibilities, that illness and even tyranny can be turned away with encounters with this beam. But we must learn how to use it with integrity, for otherwise it does not work. TREE can not be used without permission; there must be an agreement between the senders and receivers to cooperate. We can not invade each other, can enter only with permission. Here we must be most sensitive to the civil liberties of the psyche, and even in matters in love and grave concern, even in matters of life and death, we must not impose upon another in the body, psyche or heart without an invitation. But once accepted, we can begin.

\*                                \*                                \*

How is it that this woman, who happens to be myself, is being healed? There is one gift I think I have: The ability to recognize and appreciate TREE. I had an intuition it existed, was attentive to the love, believed in its existence, recognized the possibilities, saw it in a thousand forms in a thousand different persons, was/ is willing and able, it seems, to take it in.

And how did I encounter TREE? Sometimes in a circle, and sometimes from a distance. Sometimes the sender was with me, a hand in my hand. Then I noticed the sender was not depleted, went home sturdier. Sometimes we were not in each other's presence. Students chanted my name, fifty voices in unison, at a meeting some miles from my house. Sometimes the healer didn't know she was a healer, didn't know she carried TREE. Sometimes he was far away as Ariel who sent it long distance from Europe, or the sender was in New York like Robert, Corey and Susan. Sometimes, like Burke, he didn't even know he was involved in this messenger service. But he was. And is. And once it came in the form of little slippers woven out of grass which Tina brought remembering I had long ago said I liked them, by which I meant, her feet were beautiful wrapped in those grass slippers which are similar to those worn by the woman in the poster, the Vietnamese woman who is moving grain and soldiers down the river who resembles the other Vietnamese women who are building a dike together which is like the walls we are building in the Woman's Building, who work like my students work together, shifting bricks and singing. Making walls when there is nothing to make walls out of, making love when there is nothing to make love out of, making health when there is nothing to make health out of, but ourselves.

\*                                \*                                \*

I want to write a poem about TREE. I want to announce that it exists to the universe though they come to get me for it. I want to announce that it is healing my body and spirit.

\*                                \*                                \*

I will tell you a secret. Robert is warning me again to be quiet. But I have always believed that quiet kills, that cancer comes from silence. So I do not want to be my own executioner. If I am silenced, it will be imposed, not volitional. In the meantime, I am going to speak my mind. Though TREE is revolutionary and in its essence opposed to defense departments, we are obligated to use it, with it we can restructure a world where it is possible to thrive.

*                    *                    *

The Secret: In the hospital I had a funny thought I had not had before. I was sitting on the bed typing and you may recall I was thinking about treason, but I didn't tell you specifically what was on my mind.

I was sitting on the bed and had a thought which shook me to my bowels. I was thinking about a little woman named Ethel Rosenberg who was, in my mind, like a *bubie* to me, recalling that all my life I had been certain that Ethel had not stolen any secrets. Because, you know, Ethel didn't steal any. And all my life, even as a kid, I was confident that Ethel wasn't a spy. It was a setup. The conspiracy was against her and against the people and Jews and communism. And Ethel and Julius were the ones they picked, but it could have been you or me. And that is why Robert warns me to "hush hush." And Barbara says, "there there." But this has to be said. It is very simple. Simple as this book which is written to you in sentences a child can read. It is a primer. Because coming back to life can be very simple. And I want everyone to know how to do it. And I want to write it as an ABC.

*                    *                    *

Robert noticed how often our books and poems failed to reach the very people with whom we wanted to talk. And I want this to get to you so I am trying to speak that language we use in common.

*                    *                    *

But I had this thought and it frightened me. She had this thought and it frightened her. And now her mother is waiting for her, patiently waiting to help her wash her hair because she cannot lift her arm yet, but she does not greet her mother, or her father, rather continues to type, desperately, to put it down, because she is afraid she will keep it a secret if she does not empty this now. So here it is.

Ethel didn't steal any secrets. Okay? Agreed.

But . . .

Would I steal them—would the woman steal them—if it were to return the stolen energy to those who owned it, to those who knew how to use it? Imagine for a moment if the Defense Department stole TREE (They can't, fortunately. It is a kind of energy which they can't handle, but if they could—just let your mind play with it), if the Defense Department confiscated or co-opted TREE and was even planning to convert it for profit or for strategic purposes into a cancer-making energy rather than a healing energy —would you steal it back?

*          *          *

. . . if they stole it, if they rationed it, or if they reversed the energy to harmful rays and were aiming it at women, at my sisters, at Barbara, or Sheila, or Jane or Naomi, if they intended the now destructive beam for men, my brothers, Ariel or Victor or Lee, or Robert or Marc or Greg, or Sharon who brought me peacock feathers as new eyes, or Paula who was so afraid of death she never lived without it and is now opening, opening, or Candace or Tina, or Burke, or David F. who is the most loyal, who watches over my life, or Corey who sent me a much needed paper elephant, or Audre who sent health without even knowing I was ill, or Gioia who called by intuitive coincidence, Susana, Louise who also writes about Ethel Rosenberg . . . I could go on. I have named names here. I will continue to name names so we will recognize each other. We are a family. We need to know it. Holly. Honor. Arlene. I could go on and on and on. I am afraid to leave anyone out.

I leave a space here. Write your name in. _____

I do not want to leave anyone out, because we need to know our network and kinship system. If any one of you were in danger— and we would all be in danger if they stole it or invented forces against it—I am asking you—whom do you think I would be loyal to? What is loyalty? Where is my country?

\*                      \*                      \*

I am naming it by naming the citizens. You. All of you to whom
I have loyalty, to whom I have always had loyalty, *"El Pueblo . . ."*
That is where loyalty is. It is not treason to take guns from the
enemy. It is not treason to take hold of TREE. I am trying to say
that I would love Ethel Rosenberg even if she had been a spy,
even if she had stolen bread to give us, even if—no, *because*—she
had tried to return to us what belonged to us. I would love her if
she did that. I love her though she didn't do that. She didn't because she didn't have the opportunity. I love her because she was
loyal to us. She was part of our family. She gave us what she could.

\*                      \*                      \*

Remember what Ariel says: We act even by being witnesses.
Alida says, "The loving witness is a force for health." We are the
hands against the wall for each other. When the bullets come. We
do not choose our battleground or which bullets come. Some of
us are on the firing line and some of us are hands and some of us
change places. No one is safe. Everyone is safe because we have
each other.

\*                      \*                      \*

I wanted to write a poem about TREE. And I think I did.

\*                      \*                      \*

TUESDAY, MARCH 2, 1977
    Mudslides. I am an ordinary woman. Afraid and overwhelmed.
I remember TREE. I am altered. Then I forget, slide back. Sometimes I think the changes will last forever. Sometimes I know
forever is today. I ask for more, knowing none of us can ask for
more.

\*                      \*                      \*

The woman is recovering. She is surviving. Yesterday, she
returned to work. It is now over three weeks ago that she learned

that she had cancer. And two weeks since it was cut out. And two weeks as well since her sons' father had a heart attack, Marc and Greg careening wildly between hospitals, both parents shot down and who was to stand by them? And it was only a few days ago that she had been wheeled into surgery to be "reconstructed" as they put it, to have a little sand castle breast (that is how she imagined it) erected upon her chest. Perhaps it was like filling a paper cup with mud, careful not to add too much water, but having it fluid enough to pour, and turning it upside down on the beach so the mud made a conical mound. Only it was on her chest and she was not going to have to worry about whether she was funny looking anymore, but only about life and death.

But you know, things don't work out as you think they will. She discovers that every day. She is neither in charge of this society nor of her own life. She may persist in giving orders, but life doesn't listen.

Recently she was wheeled into surgery again, her chest opened up once more with a knife and then "due to mechanical difficulties beyond our control," due to the failure of electricity, of generators, of autoclaves . . . There was to be no new breast for nine months at least and if the reconstruction were later to be attempted, it would be a long process, not instant as she had been promised, but painstakingly slow, requiring the careful stretching of the skin back to its former shape.

No sand castles today. And she was sewn up again and looked exactly as she had looked when she was wheeled in except now there was another fine row of stitches on her chest and a sadness in her.

*      *      *

And there's nothing to say and no one to say it to. The woman paces up and down in a cell and maybe she rattles the bars and yells, "Let me out of here." But no one answers. There is no one in charge. I ask you what crime has this woman committed? Is she not a political prisoner? What are the number of political prisoners in your town? And what is the motivation of such crimes? Ché said, "It may surprise you, but the revolutionary is motivated by great feelings of love."

\*                    \*                    \*

They had promised her a new breast just as good as the old one.
They had promised it, but they could not keep their promises.
She had promised herself to live till eighty years; she does not
know if she will keep that promise. When Barbara's friend, Ruth,
died, she had promised Barbara there would be no more losses,
she had said she would live a long time. She does not want to
leave Barbara alone. But she does not bank on promises.

\*                    \*                    \*

When Ariel called it was important because suddenly it was so
clear that he was protecting her from cancer as she had protected
him from the Junta and both were effective users of the weapon
they had in common. And it is not unlike the weapon the women
have preserved and that is why this is called a feminist manual.
It is the women who have carried this weapon all these years,
since the beginning of time. Barbara, maybe it began with shaman,
but there are few shamans left, and since then the women often
unconsciously have assumed the larger burden of carrying it in
their breasts. That is why it is a crime to cut off breasts. And we
must find somewhere else to hold it. I will always have a pouch
ready, between my legs, in the soft flesh in the inner cheek of my
mouth, in my elbow, in the foreshortened muscle in my arm, in
my heart—oh yes, especially the heart because the heart is the only
organ which is immune to cancer.

\*                    \*                    \*

Sharon sends me a little bit of poem, like a bit of a wall, but not
the kind of wall Ariel was talking about, not the kind of wall we
are up against with the bullets comnig at us, another kind of wall—
or as Sharon quotes Angela Davis, "Walls turned sideways are
bridges . . ." Hasn't the woman been talking about bridges for the
last two months? (This book is a bridge between us.) About bridges
between women and men, between the evolution and the revolution, between healing and politics, between my hand and yours,
between TREE and you, between . . .

                    *              *              *


She is thinking of the little bit of poem by Wallace Stevens that
I sent her.

> The hand between
> the candle and the wall
> grows large on the wall . . .
> It must be that the hand
> has a will to grow larger on the wall,
> To grow larger and heavier and stronger than
> The wall . . .

Of course, Sharon did not know consciously about Ariel's tape
when she sent that poem. Of course, Sharon did not know what
Ariel said about the hand we reach for when we are against the
wall. Of course, Sharon did not know that we have been writing
about building bridges.


                    *              *              *


WEDNESDAY, MARCH 3, 1977
She cries every morning when she gets dressed. She looks for
gathered blouses, bodices and tunics which will not display or
thrust her loss too visibly in the stranger's eye. Or in the eye of
the friend.


                    *              *              *


Oh listen, it is not the loss of an appendage, it is not the loss of a
bit of flesh we are mourning here. It is not only as Alice said, that
she had returned to a normal life except there were moments,
unexpected, which reminded her of loss, and she was flooded with
a sense of irretrievable, irrevocable loss. It is not that we are
mourning here. It is something about women. It is somehow an act
against all women that we are being witness to. But she had written
about this before.
   These are her own words:

> There have been three kinds of death essentially. Death by
> hunger, death by cancer and death by madness. Everyone
> who says it is a plot is executed or incarcerated or committed.

So there are four types of death essentially. Death by hunger. Death by cancer. Death by madness. And murder . . .

. . . You must understand that what is discussed here has to do initially only with women . . .

. . . I want to write about us so it will be remembered, the strong parts which act against the death and rape and madness.

"You've added rape," Arda says.

"Why not, since I am thinking about that, too, and making lists and gathering statistics. One out of three now dies of cancer, almost everyone I meet has been raped, five out of nine in my class last year had been institutionalized for madness. Rape. Cancer. Madness. Rape. Cancer . . ."

\*          \*          \*

How did I know all this a year ago?

\*          \*          \*

And why did I say in that book, "This is the book I would write if I were to die in a year."?

Look it's difficult to understand that a young woman can sit at a typewriter in a beautiful blouse gently gathered at the neck and simultaneously hide a wound upon her chest and write: "Listen, this wound is a political wound. I am a political prisoner. I am a soldier wounded in a war you didn't know we were fighting." And at the same time, she is somehow ashamed of her bandages, of the thin little strips of adhesive which hold the flesh together on an almost absolutely flat chest. But a soldier should not be ashamed that a bullet has struck her.

\*          \*          \*

Oh, the enemy is wise and strong, *brujas*. Not as wise as we are, but strong. And he strikes at that place which leaves us breathless and we cannot fight him alone.

And don't you see how it is starting, even here, how even here, the enemy is present, because this is supposed to be a book about Toots, about TREE, about living, about courage and it becomes a book about fear.

\*                    \*                    \*

I tell you this disease is not accidental. It is untimely and unexpected—but that is not it entirely. The important thing for all of us to know is that this disease is not accidental, this is not what is meant in the insurance policies as "an act of God." This disease is a consequence of deliberately enacted economic, political and social policies.

\*                    \*                    \*

But you know all about corruption and war and poverty. I want you to know as well that this is an act against women. That I suffer not in my body alone, not in my lonely self, but in my womanhood. That what has been taken is what I loved dearly, and is too often suppressed.

\*                    \*                    \*

This is not the same as the loss of a finger. This is not the same as an ordinary loss, though too often cancer follows loss. That there is often a death in the family, a terrible blow, a loss and then there is cancer.

But what loss did I suffer? Everyone close to me is still alive. Except Anais, who died the day after I discovered I had cancer. At exactly the same moment that Anais was placed into the ambulance in Los Angeles, I was walking down a New York street in a snowstorm and slipped and fell.

\*                    \*                    \*

"We have not had enough time together," Anais had said. She was so frail she could barely rise from the bed to drink. I held her hand and she whispered, "You are my sister," and cried a little. "You think I am brave, everyone thinks I am brave. I'm not brave." She was a tiny French gamin in the large bed. In a moment she fell asleep and then put up her arms still seemingly in sleep to kiss me. I barely heard her voice, "The body is so low. The spirit is high and the body can not keep up, falls lower, lower."

&ast;   &ast;   &ast;

A man ran out of a building and stood at the corner shouting commandingly while pointing his finger at two other men approaching, all strangers, "Pick that woman up."

And in a few hours everyone's fate was sealed. Anais was dead. And I was preparing for an ordeal. Even a trial.

&ast;   &ast;   &ast;

And fall into mourning again.

&ast;   &ast;   &ast;

SATURDAY, MARCH 5, 1977

I cannot stay too long in the dark. Sometimes I think, I will be here forever, but the moon comes up, or a little star casts enough light to see by. Not very much light is required. Even a candle will do in the darkest night if you put your hands around it. Barbara stays by me shouting even when I am deaf but never so deaf I cannot hear her.

"Listen," she demands, "I want you to remember you are alive. You are alive. That should fill you with joy. You are among us."

The woman leans back into the circle of arms which have kept her safe, feels the soft limbs against her back, allows herself to be rocked by all those arms. She is happy for a moment, she knows that no one has more than this moment, none of us have more than a while. Forty, eighty years is only a while. Whenever we die, it's today. Whenever we live, it's now. Anyway, at this moment, it is very clear that she is very much alive.

&ast;   &ast;   &ast;

SUNDAY, MARCH 20, 1977

Spring has come. Nothing has listened to me and my cautions. Three weeks too early, everything was in bloom. Not only the importunate apricot, but the peach and plum as well. The nectarine is comparatively cautious, beginning not with blossoms but hesitantly with leaves while the apple displays conservative tendencies.

It is still asleep. Well, you see how quickly I have changed my stance. If it wants to be Spring, well then let it be fully, exultantly Spring.

*             *             *

I wake before dawn, when it is still dark, to meet Holly to welcome spring. I push my arm straight up for the first time, and write a poem. Something in me lets go; something becomes less relentless. I have moved out of the surgeon's path. I am no longer thinking in simple terms of cause and effect, power and control. I have decided to unleash Toots, to let her gambole and roam, to follow where I can. I have had her on a tight rein, afraid to lose what I have gained. "To give your sheep or cow a large spacious meadow is the best way to control him," Suzuki said. The sheep is my life. Watch it run. Have you ever watched a cow run from close up? Did you observe the grace in those large awkward limbs? When you get close, you know the cow was invented by Picasso. Things are not as orderly, anywhere, as we think.

I have been trying to gain control. Have at moments behaved like the medical people, looking for simple actions to lead directly to clear results. But that is not a cure. Still, I did not simply give my body over to the doctors. I have not locked myself exclusively onto the path they designate. I don't think they have any complete notion of health. So, I get up before dawn, gather kumquats, heather and eggs, go to meet Spring as she enters, moving toward health.

*             *             *

Robert says the ice has melted in the New York rivers. The ice is melting under the bridges. We can see that what is between us is water, 98% of our bodies is water. What is between is what we are and what has to be bridged is ourselves. When we forget we are water, we are ashamed to cry.

*             *             *

Everything reminds me of silence, of telling secrets, of protest, of screams which have to be uttered. Sometimes the briefest conversation is seditious, anything which posits love is against the state.

\*        \*        \*

This is a book about silences written by a woman who never thought of herself as silent. "Too outspoken," everyone always says. "Impolitic. Intemperate." So now, despite contradictory consensus, I have to look for my silences, for the places where the energy is stopped. You see the task, don't you, the dialectic—looking for the public causes for disease but looking also, always, for our own complicity. Where even I have hesitated, have been stopped. Do you know why the police system is so relatively—mind you only relatively—mild here? It is because we are our own gestapo. We internalize the oppressor. We call privilege, law. We are the cops against our own selves. In the heart of almost everyone I know there's a hide-out, a power struggle, an ambush starring John Wayne, Dick Tracy and Daddy Warbucks. Smoke 'em out.

\*        \*        \*

When I ask the questions that relate to our health, you see immediately that they relate also to politics. Where and how do you stop your energy? Where and how and why do you inhibit your power? Where are you restricted by the society at large?

\*        \*        \*

She was lying on a table in the center of a circle of women and she was thinking that she didn't want to be there in that room not only because she was angry at being ill, but she knew how recently Anais had lain there in a similar circle while strangers held their hands over her heart, sending TREE. And Anais, had she known how to take it in? And now, she, did she know? She didn't know. She felt her body was like a shield. She was accosted by the cynic, the skeptic. Her eyes were closed. Everything shut down and then in a brief moment, but it was sufficient, probably when Edith stood over her, she felt her heart breathe. That is, it occurred to her, the heart was a valve, it opened and closed, she could breathe in and out with it. Someone was sending TREE. For a moment, she was embarrassed for needing it. Need. Need. Need. She had once heard Robert cry out, "Need." It reassured her. She allowed herself the need. She could feel her heart opening and closing, Edith standing above her and TREE entering her like a breath. She had always wanted only to be the sender, perhaps because she had wanted to be safe.

*    *    *

This is where I lose my way. This is the place of chaos and confusion. Is the cancer the result of trying to be the wounded physician, to share a condition in order to learn how to heal it? Or do I endure the disease out of unwillingness to be safe at any cost?

Barbara says a sacrifice has been made. Once in a poem for Holly, I wrote, "I believe in sacrifice."

"You have given up a breast for your life," Barbara says. Everywhere I look there are explanations and interpretations. Everyone is a sybil. I read the universe in tea leaves and the configurations of crows. Alida said, "Giving meaning to everything is a form of madness." But living without meaning is a form of madness too. I am a battleground, the muscles in my arm foreshortened in the struggle between the forces of light and darkness. There has to be a truce, a reconciliation, a transformation of both into another state. I have let the horses of the sun lead too often, have followed Apollo and his reason, instead of running with the Dionysian dark.

*    *    *

A combination of factors: Collusion with the enemy, hesitancy when I could have been braver, compromise when I could have avoided it, unwarranted genuflection toward authority out of ignorance, out of habit, out of fear. A combination of factors: Commitment to community, an audacity, hunger for experience, desire, a bodily need for intensity, a refusal to compromise. An allegiance to the woman in me, the woman knowledge, the woman song, the woman talk.

*    *    *

The rub between them perhaps. The difficulty of maintaining the balance. The fragility of skin and tissue. The enormity of the battle. The desire for encounter and victory. The need to survive.

*          *          *

In September, Connie gave me a flower sealed perfectly in glass, a dandelion turned white, ready for wishing upon. Her card said, "At forty I wish to help you say 'yes' to the consequences of your life."

So I say, "Yes," even now when I know the consequences. It is only a breast, after all, which I have lost in order to have my life. I have not lost my life. I will not, can not lose my life. I have had my life more in the last years than ever, more in the last year than ever, more since I was forty than ever, more in the last days than ever. More every day, than ever. So I cannot lose my life.

I reach for new openness. Nothing can be covered up again. Nothing can be masked or disguised. Under a silicone breast, a cancer can grow undetected. David F. reluctantly warns me, not wishing to increase my fears. Life conspires to keep me open to the elements. I refuse reconstruction. I claim my body, such as it has become, as my own.

*          *          *

When Elaine calls from North Carolina sending hugs in her dark warm voice, she says, "I could think of a dozen people so full of spleen you would think they would die of it."

Somehow it made me laugh, the trick that was played on them, as they walked around in their perfect but dead bodies thinking they were living their lives.

*          *          *

She was on the table, breathing in the energy from the surrounding women, thinking of Anais, of the moments they had spent hand in hand, Anais sleeping and this woman sitting by her watching her breathing, trying to pass her own energy into Anais' heart. The last time she saw Anais she tried to pull her hand away because it was chapped from wind and dishes and Anais' hand was so soft, she was afraid of bruising it. "In the end," Anais said at that moment, "it isn't the world that matters; it is always only a few people."

\*              \*              \*

Yes, a few people, a network, a cadre, but there are more than a few of us. We intertwine when necessary, the accident of the net we weave, Ariel will never meet Elaine but they are in the same battle. And each can depend on the other. When it became clear that the energy in each case, of healing, of revolution, of feminism, is energy, the same energy which comes from the heart, the path became clear.

\*              \*              \*

I will tell you a secret now which I had hesitated to tell before. I am going to let you read a piece of Gloria's letter. It is the part I looked at and turned away. I was not afraid so much of the effect on the ego, I was rather afraid of how it might push me too fast and too far. So I ask Gloria's permission to change a few words, directing the letter to all of us.

> What is most difficult about writing this letter is the knowledge that you have been where I am, seeking the words of comfort, and working to give Anais, as I would want to give you, the energy to recover quickly for all that you have yet to give us, and yet the space to experience your own pain and rebirth in your time and on your own terms . . . I remember your reading when you described putting your own dark-skinned hand next to the pale white hand of Anais' and saying, "Look, we are sisters," and I feel that if we could put all our psyches together in just that way, one might say, "Yes, look, we are sisters." There is no physical mutilation or suffering that can make us less identical . . . I know that you know the space out of which this letter is written.
>
> We have ventured to energize that great pain and to devote our lives to healing the suffering of our century that we are equally powerless to combat without the spiritual trailblazing that must be done.

\*              \*              \*

THURSDAY, APRIL 1, 1977

I write this at the end of the afternoon. Greg is curled up napping near the typewriter. My energy is good. My spirits more stable. In February, I learned I had cancer. In March, I recovered. Today is the first day of another month. A kind of nightmare is over. As I once wrote, "I am a survivor. We are all survivors."

\*                    \*                    \*

The wind whirls the trees around, but the blossoms persist. In a moment, I am going to go out and pick the kumquats, the largest harvest we have had yet. Small golden fruits which grow among thorns. Toots whirls her body through the house, whirls his body through the house, two wolf pups at my feet, like the poem that Bert sent, full of the ferocity and softness of the beasts we are.

Robert and I talked this morning when it was dawn in Los Angeles and the sun passing through the prism Barbara brought last week was casting Robert's messenger rainbows on the wall.

\*                    \*                    \*

SUNDAY, AUGUST 1, 1977

I am no longer afraid of mirrors where I see the sign of the amazon, the one who shoots arrows. There is a fine red line across my chest where a knife entered, but now a branch winds about the scar and travels from arm to heart. Green leaves cover the branch, grapes hang there and a bird appears. What grows in me now is vital and does not cause me harm. I think the bird is singing. When he finished his work, the tattooist drank a glass of wine with me. I have relinquished some of the scars. I have designed my chest with the care given to an illuminated manuscript. I am no longer ashamed to make love. In the night, a hand caressed my chest and once again I came to life. Love is a battle I can win. I have the body of a warrior who does not kill or wound. On the book of my body, I have permanently inscribed a tree.

\*                    \*                    \*

All the forms I know originate in the heart. The tree which grows in the heart depends on community. We cannot do anything alone. I am well because you take care of me. Ariel is also alive because we took care of him. A woman brought me a feather. When I caught her eye, she acknowledged it was a political act.

I am no longer ashamed of what I know, nor the scars I suffered to gain that knowledge. I am not afraid of the power which is in us. I am not afraid of the dawn, of being alone, of making love, of announcing myself as a part of the revolution.

*        *        *

And now I want you to join me in a little song . . .

# THE WOMAN
# WHO SLEPT WITH MEN
# TO TAKE THE WAR
# OUT OF THEM

Let no one tell me that silence gives consent,
because whoever is silent dissents.

> Maria Isabel Barrano,
> Maria Teresa Horta,
> Maria Velho da Costa,
> *The Three Marias: New Portuguese Letters,* 1975

Gonzalo came to life. War makes him feel alive.
He would love to be in a fight.

*The Diary of Anais Nin, Volume III,* 1969

Bang!     Bang!     You're dead.
Aaah!
I gotcha.     I gotcha.

. . . Eden subverted by outcast sons who prefer to
march off across the deserts of the world armed
with the jawbones of asses to being shut up in
safety, who march forth wearing boots and return
home on stretchers bleeding with the prodigal open
wound of the subtle whore Malinche, traitoress
mother who fucked the enemy that you and I, my
compatriots, might some day be born.

Carlos Fuentes
*Change of Skin*, 1967
(translated by Sam Hileman)

You want to know what was the most awful thing?
The disillusionment was the most awful thing—the
going off. The war wasn't. The war is what it has
to be. Did it surprise you to find out that war is
horrible? The only surprising thing was the going
off. To find out that the women are horrible—that
was the only surprising thing. That they can smile
and throw roses, that they can give up their men,
their children. . . . That was the surprise! That they
sent us—*sent* us! . . . No general could have made us
go if the women hadn't allowed us to be stacked on
the trains, if they had screamed that they would
never look at us again if we turned into murderers.

Lt. Andreas Latzko
*Men in War,* 1918.

ADA!

THE WOMAN. That was the beginning. The sound of a name. Nothing but a name. Then I thought a name must have a woman to it. But that came later. In the beginning, when I began writing, there was only the name. "Ada!" They call her and I hear the voices calling her before anything else. I do not even know whose voices they are. But also I do know them even as I know their breath. It is the same air we live on that they take into their bodies and make a name of. Ada. It is the breath exiting slowly from the body. That is the beginning. The different voices. The sound of her name. And the women calling her. The call is in my own heart. That is where I hear it. How else could I hear it? I have lived alone so many months.

ADA!

THE WITNESS. A woman walks down the main street of an occupied village to present herself at the General's door.

ADA!

THE NARRATOR. The Woman left her home and came to the North country to write and to find the silence of winter and a simplicity of living conjunct with snow and because she had come to be more afraid in the company of the world than in living alone. Still, though she cultivated solitude and visited regularly only with her Friend, it was as if she was never fully alone. She said she heard voices, and her task, it seemed, was to write them down, to record the voices she heard, and also her own.

THE WOMAN. And Ada's voice, as well, remember that.

THE NARRATOR. I didn't forget. I know all this. How do I know? I'm the Narrator. I know the whole story.

THE WOMAN. Only what I tell you. Only what I let you say.

THE NARRATOR. Do you know the whole story then?

THE WOMAN. Hardly. Ada knows more than I. I know nothing at all; I, more than anyone, am completely in the dark. I am not even a witness.

THE NARRATOR. Let me tell the story, then, as I can see before you and behind.

THE WOMAN. Do what you can.

THE NARRATOR. A story: Once there was a Woman who came to the North country to write. Here she spent the winter comfortable in her isolation broken by occasional visitors and the frequent company of her Friend.

THE WOMAN. Let me tell you a dream. I find myself in a formal garden where everything is made of marble, even the water cascading down white rocks is carved stone. Everything in the garden is white, even my breath, and the cold stone takes the heat of my body from me ever so gently. Ever so gently, I give it up. In this garden, death, a white flower, is growing, is the curve of an alabaster wave at the moment of breaking. My hands are extremely delicate and I move them over the swell of the water looking for the word which names it. And I can't find the word on the stone no matter how I look with my hands. And I try to read my palms. I look at my palms for the word. But my palms are also empty. My hands are white as the stone and there are no lines on them.

HER FRIEND. Is there more?

THE WOMAN. No. That is it. The dream. The garden. The dream is white. The garden is made of stone. My breath is limestone. My hands are cold. There are no lines on them.

HER FRIEND. And?

THE NARRATOR. And when she had awakened, there was a line in her mind left over from the dream, the writing on the wall perhaps. The handwriting. It said: THE WOMAN WHO SLEPT WITH MEN TO TAKE THE WAR OUT OF THEM.

HER FRIEND. And?

THE WOMAN. It frightens me.

HER FRIEND. Why?

THE WOMAN. I don't know how. I don't know how to take the war out of them.

HER FRIEND. But you know how to make love.

THE WOMAN. Yes. It isn't enough.

*             *             *

THE WITNESS. A woman walks down the street of an occupied village to present herself at the General's door.

ADA!

HER FRIEND. Who's Ada?

THE WOMAN. You hear her speaking, don't you?

HER FRIEND. No, I don't.

THE WOMAN. How can that be? I hear her so plainly, her voice is so distinct.

HER FRIEND. Who is she?

THE WOMAN. Ada is Ada. That's who she is. She's the one who goes to the General. She's the one who opposes him. There must be one like her in every war.

THE NARRATOR. Some miles from a small town in the North country, the Woman found a cabin on the grounds of a lodge that was closed for the winter. This lodge, or compound as it was called, once belonged to the Green Dragon Ladies at the turn of the century. The Ladies are long gone but it is rumored that one of them survives in the old age home in town. It amuses the Woman to think the cabin she lives in now was once a bordello.

When the lodge was rebuilt, the screen porch of the Woman's modest quarters was glassed in, restoring some of the earlier elegance.

THE WOMAN. No feather boas now. There's only a drying sprig of wild grass for plumage. And the roof leaks. So much for grace.

Grace was an old whore.

THE NARRATOR. Ssh. You don't know anything yet.

Against the cold, there is only a wood-burning stove.

ADA. Nothing defeats the winter.

THE WOMAN. Who said that?

THE WITNESS. Ada.

THE WOMAN. Ah! Has she come again? Is it still winter?

THE WITNESS. The occupation of the village coincides with the onset of a bitter winter.

THE WOMAN. Is there no end to it?

THE NARRATOR. Let me tell this: The Green Dragon Ladies placed this cabin directly under the redwood trees, so especially in winter, it sits mostly in the dark.

THE WOMAN. Well, they were dark women, weren't they?

THE NARRATOR. The cabin suited the Woman's needs perfectly. Far from town and company and distractions, it satisfied her desire to write and to be alone.

THE WOMAN. You go away to the woods to be alone. When you don't hear your friends' voices, you hear other voices. At first you say, "It is the squirrels I hear." Then you say, "My dreams are loud." Then you think you're mad. Then you spend your time eavesdropping. The voices hover about you, locked like flies in the circular air. I had forgotten one could overhear time. I assumed words once spoken died and dropped to the ground. Now I consider that all conversations are dormant spores waiting. I become aware of the indestructibility of matter, of the obdurate endurance of language. I come to know that everything, even that which was secretly whispered, remains, and that every unanswered question is

still to be answered. I remain puzzled by the terrible persistence of flesh.

ADA!

THE NARRATOR. During the long winter, what the Woman usually
called chaos differentiates itself.

THE WOMAN. Don't you know what a familiar is?

HER FRIEND. I thought you were writing a novel.

THE WOMAN. I am.

HER FRIEND. It looks like a play.

THE WOMAN. I know.

THE NARRATOR. Silence provides what is lost in the normal din. The
Woman comes to know possibilities as she comes to know
the trees: fir, pine, birch, redwood, sequoia, spruce, manza-
nita, madrone. Trees are not so difficult to distinguish, yet in
the past when she walked in the woods, she was ignorant
and blind. Now she is happy to be alone.

THE WOMAN. You can hardly call it being alone.

HER FRIEND. Where's your lover?

THE WOMAN. Away.

HER FRIEND. To the wars?

THE WOMAN. No.

HER FRIEND. And if he were?

THE WOMAN. I would have left him.

HER FRIEND. Is that all you know to do?

CHORUS. Ada!

THE NARRATOR. That is what the Woman has in the beginning. A
call. The sound of a woman's name before she knows the
woman, the sound of a woman's name being called in the
streets. The call.

THE WITNESS. Is it an invocation or is it a rebuke? Maybe it is merely the muffled clucking of tongues practiced by women hidden in black veils behind the night doors, who whisper the name of the woman who walks past their keyholes. And in this village, there isn't a single door which hasn't been opened by force. The call: "Ada." Or is it a warning?

On Sunday, Ada walks through the center of town.

There are no Sundays. Sundays have been cancelled. In a state of siege, of war, there are no days of rest. There is only the interminable waiting, which puts a man's stubble on the women's faces. The sign of the widow—a prohibition against cutting her hair. And there are no widow's walks.

THE WOMAN. Why do you walk the streets, Ada?

THE WITNESS. And Ada? Ada is what moves. The hens sit fixed in straw, the roosters dare not crow and shamefully peck in the shadows of the barn wall. There has been a general conscription of everything which is both masculine and alive.

CHORUS. ADA!

THE WOMAN. I can't bear the sound of it. That terrible calling like the baying of dogs caught on the wind. Have they found her scent and will they chase the only bitch in heat, tearing at her cunt until they find what makes her sweat, what makes her sweet?

CHORUS. ADA.

THE NARRATOR. And the Woman also calls her. She is not adding her voice to the others but using her voice as one who wonders out loud how a word sounds, opening the teeth and pressing the tongue down, but only momentarily, as the tongue must move toward the palate to seal the passage and then will open again. And in a whisper as long as her exhalation—

THE WOMAN. Ada.

THE WITNESS. Ada answers to no one.

THE WOMAN. Why does everyone talk at once?

THE NARRATOR. The cabin where the Woman is writing is small and easy to maintain and does not preoccupy her much and in winter there are few visitors to the adjacent lodge to distract her. This cold season stretches immoderately and shows no signs of diminishing. Nothing opposes it. The air is crisp and unimpeded, ideal for the carrying of signals.

When the Woman goes to town, someone always reminds her that she lives where the Green Dragon Ladies lived. Green Dragon because pleasure is not native here and must have been brought in from across the ocean. The inhabitants are certain the women were brought up the river which is itself a green dragon, a cold green fire licking at the roots of things.

The Woman learns it was the prostitutes who built the road. And she takes this knowledge as a gift and makes it part of her tradition. Recently, the state attempted, but failed, to take the road away from the lodge, claiming it as public property. But the land had been deeded to the Green Dragon Ladies almost eighty years before the Woman's arrival and they had created the road with their own labor. The right of way belonged exclusively to the compound and anyone who passed over it did so at the Ladies' express or implied invitation or at his own risk. The Ladies hadn't let the loggers who came at night, or the railroad builders, or the fishermen who came in season, help, not any of them, not in any way. As they cleared and graded the road themselves, they also decided who had access and who didn't and they could put up a "No Trespassing" sign whenever they wished. The prostitutes were businesswomen who managed their private incomes, had a highly developed sense of property, knew the value and cost of what belonged to them and treated it accordingly.

THE NARRATOR. It is told that the French following the Spanish into Mexico, cleared the hemp fields of all the stones in order to increase the yield. But afterwards the hemp had no strength. The resistance was only in that hemp which had pushed up out of the earth against the stones.

THE WITNESS. The General walks in the winter garden. The winter sun hits him on the shoulder and glances off. His stride is regular for someone so confined and when he stops and stands motionless, his legs spread into the absolute triangle of force. His shadow extends into the afternoon. Sunday. Outside this little winter garden, there are no longer any Sundays, but no one has apprised the General of this. And why inform him when he might, in spite, proclaim a perpetuity of Sundays? He may declare Sundays, but he can't annul winter. Not even the General can cancel winter.

The sky is gray and there are shadows. Long triangular shadows. A winter squirrel settles back into the trap. First it rests, then it tries to escape. Is it the foot which is caught or is it the entire body? Thick gray fur is not enough protection against the teeth of the trap. It nuzzles against the metal and then attempts once again to escape. It does not call to the other squirrels. A trap is so like an embrace. The pine tree blooms unintimidated by winter. Hundreds of triangular cones. Little seeds pressed into the base of the cone in skin-thin sockets, against the winter. If there will be an end to winter.

The squirrel calls to the others. A little cry only as of nuts rattling against each other. A little alarm. In that species even a little sound is heard as danger. Otherwise the sky is clear.

All soft creatures wait for the steel to soften. They do not comprehend the persistence of metal. The winter garden is silent. There is no one who speaks to the General. No animals come to the spring. There is no spring. The sun sits implacable, imperious, immovable. There is no spring this year.

CHORUS. Ada.

THE WITNESS. Not yet. It is not time for Ada. She has not yet arrived at the General's house. You do not yet consider her name. You do not think about her much. She is still living with the dead.

But Ada. aDa. AΔA. aΔa. Alpha Delta. Delta; something shaped like the capital. Especially the alluvial deposit at the mouth of the river. It is winter. The mud is thick and sluggish.

THE WOMAN. Why doesn't spring come, Ada? For God's sake, why doesn't spring come?

THE NARRATOR. There is only silence.

THE WOMAN. Ada, for God's sake, say something.

THE WITNESS. Less and less chatter. Every morning there are fewer squirrels. Which ones are caught in the trap, the males or the females? Does it matter? Yes, it matters which die immediately and which die lingeringly, which are killed and which die of longing.

ADA. It's all lies. It's all talk.

THE WITNESS. Night follows day but spring does not come. The General sleeps late on Sundays ignoring the state of metallic alarm, the clatter of metal, the continual chill. During a state of war, the weather is cruel.

The winter creature is soft against the trap. The winter creature does not become hard. The winter squirrel remains a squirrel. Even the General may not be able to alter his nature. In another tree another squirrel chatters. Little creatures have secret nests. They do not forget their songs. The females do not become doors.

Ada combs her long hair and ties a scarf about her head. Her body falls into a triangle, breast cones bearing little unused seeds. A delta full of frozen mud. A woman who says she never heard of spring. She is a woman who sleeps alone.

The General is not at ease in the garden. He is too exposed to the elements. He is not at ease in his sleep. Under a feather quilt, he stirs uncomfortably at the howl of each dog. The sheets wind about him and animals enter his dreams. Whenever he sets a dream trap, the little beasts escape. The dream squirrels raise their winter tails. The winter squirrel scampers freely across the dream garden eating the General's dream plums and white, white dream eggs. In the morning, the squirrel has escaped the trap. The General returns to his duties.

THE WOMAN. Stop it! Leave me in peace. Please, I am not interested in the General.

THE NARRATOR. The Woman stands in the center of the little room at the furthest point of the shadows of the dark trees and satisfied that her privacy is secure and no one is about to call her mad, talks aloud. When there are voices they must be acknowledged. It is more than politeness to be willing to respond in a conversational tone. It is absolutely necessary if one wishes access. Yet it is also necessary to be cautious. Not of the voices.

She stands in the center of the little room at the furthest point of the shadows of the dark trees and satisfied that her privacy is complete and no one is around to call her mad, cries out.

THE WOMAN. Ada!

THE NARRATOR. The Woman rises from her typewriter and speaks aloud to the empty room.

THE WOMAN. We are not talking to ghosts here. I know Ada by the way she walks and the dress she wears which is black and white but ought to be red.

And the General? What do I know about him? What everyone knows about generals. Let us say at the outset that he is not the worst of the species. If he were, even Ada would, I think, have used the available knife. There are times when such actions are necessary. Though they perpetuate the status quo and a primitive resort to violence, they provide time. I can't speak for Ada. The truth is, I barely understand her, but I assume—and I could be wrong—that she is not absolutely opposed to the use of summary execution for certain war criminals, even execution without trial and without mercy. I assume . . . How dare I assume anything about Ada, that she recognizes that certain crimes against us are so extreme, that certain individuals are so unconditionally opposed to our survival, that they must be eliminated though nothing else is altered in that act. An eye for an eye. Don't you agree, Ada?

The General? Is familiar. You know him as well as I do. He is a stock character in our lives. I don't propose to examine either his guilt or his crime here. All that is commonplace and known. This book is not about him.

Ada does not dwell upon any of this. She does not know what is coming. She is not an analyst of military affairs, nor is she intellectually preoccupied with the current ethics of the *politic real.*

THE WITNESS. Ada rises in the morning and does what she must.

A woman whose name is Ada walks down the street of an occupied village from the cemetery, passing her own house, to the General's house which she enters without a word, to lie down unashamed on his bed, She does this—

THE WOMAN. —with the full cognizance that she is committing a political act.

THE NARRATOR. A story: There is a woman. A man stands outside
her house with a gun. But she doesn't do anything. What is
the story of the woman who lives in the house while the man
is outside with a gun?

She says, "Get out from under the lamppost. If you are
going to carry a gun, do it in the dark."

THE WOMAN. I know that story.

HER FRIEND. How would you know it?

THE WOMAN. I know it very well. It began innocently enough. Little
white envelopes arriving in the mail. At first, I didn't know
whom they were from. I couldn't read his name and was confused by the glyph on the envelopes which he used as a
signature. It reminded me enough of Kilroy to know that he
had been in the war and had learned to leave that signature
on a tree as if the bombs weren't enough. Weren't there any
lovers then who could carve their names in a heart? I had
hoped there were messages that trees accepted and messages
that they refused. Why, I wondered, why would anyone want
to remind me of the war?

HER FRIEND. Because you're smug. Maybe you think it has nothing
to do with you.

THE WOMAN. The letters filled me with shame. There was nothing
in them which shamed me. Simply their presence. They were
fat, white, and uninvited and there was nothing I could do
to keep them out. They were unstoppable, marching through
my house, a thick column of white ants. And when I discovered finally who was writing them, then I was more

deeply ashamed. When something we do best turns awry, when someone to whom we've given some attention turns against us . . .

HER FRIEND. Had you loved him?

THE WOMAN. The way you love a child when he comes in shining one morning. The way you love a poem which comes to you by surprise. It was nothing personal.

I should have been suspicious in the beginning when the letters began coming, each with such intensity and each so confusing to me since I didn't know who had sent them. Yet, he clearly knew me quite well and thought about me a great deal. He said we had been intimate in our thoughts. He said I had probed his psyche with my eyes. He said I had entered him unannounced. He said I had committed indecencies with my mind. Sometimes he included poems but more often he wrote long confused harangues. Shell-shocked, I thought, always thinking of the war. But I had never known anyone who had been shell-shocked. It's not something I would have ignored in someone. Wounds of that nature never heal.

And each envelope had a return address and this little logo, the drawing of a long nose peering over a wall. And a warning. "You owe me," he wrote, "I'm going to get you for this." Was I supposed to answer him? The thought made me afraid. That's putting it mildly. I felt the chill of a perverse and misplaced affection under the grim threats and my heart receded into a hard burl. I hated to touch the envelopes in the mailbox, taking them out by the tips, then placing them with distaste on my desk. How could someone presume to know me so well when I could barely remember him? One afternoon, he had brought me a story to read. He rewrote it later and dedicated it to me. It was much improved. Did he want me to acknowledge him? If so, what was I to say? I didn't want to encourage him. Encourage him in what? "Don't talk to strangers," was my mother's most frequent warning. Traveling alone on the subway when I was eight, I sat immobilized as the man next to me spread a newspaper over both our laps and ran his fingers into my cunt. The story he pretended to read followed the American army advancing through France. I didn't know what to do. The map of Europe confronted me; crosses for the enemy and rising black arrows for our side.

I sent one letter back, marking it REFUSED in bold black letters. Afterwards I felt I had overreacted, could have, at least, used a normal pen instead of that obtrusive marking pen. REFUSED. Angry and dark. It didn't stop him. There was another letter in the mailbox several days later. I didn't dare send this one back and when I opened it, I found exactly what I had expected. One envelope inside another. A new letter and the old envelope unopened beside it. Next to my black marks was a baroque question mark in colored inks which he had turned cleverly into a heart.

Why? Indeed, why?

The letters pretended to be about me. Outrages about the kind of woman I was, always leading a man on and then unwilling to open my skirts. He said he asked me for something once and I had turned him down. But I couldn't remember what it might have been. He said I had had no right to refuse him, given that I had probed him so far. "Bitch," he clamored, "I'll expose you now. I'll tell them who you are."

Yet the letters were not about me at all. Nothing I recognized about myself. The image of a woman seen from far away blurred and indistinct. It could have been anyone he was talking about, the image of a woman seen through the telescopic sight of a gun, an image of someone seen from a great distance, her movements both clear and incomprehensible.

A single drop of water slides down from a leaf on a tree outside. It is so small and far away. It's a wonder that I see it. From here I can't tell if the tree is still wet or if that is the last of the morning falling away.

Maybe he was only a nuisance. I didn't read the letters. I read the letters. I tried to decipher what he wanted. He didn't want anything. He wanted everything. He didn't want anything I could give him. It was just the same as when we met, he sat hunched and silent and unresponsive across the table. He was an older man. Older than I was. He surprised me being there. I thought his words were written with a knife. There was so much blood in them.

Soon I could barely face the mailbox in the morning. It was stuffed with so many white envelopes there was no room for anything else. I would open the front door with apprehension, looking at the whiteness gaping out at me, the little funny man who was no longer a little funny man with his nose hanging down over the wall.

Then the telephone began ringing and there was no one there in the middle of the night. Not even a heavy breather. That would have been a relief. At least I could have given him something. But there was nothing. "Listen!" I would scream, "I'm going to report this; it is against the law." Perfect silence. I wrote him a note. I simply said "Stop." It was returned, "UNKNOWN AT THIS ADDRESS." I recognized his handwriting on the evelope.

In the morning, the mailbox exploded with white envelopes, the letters becoming more distraught and vituperative. "J'accuse," he wrote, "J'accuse." But of what? Of what? And in the night, the telephone calls. The phone ringing and then silent or sometimes he hung up just as I picked up the receiver, my sleep gone. "Listen," I shouted into the phone, "I know who you are." But there was only silence. The phone calls multiplied. The letters multiplied. Then he sent telegrams. "Watch out." I couldn't trace any of it. The police were disinterested. They said he was not doing me any legal harm.

One day he was standing outside my house. Smiling. A small man on a black motorcycle. I walked toward my car scarcely breathing, afraid he would come after me but he didn't move, except to follow me with his eyes. He didn't say anything. I was very frightened. When I returned, he was gone. The next day, he was there again. Once I got up the courage to ask him to leave, but he only smiled.

I've always wondered how an army advances. Is it in the width or the length? He had been a paratrooper. I remembered his description of being dropped down without announcement into the very heart of things, white frost descending into surprised sleep.

I've had many lovers who went to war.

HER FRIEND. It's hard to have one who didn't. There've been quite a few wars since we've been born. And some wars, they say, were rather hard to resist. That old friend of yours . . .

THE WOMAN. Oh, yes. He as well. He said it was—

A MAN. —because I wanted to test myself, to finish something, to discipline myself to the ultimate, that is why I joined. And to be completely other than myself. I joined the marines as a non-com. But I was too handsome and too smart and before I knew it I was an officer. Intelligence, of course.

THE WOMAN. I lifted my glass and gestured wtih what you might call a wry smile saying, "You are still handsome—"

A MAN. —and intelligent.

THE WOMAN. Was he warning me? He lifted his glass in return. His movements were precise. I would not have thought to call them military until then.

HER FRIEND. And you loved him?

THE WOMAN. Yes. But earlier. Twenty years ago.

HER FRIEND. And did you love him for a long time?

THE WOMAN. No, but for as long as he would let me.

HER FRIEND. And did it make a difference?

THE WOMAN. None.

HER FRIEND. When did he go into the service?

THE WOMAN. At the same time. Twenty years ago. You see my love made no difference at all.

*          *          *

LA MALINCHE. In the night you lie down. Your body is dark as earth. There is a river of blood flowing and you are the only dam. He says you are slim as a reed. He has loved thin Spanish women with delicate wrists and gold on their breasts. You are too thin, you think, you are too slight. The river flows on and you bend.

THE WOMAN. Malinche. La Malinche. Malintzi. What were your purposes? Did you plot in the night?

HER FRIEND. Do you know La Malinche's story?

THE WOMAN. It's all the same story. Nothing ever happens to women. Things only happen to women. Women rarely make anything happen. Isn't that what they say? What can they stop from happening?

I sit in a room at the typewriter and make something up. I go to the store and buy vegetables because I have no imagination for killing. Then I come home and shut the door. What is it that women do? Ada, for example.

HER FRIEND. Who is Ada?

THE WOMAN. Ada? She is the most important one. She is the woman who sleeps with the General to take the war out of him.

HER FRIEND. Oh, you mean this book isn't about yourself?

THE WOMAN. Hardly. I am not brave enough.

THE NARRATOR. From her window, the Woman watches a man and a woman, two rare winter visitors to the lodge seated on the lodge porch enjoying the winter sun. The Woman brings them into her book, accepts their presence as a gift, a sudden and appreciated thaw. The man is like a winter bird, precise and distinct against the snow. The woman is like the light, both at rest and moving.

THE WOMAN. A story: A woman was lying on her bed and thinking. You tear it up and begin again. A man was lying on his bed thinking. Or was he planning a war?

HER FRIEND. Is that all you know?

THE WOMAN. Someone passes by. Someone waves to me through the trees. I pull down the blinds. I have come here to be alone. There are far too many sounds in this room. I drink a glass of wine. And then I worry about it. Drinking in the afternoon. And while working! A woman drinking alone . . . No wonder she hears . . . No. I continue working. My efforts feel aimless. Still I think this may be the quality of life which is not premised on combat. Is it flaccid? I don't exercise enough. I don't exercise as much as my lover. But that isn't the point. I don't need my body so hard, so ready. I wanted to laugh when he said, pointing to the solar plexus, "Here, hit me, hit me here, with all your strength." This is off the mark. Many of my women friends exercise as much as men. And are in better shape. But the surface tension is different. He keeps his body in a state of preparedness and she, the one on the porch let's say, the one who is stretched out so indifferent to the entrance of the sun, she who is not so different from myself, she is made of a looser thread. There are certain cloths, certain tight fabrics you might even carry water in. She is not of that weave. The water flows through.

LA MALINCHE. I carried all the Spanish blood and all the Indian blood. I didn't spill a drop.

THE WOMAN. What is a story?

THE NARRATOR. A story is: Once upon a time there was a woman who lived in the shadow of a man who was trying to kill her and she took a gun and shot him.
     Then you put in all the details in between.

THE WOMAN. I see. Is it: Once upon a time there was a woman who lived in an occupied village and who, with deliberateness and forethought, after her husband was killed . . .

HER FRIEND. How can you write that? How can you possibly know about that?

THE NARRATOR. She shakes her dark head. Her voice is as dark as her hair.

THE WOMAN. I know that. I have lost people, not to war perhaps, and not to murder. Nevertheless: Once upon a time there was a woman who lived in an occupied village . . .

HER FRIEND. How do you know what that is? How can you even presume to know?

CHORUS. Every country is an occupied country.

THE WOMAN. That's not true.

CHORUS. Every country is an occupied country. Every woman is an occupied territory. Every woman knows the enemy. Every woman who sleeps with a man sleeps with the general.

THE WOMAN. It's not true.

CHORUS. You know it's true. You've volunteered for the enemy's bed.

\*                 \*                 \*

THE NARRATOR. Tossing feebly in the hospital bed, the bars up—a fortress, a jail cell, the old woman can't tell which—is that first little boat going up the green river. "Where are we going, Pearl? Can you tell?" She tosses in the wet bed, scratches under her breasts, puts her old hands under her buttocks to change the weight.

GRACE. Where did you go, Pearl? Know what they think? I'm a camp follower. Was I? And why not? "Love's where you find it." Silly song. Pearl, you used to dream of going off. Where'd you go, Pearl? Not me. I stayed right here. I was my own woman. Got the pleasure I wanted, and paid for the trouble, thank you. My poor white little breasts. Need a proper corset. Nurse. Nurse! Can't leave them drooping like this. Gravity likes to pull everything down to itself. Hungry little bastard. My best customer was . . . which one? . . . I think it was Alf. Yes, it was the sheriff. He was reliable. And no one rushed me when he was around. We could sit and chat, having a glass of wine, after as well as before. Pearl. Did you really want your own house and everyone having to knock at the door and you not home to anyone except as it pleased you? You wanted Sunday every week, I remember, more than anything you wanted Sunday. You'd be happy here. There's a thousand damned Sundays in every month. And no one coming beside that damned hussy of a nurse saying, "Evening, Grace. How's tricks?"

THE WOMAN. Once upon a time there was a woman who lived in an occupied village.

HER FRIEND. How can you know what that is?

THE WOMAN. A village isn't different from a city, and if my house were not occupied, why do I live now in such retreat?

THE NARRATOR. She sometimes hears things she thinks she hasn't heard. It isn't exactly the voice of the tree, but it is not far from it. She can not speak the language of the bird. Yet. But she speaks some language not spoken in these parts. Otherwise how explain how odd she is? She has not lived in this part of the country for a long time. She has not learned to walk for days without getting lost. She has been afraid to sleep under the trees alone.

HER FRIEND. I told you, you're too sophisticated.

THE WOMAN. I can imagine what it's like to be someone else.

THE WITNESS. A woman was living in an occupied village and one morning, she got up and went to the Commandante.

HER FRIEND. What do you mean? To the Chief of Police? To a senator? To the President of the United States? Where would you go?

THE WOMAN. Some of my friends say . . .

CHORUS. She simply goes to the man she loves.

THE WOMAN. Let me imagine it. If I were Ada, to whom could I go?

CHORUS. We are an occupied village, city, country. Yet you choose to live with the enemy even in the same house, in the same room, in the same bed, even in the smallest spaces.

THE WOMAN. I could go to the Chief of Police. But I think he would have to be a man who lives alone. A man who is not too ugly and who lives alone.

HER FRIEND. If he is married, why doesn't his wife do the job?

THE NARRATOR. And in the meantime, she pours herself a glass of wine and walks about the room in which she feels very safe. She says:

THE WOMAN. For me, it's a moot issue. I probably won't go to a general. I can always say there is no enemy here. I can say it isn't possible to make a change. I can say the circumstances aren't right. I can say we work differently here. I can say the writer uses other weapons. I can say it's an old technique and it doesn't work. It never has.
   But Ada, what of her? She says none of these things.

THE NARRATOR. The sun fades. The green is less green. The river is cold. In the rest home, Grace turns on her side, has bed sores and bad dreams.

The Woman foolishly sets weeds in water though this wild grass will survive better dry. This way it will rot, without water the grass will last forever. The evening stretches out into the dark and the green fern she picked yesterday wilts.

*         *         *

THE WITNESS. The woman who lived in an occupied village went to the General. She knocked at his door with the pretext of selling him eggs.

In the morning she washed herself and in the shower as the water fell on her she asked:

ADA. May I be like water. May I bend over rocks. May I not break. May I flow. May I endure.

If I die, may I go up and come down again, may I not be gone forever. May I find a secret hiding place under the earth. May I be a well. May I move under the feet and over the houses. May I be strong. May I be white. May I be pure.

THE WITNESS. And the water fell on her in great hot sheets and she soaped her long dark hair and piled it whitely on top of her head. The soap curled under her arm, in her groin, on all the covered places of her sex and then was rinsed away.

And she went to the house of the General and knocked at his door.

THE NARRATOR. The Woman thinks about La Malinche.

THE WOMAN. Maybe we all think of her during these times. Maybe we all think of the same things.

When we make love, he says to me:

THE LOVER. I want to fight with you. I want you to be strong and cruel. I don't want to know at the outset who will win.

THE WOMAN. Everything soft in me readies itself, receding into a hardening shell. We wrestle in the bed. It is an easy battle because he can and doesn't win. I say to him, "I want to cause you pain." He says:

THE LOVER. I wouldn't dream of that.

THE WOMAN. I tell him, "You have the choice." What do I mean?

Do I mean he can choose? Do I mean he will?
A mock fight. Yet, I love him.

CHORUS. Is that difficult?

THE WOMAN. Perhaps. What do you think?

CHORUS. We think it is more than difficult. We think it is danger-
ous. To you and to us. We think you will betray us. We
think when you will have to choose, you will choose him.
We think this is not the time for women to be with men.
We think it is more than difficult. We think it is dangerous.
To you. And also to us.

THE WOMAN. Is it that they fight? Or . . .
Is it how they fight and whom they fight and when they
fight and why they fight?

CHORUS. They fight; they fight; they are fight itself.

THE WOMAN. We were sitting in the garden, my lover, myself, some
friends, during an inconsequential rain. A man was telling a
story, and I envied him his ability to smoothly narrate events
from beginning to end. He was discussing a friend who
wanted to be a christ, by which the storyteller meant, the
man was trying to find a quick and useful death.
"That is not the way it has to be," I argued with him. The
rain was very fine, perhaps more of a mist beading delicately
on our hands.
"Christ is the one who must be killed," he insisted. "The
crucifixion is at the heart of it."
"Is that the heart of it?" I felt at odds. "The story has alter-
natives. The plot invites a variety of endings. Anything is
possible."
"He is betrayed and dies. To be reborn, he has to die. That
is the essential part. He is betrayed and dies!"
"And what if Christ had lived?"
"It wouldn't make a good story."
"And your friend?" He only shrugs.
Perhaps his friend is dead by now.
I think about La Malinche. About betrayal.

THE NARRATOR. In the late afternoon, the Woman stretches across
the bed, reading. To the author, it seems the successful con-

quest of Mexico resulted from the betrayal of Malintzi, the one they call La Malinche, the Indian girl who became Cortez's mistress and interpreter. She and twenty beautiful slaves sent to Cortez became the mothers of a new mixed race on the American continent.

THE WOMAN. Who protected you, Malintzi? When you were given as a gift, who taught you not to be the gift? Who accompanies you on that terrible march? Who holds your hand as you enter his bed?

LA MALINCHE. A scrofulous man and arthritic in the knees, bent over. Ugly. Vicious. Cruel.

THE WOMAN. Who betrayed you, Malintzi? What happened in your bed? What happened to your tongue, Malintzi, you who could speak the language of birds? Did you lose the cry of the eagles? Did you forget the whistle of the quetzal?

THE NARRATOR. And the *cacique*, the chief who gave her away, died at a ripe old age and with much honor and protection from Spain. He was one of the few that Cortez spared, since this man, at the least, had given up all his gold.

THE WOMAN. And your brothers . . . Why didn't they steal you away?
    They call you La Malinche. *La Chingada*. The slit. The open one. The traitor. The wound.

LA MALINCHE. Why was I sent? Why was I sent alone?

THE WOMAN. Who defends La Malinche now? Who defended her then? How lonely was her job in the bed?

LA MALINCHE. In the morning the gold of my breast is not enough. And in the morning the hills of my body do not suffice. And in the morning my blood is not red enough though when he enters for the first time it flows. But it does not make a river by itself. And these are the only weapons I have and the only tools I have ever been trained to use. The jaguar who comes in the night teaches me nothing. And the flowers of the floating gardens of Xochimilco are sweeter to him than the flowers I twist in my hair. And in the morning, he already knows this country which I am, and being an explorer, he decides to move on. With all my beauty, I could keep him motionless only for one day.

THE NARRATOR. A story: Once upon a time there was a woman . . . who took a gun and changed the world.
    Just fill in the details.

THE WOMAN. That's an old story. It doesn't work.

THE NARRATOR. A story: Once upon a time there was a woman. She changed the world without taking a gun.

THE WOMAN. How did she do it? I haven't the faintest idea how that might be done.
    If La Malinche had access to guns, how many guns would she need? A thousand guns and a thousand slave girls to fire them? Neither prayers nor jaguars nor eagles nor serpents nor fire ceremonies nor gods sufficed against Cortez. What could she do to stop him? And even if he had been killed, weren't there others to replace him? Countries of them, millions she couldn't even imagine, from worlds she never conceived of. They came on the wind. She could not make herself storm enough to destroy the ships, not even the moon could impede the continent which drifted inexorably toward her. And she was open. They passed right through her.

               *               *               *

THE NARRATOR. Once upon a time the moon gave a gift of a flute to a man on the condition that it be played continuously. The man played it without ever tiring, so beautiful was the music and so grateful was he for the task. And whoever heard him play, learned to sing and the song and flute accompanied them also in their labor. Those who worked to the flute's song never suffered the pain of their efforts; and the man did not tire either, for the song eased his labor as it eased others. And so he played and so the song lived and it traveled. And with this single flute, the air was filled with singing.
    One day a man came to the village who did not want to hear the flute, nor to learn to sing himself, but intended to take the flute back with him so as to increase the labor of those

who worked for him by diminishing their pain. It was not enough for him to bring back the song; he wanted to bring back the source of the song as well. He wanted its full power for himself.

Whatever the man offered, the flutist refused, shaking his head, the trill passing into his song, for he couldn't stop, though the gold coins clanked at his feet. The flutist continued playing but with great difficulty, for the shadow of the man was heavy upon him and the notes almost inutterable in the darkening night. And for the first time, the flutist faltered, and faltering, sighed, and sighing took a deep breath before playing again. Then the man demanded the flute again and lifting his knife as the flutist shook his head tremolo, struck with his knife and cut the flute out of the musician's hand.

Is the knife stronger than the song? Is there nothing to be done? Is the gift given without the means to preserve the gift? Or is it in the moment when the flutist sighs, in that slight pause, that everything is lost?

A friend told me:

THE MAN. In the last analysis, a threat is always between men. The threat is not the arena. It is not outside of them. It is between them. The last step. And, therefore, the most basic.

THE WOMAN. Have you noticed that those who fight wars tell war stories? And finally all the stories are war stories of a kind. And even this story is about the battle between a man and a woman. And so at the onset he has won.

\*        \*        \*

THE WITNESS. She goes to the General. She knocks at his door. In order to offer him eggs. It is in the morning. Her knuckles become red from knocking.

He hesitates a long time before answering, refusing to move the curtains to see who is there, for he thinks it is a woman's gesture to edge the cloth away unless it is done with a bayonet. But he is not going to be caught in that trap; he would laugh at himself if he ran for a rifle at the slightest irregularity. So he waits. Not liking to be surprised, as she is surprising him, nor to be interrupted, as she is interrupting him. He does not know who she is and she remains adamant, knocking, knocking each time as if it is the first time and renewing her bravery with that device. She says:

ADA.  I hear the villagers have refused to sell you eggs.

THE GENERAL.  And why would you bring me some?

THE WITNESS.  Naturally he is suspicious of her.

ADA.  Maybe I think you deserve worse than starving to death.

THE WOMAN.  Ada, I am afraid for you.

THE WITNESS.  She has a full laugh and she allows it to bellow from her. Her body shakes and she permits the full provocative trembling. The General hasn't heard laughter for a long time. And if it is nervousness that shakes her so, she keeps it in disguise.

ADA.  Do you know the story of Hansel and Gretel? Do you remember the witch? I like my victims fat.

CHORUS.  Ada. Do you know what a general is? This is no fairy tale.

THE WITNESS.  She stares at him appraisingly. There is no hint of fear in her. All of the nervous laughter has vanished and she smiles at him with her large mouth open, her wide teeth exposed.

ADA.  Let me see your finger. I want to know how thin you are.

THE WITNESS.  And while standing in the doorway, without asking her to come in and without moving himself over the threshold and without speaking and without consideration of any passersby, but staring at her, he slowly unbuttons his shirt and lets it slide to his waist and then to the floor. Perhaps if he were ugly she could not have gone through with it. The fact pains her, but that is how it is. She hopes her husband will understand. She believes the dead come back. And watch.
  She says:

ADA.  I will come back tonight.

THE WITNESS.  He offers to come to her instead but she refuses, stating:

ADA. I will come to you. This is my choice.

    I want everything that I do to be clear to those who are watching.

\*          \*          \*

THE NARRATOR. A radio news bulletin: A housewife is being held on charges of killing a rapist. This is the fourth such incident to come to national attention within the past two years.

THE WOMAN. So it is not enough, Malintzi, to learn to use the enemies' weapons, you must use them with cunning and disguise.

HER FRIEND. What are you thinking?

THE WOMAN. I am not as brave as Ada. I am not brave enough. I couldn't do it.

CHORUS. Couldn't you? You do it all the time.

THE WOMAN. He is the kindest . . .

CHORUS. Just so.

THE WOMAN. I came to this compound to be alone, but my lover drives up with me to help me set up in these woods. Before we reach the dark trees, the land is hot, ugly, and fast; and the highway spews open without a single curve. The ruined land bleats, is spread out like a dead sheep. What can be gathered from the hide is already gathered. This dry landskin stretches as far as the eye can see. The heat alone is a funeral for the stripped soil. My lover looks about him, thinks: Too much grazing; too little regard; this lady's old; this bit of earth is old and mean.

THE LOVER. Used up. There's nothing left.

THE WOMAN. It never amounted to much. I bet they did the best they could.

THE LOVER. Is that what you think?

THE WOMAN. It's what I think.

THE LOVER. You're wrong.

THE WOMAN. Well, that may be. It doesn't matter much.

THE LOVER. It matters. These things matter, how something's used.

THE WOMAN. His body's stiff. The muscles in his chest are tense. He leans against the car door, gray leached twist of desert wood.

THE LOVER. Let's fight.

THE WOMAN. I won't fight with you.

THE LOVER. Why not? Take any side you want. The day is made to fight, the heat is in it.

THE WOMAN. I want to fight. I do not want to fight. The anger weed is a quick flower, comes up after the fire, fertilized in the hot ash. Nothing prevents its spread. The spores catch in my throat. I say, "We should make love." It is a euphemism. He's full of battle; we'd rather kill.

THE NARRATOR. He wrestles her playfully to the ground.

Nails and teeth are small weapons not only for defense. Each invites the slap of the skin. They pummel each other at the hips, there is a retreat and an attack, one mounts the other, counterattack, the neck is offered and then they roll away. The blood is on the alert. No one deserts. The body screams. They fight to win and then they sleep.

Later he says:

THE LOVER. You did that to take the fight out of me. You were writing your book on my back.


THE WOMAN. La Malinche was not as fortunate as I. She says:

LA MALINCHE. *Ellos me casaron con Cortéz. Yo era joven. No tenía derecho a decir sí o nó. Ellos me entregaron a el como si fuera una gran ave maravillosa y cantante y domada.*

He was so ugly, I thought he was a god in strange disguise. Nothing in the jungle resembled him so much as jackals and the hairless dogs we used to warm our feet in Tenochtitlan. Before Cortez, I thought the gods were jaguars, eagles, were snakes of lethal beauty. I always thought the gods walked about with grace and that is how you recognized them.

My breasts hurt when I was pressed against his strange clothes. He wore something harder even than the necklaces my mother wore. There was no love in his crooked fingers as he opened me. He passed through all gates in the same twisted way. No one who thought of retaining a single nugget of gold was left alive. And those who gave all they had died also. I was spread-eagled before him, though the eagle is a sacred bird. But nothing held him back. He had no awe. He did not answer to the gods and the sun could not drink any of the blood he spilled. To him I was simply a gate and a thousand men walked through me.

And they, my brothers, gave me to him. As if I were a fruit picked in the garden to be exchanged in the marketplace. Or a flower for the table. As if I were a stone to be swept from the doorway. And in the end, I am remembered because he entered me. And no one asked if I wished to remain closed. The gate is not permitted to speak, never tells what it knows.

*          *          *

THE WITNESS. Ada sits at the edge of the bed. Weary. Weary she sits by the edge of the bed. Her entire body hanging heavy, the flesh pulling down off the bones toward the sheets as if she were sheets, wet sheets hanging on a line pulling down with the weight of water. And what is whipping her to go on? Flesh beginning to gather itself in wrinkles as it is filled with water; and water which must run downhill wants to regather itself in the earth pushing as if against mud, scales of mud, mud imbricated by the wind, by the push of water, folds upon folds; she is a fish, the scales of weariness push push one bit of flesh on another as mud is pushed, a delta forming in her body. Watch the water come down and push everything which it is not, before it. It layers in thick sweet muddy yellow layers. The flesh pulling down toward the sheets and beyond down to the very soil.

Her feet are bare on the rough wooden floor which she traverses with great care so as not to get splinters in her soft feet which are still soft. It is because she wears shoes. Heavy high-heeled red shoes. The kind flamenco dancers wear.

HER FRIEND. Was she ever a dancer?

THE WOMAN. If you like.

CHORUS. Ada!

ADA. Leave me alone.

CHORUS. If we are twelve women and one leaves the circle, then how many are we? Are we still twelve women and one woman out of the circle? Or are we diminshed?

ADA. If we are twelve women and one woman leaves the circle then how many are we? Are we still twelve women and one woman out of the circle? Or are we increased? Are we twelve women, and one woman outside the circle, is she the thirteenth?

CHORUS. You diminish us.

ADA. You increase me. How could I fail to do likewise?

THE WITNESS. Perhaps it is . . .

ADA. Quiet. I want to tell this myself. I have my own voice and I am sick to death of intermediaries.

I lay in the bed with my head against his shoulder and his arms about me so that nothing, not even wind can enter and tear us apart. In those moments even the largest room must close. When we were under the stars, the sky bent down to complete the embrace. I did not have to close my eyes to make the world into a nest, night or morning. We crawled into this safety with each other.

When we leaped into the sexual sleep, the world contracted to a point and then exploded and we sped out to . . . I don't know . . . sometimes I was lost . . . farther than I had ever traveled, beyond the planets, perhaps to that place where they say the world speeds in order to return, the foam end of the universe where the invisible waves break and retreat back into the original sea.

THE WOMAN. Are you talking about the General?

ADA. Silence. Please. I told you, I have to tell you the story in my own way and in my own language because otherwise you can not hope to understand.

THE WOMAN. Do you understand it?

ADA. How can it be understood? But you may be able to piece it together. It will not lie on your heart as heavily as it lies on mine.

THE WOMAN. But, I must know: Are you talking about the General?

ADA. I am talking about the man I love.

THE WOMAN. I know, but, this is also my story. I must know. Is he . . .?

ADA. You make me angry, I begin to forget myself. Remembering is taking one little grain of sand and adding it to another in the quiet tedious task of bringing sand into some shape. I would have become a woman for you, not in a day as God made a body, but more slowly and with less confidence . . .

THE WOMAN. But . . .

ADA. All right. All right. But if I tell you, will you keep quiet afterwards? Don't you see that questions answered make their own story? Your story? This is my story. Later you can retell it, can make it your story. Or, you can say, this is how it happened to her. Nor is it to me alone that this occurred. But this is how I know it.

I know . . . please . . . don't interrupt. I'll tell you . . .

It wasn't the General. It was the man I loved. He's dead now. I took off my wedding ring when he died. It was green jade. I wanted jade because stone is older than metal. And looking into the ring, I could see what I thought were traces of life, the smoke of tiny old bones, the darker haze of reptilian breath.

He is dead now and buried. I buried his ring with a lock of my hair near his grave, though I was afraid to give him more power over me than he already had. I want the power of his life, not of his death. I don't like to meet his ghostly eyes in a corner of my room at night. He watches, I know. But I resist catching his eye. Yet, I do not look aside. If I am to be caught and dragged down, it will be by a familiar. I buried the ring two feet from his grave and at the same level as his coffin. It took me all night.

After the funeral I tell my sister I want to sleep in the house alone in order to test our bed and see how cold it has become. She stares at me with her terrible brown eyes which see everything and I hold her apart.

SISTER.  You must spend the night with me. Don't refuse. Or I'll stay with you if you wish. I'll sleep in the bed with you. On your side or, if you wish, on his. We can put a pillow between us to save you the surprise of a body touching you at night.

ADA.  To say goodnight, I move cautiously away from the circle of her arms. How deeply she wants to hold me and I have made her go home with that emptiness in her hands. But how can I relieve her when my own arms have the same burden and I can let nothing come into them because that is how I must now hold my love?

When she leaves, I take the ring from my finger and wrap it in a piece of hair cut from the base of my skull, from underneath so it will not show but where absentmindedly he used to rub his fingers, his elbow on the back of my chair, stroking so unthinkingly, he may have thought it was his own skin. When he pressed his fingers down my spine toward the shoulders, and I stretched my neck up and back in pleasure, he was surprised. We would often get lost in each other. I had given him my body as his own house.

THE WOMAN.  And did he give you his?

ADA.  Why do you persist?

THE WOMAN.  Did you have a child?

ADA.  No. Only the idea of a child. The thought that we could make a child held us for a long time.

THE WOMAN.  And then?

ADA.  And then he was dead.

THE WOMAN.  Did he give you his body, since he did not give you a child?

ADA.  There were gifts between us. He opened his body to me when he could. It was not his way. I came to understand our differences. But sometimes I lay wondering, what kind of creature is a man? What kind of creature am I? He died too soon. If I knew more, it would serve me better in what I must do. I would know what part is war and what part is man.

THE WOMAN.  Perhaps they are the same.

CHORUS.  Exactly!

ADA. Quiet. My life is difficult enough.

    I return to the cemetery at night. The grave is fresh and raw. I invite him home, but he does not stir. I scratch the grave to give him air to breathe. Lying down, I put my ear to the ground, but he does not speak. It's a cold bed. In time there will be grass, but now the covers seem too hastily pulled up as if to embed some shame. "Here's your gun," I slip it under the earth. "Perhaps you will have need of it." Maybe he stirs a little. Surely he wants me to keep it. I know how he thinks. "At the least hold on to it," he would say, "for me to use when I return." My sister had asked me for it, but I said it wasn't on him when they brought the body back. They had risked their lives to escape with him, not knowing how soon he would die. "One of his buddies took it," I lied.

THE WOMAN. Were you against him then?

ADA. No. I only wanted to know how it would be to do without. He said he had no choice, that guns were given to him like food. I wanted to impose the opposite on myself.

CHORUS. You only reimpose the woman's condition. We have always been without guns. What new can you learn from this?

ADA. I wanted to know what I could do with my bare hands.

THE WOMAN. What did you do?

ADA. I held them open. And at the end, the emptiness was neither greater nor smaller. On the six-month anniversary of his death, I put a stone on his grave. Because of the General, we couldn't be overt. It read, "He was a good man and loved his people." Even the General couldn't object to that. And everyone knows what that means. The grass had grown thick and his body was feeding the wildflowers. That night, I let my sister hold me in her arms and then she combed my hair and we slept together the first and only time since we were kids in the same bed.

THE WOMAN. And then?

ADA. And then I went to the General's house.

CHORUS. Ada!

THE NARRATOR. Before the Woman came up to the compound, she was living with her Lover and one night he asked her for a story.

THE WOMAN. The mermaid . . .

HER LOVER. The mermaid?

THE WOMAN. Yes, you asked, remember? The mermaid is the one who goes down, he watches how she sits on the rock and then she dives and he seeing her . . .

HER LOVER. Who?

THE WOMAN. The mermaid, I told you. You asked, remember?
    She's impatient, irritated, for she has already dived and is under water and he's fishing from the shore with a thread and a sharp hook and calling her back. But after she swallows it she always goes down—so far down he does not have enough lead, yet he doesn't want to follow her . . .

HER LOVER. Oh, the mermaid. Is it that story again?

THE WOMAN. Of course. You never listen. I must always start it again.

THE NARRATOR. It is difficult to go on. He is naked on the bed. The man's body is simple. She glides her hands over the skin and meets no scales. Everything is smooth. Is it like marble? The Woman is afraid of that stone.

HER LOVER. What are you looking for?

THE WOMAN. You.

HER LOVER. Hidden.

THE WOMAN. They say women are hidden.

HER LOVER. It is only a subterfuge. A device. You fire a shot in the other direction to confuse the enemy.

THE WOMAN. Everything between us is always couched in war images.

HER LOVER. No. It is not couched in war images. You would like to couch it. I embroil it in war images.

THE WOMAN. Would you embed it?

HER LOVER. Hardly. Enmesh. Enshroud. You, my dear, would embalm it.

THE WOMAN. I'd know you anywhere.

HER LOVER. You were telling me about the mermaid.

THE WOMAN. She . . .

HER LOVER. She?

THE WOMAN. She!

HER LOVER. Oh yes, you were telling me and I forgot.

THE WOMAN. Always.

HER LOVER. No. Not always. That's too simple. Most of the time. But not always. After all, we are here together.

THE WOMAN. I take a great risk.

HER LOVER. And I?

THE WOMAN. I'm not sure.

HER LOVER. I take a great risk as well.

THE WOMAN. Why then?

HER LOVER. I think I can survive it.

THE WOMAN. It?

HER LOVER. You.

THE WOMAN. And I?

HER LOVER. You are not so interested in such things. But go on. You were telling me a story about . . .

THE WOMAN. The mermaid. She dives quickly down into the dark
and he standing on the bank wonders if he can follow her
and there she speeds, her tail scaled with a thousand colors
flashing at him as he pounds the water and she makes a white
nest so that he can enter. He is afraid he can not breathe
under water and she is afraid she can not walk on land. She
is wondrous in her beauty, fast and lithe and full of those
colors which can only be seen in the dark, the phosphorescent
glints which carry their own light.

She gives him what he needs and he is afraid. Puts out her
watery arm and offers him a shell. The shell is closed and
the muscles seal it from within.

What do you do, my lover? Do you pull it apart? Or do you
enter the water and wait for it to open in its own time? What
if it resists? Do you, with persistence and determination, take
that knife from your pocket, the knife you've honed yourself,
to pass the most stringent test, and slide the blade into the
dark shell? What if it still resists? Can you wait for it to open?
The blade moves in, or the shell opens itself. Opens . . . I
have . . . you have . . . opened . . . so.

HER LOVER. You were telling me about the mermaid.

THE WOMAN. She is the color you dream about when you sleep
under the sea where the fish of the very deep glide through
your brain, cobalt blue and phosphorescent yellow, steel,
silver, gold, platinum, copper . . . And you sit on the bank
afraid that . . .

HER LOVER. . . . that you will not be able to mate.

THE WOMAN. That I will.

\*          \*          \*

THE WITNESS. Ada is weary. And wary. And the flesh is falling
toward the sheets. This is how we age too early, what wrinkles
are, a fullness which can not sustain what it holds and slides
down upon itself. She is not old, but the tired inner flesh
removes itself from the bone on a thousand invisible feet
and begins a descent to the earth.

She sleeps alone in the bed in the afternoon. During the day she is not afraid to sleep with her feet apart reaching from one side to the other and nothing encountered in between. Arms out and asleep on her back, her legs stretched open and only a thin sheet over her. The hairs on the labia moving out toward the thighs and her lips parted just enough for the breath and her eyes open or closed.

THE WOMAN. Oh, Ada, how tired you are.

THE WITNESS. The sheet is white and thin and pulls up in folds between her thighs like the arch of the theatre curtain pulled up from the stage. The curves fall heavy as her fingers pull at the cords. These shapes which water makes or heavy earth pushing toward a delta.

*          *          *

THE WOMAN. Well, Grace, one of your customers came by tonight. The lodge has been legit for years. He wasn't old, so maybe his grandfather told him stories and he came to find you, thought you'd live forever. What do you think, do I look like you? Does he think it's passed on in the genes? Or does he see every woman as a whore? Is everyone here fair game since your residency, Grace? Knocked on my door, opened it, walked in wanting a room, he said. I said the lodge was closed. The people out on the terrace this afternoon were gone. I don't resemble you at all, I don't think. I don't want to hear anyone knocking on my door. "All I want's a room," he said. "The lodge is closed," I said. "All I want's a room," he said. "The lodge is closed," I said. "All I want's a room," he said. "The lodge is closed," I said. He had lots of dollar bills in a big roll. I think he changed the tens to ones just so it would look thick. He started peeling them off. If you want a man so bad, Grace, why weren't you here? "How much is a room?" he asked. "If there was a room," I say, "it would be thirty bucks." "Too much," he says. "Here's fifteen." Drops them on the floor. "And fifteen more, I'll throw in when you warm the bed." "The lodge is closed," I say. "Well then," he says, "How's about fifteen just for the girl and we can make it right here on the floor?" Tell me, Grace, was his grandfather a friend of yours?

THE WOMAN. A story: A woman lives under the shadow of a gun and one day . . .

THE WITNESS. It is told that a woman who had lived alone for a year offered herself one day to the local army officer, to the general in command of her village.

THE GENERAL. What are you doing here?

ADA. Maybe I've decided to become a prostitute.

THE WITNESS. Ada is not a young woman, perhaps she is thirty. The village is a small village. Most of the men, including Ada's husband, were killed while fighting to keep the General's army from occupying their village.

Ada knocked at the General's door and when he opened it, she entered the house and they talked.

HER FRIEND. That's not what happened. That's a dream. A pipe dream!

THE WOMAN. They talked. This is what they said. This is what they would have said if they could talk. This is what was under their talk. This is what they couldn't say:

THE GENERAL. Since one of my men killed your husband, why do you give yourself to me?

ADA. I am not giving myself to you. You will pay for my services. In this way, I am no different from the woman who sells you cheese or the man who brings you wheat or uniforms. My chosen profession is just as honorable and is older. And anyway, a man is a man.

THE GENERAL. Do you think there are no differences?

ADA. I think there may be some differences. And ultimately none. Both you and my husband went to war.

THE GENERAL. He had no choice.

ADA. Yes, that is what is said. But, I wonder what your wife says when her friends ask why you are away so long. Doesn't she say, "He has no choice.?"

THE GENERAL. Yes, those are exactly the words we used to each other when I left. That is what I told her.

ADA. You see, there are fewer differences than one would expect.

HER FRIEND. And fewer differences, it seems, between you and Ada than I would expect. I can not tell you apart.

THE WOMAN. Perhaps she also tells stories. Perhaps she invokes the tradition of the hetaera. Perhaps she is Scheherazade.

HER FRIEND. And which story does she tell him?

ADA. Once there was a man who saw his own image in a pool of water and fell in love with it, spending long hours contemplating the reflection of his own face.

THE GENERAL. Oh yes, that story was taught to me as a warning against self-love. That man was Narcissus, wasn't he? He was so enchanted with his own image that trying to kiss it out of love, he drowned. Isn't that it?

THE WOMAN. We imagine that she laughs now, for to keep his attention she must twist the story.

THE WITNESS. Before she answered, Ada laughed heartily, a full-throated laugh which intrigued the General.

ADA. No, General, he was fatally attracted to the image and spent long hours contemplating the face he saw in the water, moving closer and closer to examine each feature, intrigued because he could find nothing which did not resemble himself and . . .

THE GENERAL. that was the source of his love.

ADA. No. That was the source of his contempt.

THE GENERAL. Why, then, did he move toward his reflection?

ADA. One day, filled with loathing and finding nothing in the reflection which was different from himself, he plunged through the image, breaking it as one breaks a glass, satisfied that it could never reconstitute itself. And so he died. Content.

THE GENERAL. And a flower grew where he had been.

ADA. Yes, and it did not resemble him in the least.

THE GENERAL. And what is the moral?

ADA. That you ought to have killed yourself instead of my husband.

THE GENERAL. And he likewise should have made an attempt on his own life rather than on mine.

Tell me, why have you come here? Is it because you believe there are differences between your husband and me? Or is it because it doesn't matter since there are none.

ADA. Because I must confirm a few.

THE GENERAL. And if you can't?

THE WOMAN. Then nothing will matter to me and I will probably make an attempt on your life. It is what you would do.

THE GENERAL. And if you find differences, if you find, let us say, that he was a good man and I am not?

ADA. I don't know what I'd do. Then certainly I would not like to become like you, to be a killer. Still it would be a pity to let you live when I am convinced of your evil.

THE GENERAL. Do you have any doubts?

ADA. I only wonder about my own frailties.

THE GENERAL. So what keeps me alive then?

ADA. The knowledge that I do not wish to come to resemble you . . . nor him. I don't think I am ready and willing to go to war.

THE GENERAL. So, I am protected by my evil and not my virtues.

ADA. But, General, you always knew it was your strength.

THE GENERAL. In the meantime, you will learn to be a courtesan.

HER FRIEND. It's very puzzling. Why would she want to learn to please someone who is so unlike her and who, in fact does her harm?

CHORUS. Indeed!

ADA. Indeed, it is odd that I am willing to learn to please you.

THE GENERAL. Did you please your husband?

ADA. He said I did but now I wonder about it all the time, since he resembled you so much.

THE GENERAL. So much?

ADA. Yes, so much. But not entirely. This is the puzzle, you see. I suspect the differences between you are very small and that, nevertheless, they matter. Yes. I suspect they matter very very much and that . . . ultimately . . . they matter not at all.

Once I saw a play about a German officer and a member of the French underground. The play was set some years after the war when the officer had retired to the French countryside. During the occupation, an entire village had been wiped out due to the officer's offhand command. Was the German a war criminal? After all, he had only given the orders; he hadn't actually held the gun. That's a small detail. Ultimately, he died—that is, he was executed by the partisans. But before he died, he asked the partisan, "Forgive me for what I did. Don't forgive the deed, but forgive me. We are both men," he said. "Forgive me." And in the play his wife mourned his death with grief equal to the grief of the partisan for his own massacred dead. I do not want to forgive the General. I don't think deaths are equal. I do not want to be witness to the equality of grief.

HER FRIEND. So, you don't think in essence all men are the same?

THE WOMAN. I don't know. After the play, though, I was ashamed of my refusal to accept the humanity of both men, still I insisted that the Nazi and the Partisan were different, that the Nazi had earned his death and a thousand cruel and painful deaths and the Partisan's family had not deserved theirs. I resented the dramatization of the German wife's grief. I could not bear her pain. I said the play was falsely sentimental and without morality and that the author could not distinguish one action from another.

HER FRIEND. Isn't there more to tell?

THE WOMAN. Yes, it's awful. The author said, "All men are alike, forgive them."

HER FRIEND. And you?

THE WOMAN. Sometimes in despair I also say all men are alike. But while I clearly see the difference between the actions of the Partisan and the German, ultimately, I may not be able to forgive either one.

THE GENERAL. Is it your thought that all men are alike which brings you here?

ADA. Yes. I must prove myself wrong.

THE GENERAL. What if there are no proofs, only enchantments? What if, in fact, I am Scheherazade and seduce you with my story? I can be very eloquent and I suspect your husband was not.

ADA. No. You are wrong. My husband was also eloquent. Men are always eloquent when they talk about war.

THE GENERAL. When I take you in my arms, what if you close your eyes, what if you forget yourself, what if it feels the same? Perhaps in such moments, I can be very tender, may even give you pleasure, may make you less lonely.

ADA. There is always that risk and it will give me great pain.

THE GENERAL. Will you allow it?

ADA. The fact is, I will allow almost anything to do what I must do. I'll bear the pleasure and the pain of that.

THE GENERAL. And what if in your loving, you convert me?

ADA. That is my purpose, still I wonder if it's possible.

THE GENERAL. Because?

ADA. Because you are a man.

THE GENERAL. So what?

HER FRIEND.  A general wouldn't ask that. Even ordinary men don't say such things about themselves.

THE WOMAN.  I wonder if they don't think it. If they don't in quiet and sorrow examine their lives and say it's a trifle, it's nothing, and it has caused so much pain.

HER FRIEND.  How you contradict yourself.

THE WOMAN.  I do, but Ada is steady. She knows what she knows. She does not resemble me at all.

HER FRIEND.  But she is . . .

THE WOMAN.  No, she is Ada. She is who she is. She is beyond me. Don't you understand? I long for her.

ADA.  Sometimes I doubt if I will succeed in converting you when you are the General who killed my husband and he was a good man.

THE GENERAL.  And you could not convert him,

ADA.  No, not with all my loving.

THE GENERAL.  Because he was a kind man?

ADA.  Yes, in part, because of that, and also I wouldn't leave him so defenseless.

THE GENERAL.  And what if you do succeed with me?

ADA.  I must, though it will be awful. If you change, I will have to let you live and you will escape the punishment you deserve and my husband will remain . . .

THE GENERAL.  Dead. Love did not convert your husband.

ADA.  He couldn't have lived if we had lost the war and he had failed to protect me or if he had refused to protect his comrades who were giving up their lives.

THE GENERAL.  But you say there is a choice. That they wanted to risk their lives because they love war. When your husband said, "I have to go, "what did you say?

ADA.  "I know," is what I said.

THE GENERAL.  So there are no differences. It's all a matter of love, of one kind or another.

ADA. Maybe I would like to learn that love. The love for the Widow Marina, for example, or my sister, the kind of love my husband had for his companions. But what has this conversation to do with that?

THE GENERAL. Indeed. Or your permitting me to put my hand on your thigh?

CHORUS. Indeed!

ADA. If he knew I were here . . .

THE GENERAL. He would want to die.

ADA. Again.

THE GENERAL. And when you pictured him holding a gun against my head and pulling the trigger deliberately and the bullet exiting and the brains splattering, though I was the enemy, did you also want to die?

ADA. I was relieved—and I wanted to die. And I couldn't ask him to live any other way.

THE GENERAL. In either case he died. Shall we say it was his choice?

ADA. Perhaps, even as I choose to come here. Yet, I may mean, I have no choice.

THE GENERAL. Do you admit that?

ADA. No. I want to be responsible for my actions.

THE GENERAL. Still you are compelled to come here. What in me attracts you?

ADA. It is more than attraction. Sometimes I think it is a bodily need.

THE GENERAL. Can't you control your needs, woman? Is all this moral philosophy, only sex? Can't you satisfy yourself?

HER FRIEND. He really is a general, isn't he? He is a general and a tribunal. He has all the power.

THE WOMAN. He has been well trained.

ADA. It is not a sexual need. I can control that. It is a need of the psyche. It is the attraction and insistence of the psyche. It is as if my nature itself insists that I confront this.

THE GENERAL. Then you have no choice.

ADA. Exactly. I have no choice.

THE GENERAL. In that way you are like a man.

ADA. I wonder. Sometimes I believe men can choose.

THE GENERAL. And that you can't? Do you believe that?

ADA. I am not interested in belief. I am interested in facts.

THE GENERAL. In facts?

ADA. Yes, in the facts of nature.

THE GENERAL. Are there such things? And are you at war with with nature then?

ADA. That is a terrible possibility.

THE GENERAL. And so you choose me to see if you can win that war—because I am the least likely?

ADA. And the most dispensable.

THE GENERAL. And if I don't fail you?

ADA. I will be successful.

THE GENERAL. And you will suffer.

ADA. I will suffer . . . but there will also be hope. And I will be able to say my husband and I fought the same battle with different weapons.

THE GENERAL. And will I always be your enemy?

ADA. Yes.

THE GENERAL. How is that possible when afterwards I will be someone else? You will have to sponsor me as your prize, a miraculous accomplishment.

ADA. That is what is awful.

THE GENERAL. And there is something else, even more terrible. To accomplish this you will have to let yourself love me. Not in advance alone, that's easy. It has a nobility to it. But afterwards. And differently.

ADA.  And if I don't?

THE GENERAL.  I think you must. Or else be Judith.

ADA.  I told you, I don't want to resemble you.

THE GENERAL.  There is Lysistrata . . .

ADA.  It wasn't love they practiced, but the withholding of love. And it didn't last long.

THE GENERAL.  Then there is no alternative: you will have to come to me with love.

          \*          \*          \*

THE NARRATOR.  The compound is lonely even with the voices. The winter is harsh and the Woman is not indifferent to the absence of her Lover. In the mornings, she writes, in the afternoons she takes long walks in the snowy woods. At night she eats the small meals she prepares without thought. If not for her Friend, she would have no comfort at all.

HER FRIEND.  Do you think we are all the same, that women are all the same in the way you sometimes think all men are the same?

THE WOMAN.  I like to think that women don't go to war.

THE NARRATOR.  The Woman has interrupted the reading of her book and her friend waits patiently. There is a long easy silence as exists between couples who have tested their love. Even together they can be alone.

THE WOMAN.  In the play, the German wife embraced her husband and even begged, ''Don't go,'' hoping her love would hold him. I knew it never would.

HER FRIEND.  Did you feel pity for her?

THE WOMAN.  I despised her.

HER FRIEND.  Because she was foolish?

THE WOMAN.  Because she was selfish and was not opposed to war, only the discomfort it caused her. And because—I am also ashamed of this—she humiliated me.

HER FRIEND. Because she wasn't effective? Because she couldn't hold him back?

THE WOMAN. Yes. She didn't know enough to hold him and she didn't know it didn't matter. None of it. Her love wasn't enough. He wanted to go to war. Love is momentary and war is endless. Men say it is full of possibility and even the preparations are totally absorbing to them.

   Love never matters enough. Men want to go to war. It is better than saying, "I remained behind for the sake of love."

HER FRIEND. Is it so personal then, your wound?


ADA. Isn't it generals who think love doesn't matter enough?

THE GENERAL. At the present, it appears love is limited and ineffective. Nothing comes of it.

ADA. That is why I am here rather than with my sisters.

THE GENERAL. Remaining with them, you will surely learn more about love than remaining with me.


THE WOMAN. I wonder if that is true. Do you learn it where it is easy or where it's hard, where it exists or where it's absent?

HER FRIEND. And where do you learn it?

THE WOMAN. Also here in the woods, alone.


ADA. That is true, but if I leave you, then it is possible that after you kill the few remaining men, you will have nothing to do and you will . . .

THE GENERAL. . . . kill the women?

ADA. Yes


HER FRIEND. So she goes to him to protect the village women?

THE WOMAN. They do not see it that way.

HER FRIEND. She's nothing but a distraction then, a decoy.

THE WOMAN.  When she's with him, there is less death.

HER FRIEND.  Then she is only buying time.

THE WOMAN.  That is also worthwhile.

HER FRIEND.  It doesn't change the scheme of things.

THE WOMAN.  No, but it is important to the living.

I want to tell you something. I do not forgive the General's deed, and don't think I can forgive him either. Even if Ada succeeds, I may not be able to forgive him.

HER FRIEND.  But will you forgive Ada? Will you forgive her everything?


CHORUS.  Must you go?

ADA.  I must.

CHORUS.  Don't.

ADA.  How will I live?

CHORUS.  We will help you.

ADA.  I know, but it is not so simple. It is not a matter of bread and butter.

CHORUS.  More like caviar and cream.

ADA.  It is not a matter of that.

CHORUS.  You are a creature of habits. Bad habits.

ADA.  I would like to think there are some principles . . .

CHORUS.  Is it so altruistic then your ''work''?

ADA.  And if it happens that I also sometimes forget myself and for a moment it happens . . . that I feel pleasure . . . so what?

CHORUS.  We were scattered and came together and the winds came and scattered us even further and again we came together.

So now when one separates herself from the stalk, it is as if we are scattered again and we lack the force to cleave together . . . So we beg you . . .

ADA.  To turn back. It is too late. And even so, I can not. It is not in my nature.

CHORUS. That is at issue.

ADA. I must do this.

CHORUS. Once we thought of doing it ourselves. It doesn't work.

ADA. You are lucky to be so certain.

CHORUS. Yours is the act of a weak woman.

ADA. No. It is making me strong.

CHORUS. Then you are already altered. You resemble him. You have become a warrior.

ADA. That is not easy to do.

CHORUS. Go your way then.

ADA. And you?

CHORUS. We remain here. And later? We do not know. Perhaps we will gather stones.

THE WOMAN. In the morning, the man is outside my window. In the afternoon he is gone. In the morning he reappears. In the afternoon he is gone again. He is steady as the sun. The letters keep coming steadily, as well. Nothing is acknowledged, as if he had nothing to do with them. He is so quiet; they are so vicious and wild. When I go out in the morning, he says nothing. I've made inquiries, and there is nothing I can do about his presence. He has a right to the street as long as he moves along. Every twenty minutes, I think that is what the police said, he must change position. They won't come to arrest him, saying loitering is not a serious crime.

One day, quite suddenly yet quietly, yes, suddenly and quietly . . .

THE NARRATOR. Suddenly and quietly the pattern is broken. One day the Woman goes out almost unconscious of the habits she has acquired, the involuntary shudder at the white bulge in the mailbox and the furtive glance across the street. She expects his presence by now. In a way, it is reassuring. Habits, finally, of no matter what nature, speak to the order of things. And a known discomfort can be an asset. Once we accommodate to it. Resilience. It is said that women have great resilience. She goes out, glances to the left, closes the door behind her with her left hand, looks across the street, and sees, suddenly and quietly the pattern has been broken.

The man is still there. Looking at her as he always does, he is unmoving and serene. Only this time, he is looking at her through the sight of a gun.

HER FRIEND. What did you do?

THE WOMAN. What do you expect? What any woman would do. I went to the police who said there was nothing they could do. It isn't illegal to hold a registered gun. And he had done me no visible harm. No scars on the body, you see. After the fact, they might do something. But not before. So I went to my lover. I said to him, "Well, love, this is your opportunity. You like fighting, don't you? Why don't you get a gun?"

HER FRIEND. Is that what you did?

THE WOMAN. I got a killer dog. Attack trained. It's what I did.

HER FRIEND. What did you really do?

THE WOMAN. A story: Once upon a time there was a woman who lived in the shadow of a man who was trying to kill her. She asked every man she met to kill him but they refused her because they claimed to have rejected violence. So she took a gun herself and shot him. Right between the eyes.

HER FRIEND. Please . . .

THE WOMAN. What do you want?

HER FRIEND. The truth.

THE WOMAN. The truth is: I went to my lover and said, "There is a man outside my window holding a gun." And he stroked my face so tenderly, ran his fingers down my dark hair. He held me in his arms and whispered to me,

HER LOVER. There is no danger there.

THE WOMAN. "Look," I said. "Look out the window." Maybe it wasn't morning anymore. Maybe it was afternoon. "Look," I said.
　　"No," he assured me, "There is no danger there."
　　But in the morning the man was there.
　　You get up in the morning and you drink a cup of coffee and that is normal enough. So you think you're safe. And then you open the door and go to your car and the man stands there smiling beatifically while you stare directly into his blue eye, only one eye, because the other eye is covered by the gunsight.

My lover held me so tenderly in the night and never took his arms away as if I were the egg, all naked heart beating yellow and red under his dark feathers.

HER FRIEND. And what happened?

THE WOMAN. Happened? Nothing ever happens to women. No, that isn't the way it goes. Women never make anything happen. I could make nothing happen. My lover said, stroking me,

HER LOVER. There is something in you, I don't know what it is, something even in your hands and in your skin—inexplicable, the softness of it, the darkness of it, the nudity of it . . .
Why do you think you bring out such violence in men?

HER FRIEND. What did you do finally?

THE WOMAN. You know what I did. I'm here, aren't I? I ran away.

THE WITNESS. She bends down and presses her foot into a red shoe. the heel is thick as a stump, four inches high, fat as a walking stick, heavy as a water pipe. She fastens the straps about the ankle and legs also thick, heavy, firm. She raises the other leg and bending down, picks up the other shoe, puts it on her other foot. And all the time she is sighing. Her body aches to lie down, aches to extend itself, aches to think out in the long stretch of rest. But the spinal column arranges itself above the hips and the neck bones straighten and the skull bones with their white blind smooth curves pull themselves up and forward like a long-necked beast, a giraffe, an ostrich, even a cobra, a creature with a forward-moving head, coiling or winding or bobbing, but directed ahead. There. Where? Forward. The chin rises and falls, she is riding, as on a horse, or rather, on a camel; the chin and then the chest and then the hips, wind, coil, undulate; she was trained to the camel dance and now the body doesn't rest but raises her, moves her across the desert, carrying the water with her. Look how she moves, the mouth open, the jaw loose, the tongue poised. In such a body, there is everything to be gained. She is practicing the full gait of desire.
And how many faces might these bones create? One skull, after all, is like another. Can you reconstruct the features of the one you love from that scaffolding? What animates this

face and body, what forms the flesh and causes it to extend itself out of such weariness and against all warnings?

And now she walks across the floor while her robe of black silk imprinted with a sprig of white bamboo aimlessly tied with a silk rope, falls open. She releases the belt; it falls to the floor. She does not pick it up yet, but moves, naked in her red shoes, toward a dress which is hanging on a hook. She puts the dress on. She bends down, retrieves the rope, hanging it up again. And the dress, white and black silk as well, slides down her body and covers her.

She says she wears black to remind her of death, white to remind her of life, and red to be cognizant always of blood, flowing and stilled, her husband, and her purpose. Now every action is reduced to a specific motion and characterized by a deliberate simplicity. So it will be easy to keep accounts.

What does this body look like? What does this woman look like? Who is to say? Couldn't these bones form another face? What moves her is not only intelligence, though she is intelligent, not only politics, though she is politic, not only principles, not only hunger, not only desire, though she wants, not only need, though she is needy. What moves with her now and yesterday and tomorrow is a heavy current which is like the ancient water which has absorbed into itself all leaves, fish, blood, death, sperm, rain, water as ancient as the womb's recycling water, water to feed the generations, old water pushing up through the earth.

"My shoes are always red," she thinks. She has only two pairs of shoes. Those for walking and every day use. And these. "And when I was born, I was covered with blood."

\*       \*       \*

GRACE. Slippers, damned ugly things. Quilted soles so I shouldn't slip, they say, as if they ever let me out of bed. Slippers. Snow shoes is what they are. Bed? Little gilded cage with tiny brass bars for the canary, little yellow winging bird just like you had, Pearl. Think I can sing? Or am I a blue parakeet like my blue eyes? Parrots from Venezuela. Took them in the shower because they liked the rain. Didn't have much to say. Like me. Repeat. Repeat. Nurse, let me out of her. Nurse. Nurse!

Bitch, doesn't ever come. Ugly slippers. Look at these feet,
pretty, except for the veins, of course. Alf said they were just
the tributaries to the river. "All the sweet water's running in
your little feet," he'd say, popping my toes in his mouth as
if to drink. I'd put them on the back of his thighs or cross
them just above his rump and press down. That brought a
nice warm river. Fur slippers and little pointed heels and
puffs of ostrich feathers. Rhinestones. Wouldn't walk on anyone's back unless they paid double and signed a paper first,
filed it up front, and only good if they hadn't had a drink yet.
Well, aren't I a pretty bird with this beak of a nose? And the
nurse won't bring me a powder puff. Says the bed gets dirty.
Shit in my pants to show her what dirt is. Or just take a
little pee, a teeny pee; yellow stream straight down the
sheets, just to show her. She doesn't like how my body
smells. She's all Johnson & Johnson and alcohol. Thinks I can
put baby powder on my nose. It's for your ass, my dear. She
likes alcohol a lot. I used to like Magnolia, didn't I, Pearl?
They could at least give me a mirror. All the birds Pearl kept
in the little cage had mirrors so they had someone to cheep
to. If there were someone here, I would show him my pretty
feet and ask him to bring me slippers from his next trip
round the world. Embroidered slippers like the kind the
women used to wear, oh, poor women with their bound feet,
folded back like little baby fists. Still so sweet the men who
came. We didn't allow any whips. No rough stuff. And when
they left—little lambs. Do you think the wives sent us a
basket at Christmas with a little homemade jam, for thanks?

The river, Pearl. The jays. How blue they were. Your poor
little birds lost their color staying indoors all day. But those
jays were a fierce blue. Look at these bird feet. Still pretty.
Remember the river, Pearl?

\*　　　　　\*　　　　　\*

ADA. Of course, I was tired, tired of death and tired of sleeping in
the cemetery and tired of the tomb which my bed had become, the sheets frozen. I never had to change them, simply
wiped the surface off as if they were marble.

THE WITNESS. Her own body now so cold had become like the stone angel on the church sepulcher protecting the dead.

ADA. And I would talk to him for hours, but all that answered was the grass that slowly covered the grave and the wildflowers which took hold where I had dropped seeds. I wanted the daisies to sweep over his grave in great white fires. My sister came and visited and I felt sorry for her. She would come into the house, hesitant but full of energy. Everytime she came she built a fire watching me from the corner of her eye as she carefully stacked the paper, chips, branches and logs. Warmth was in her nature. Her fires took immediately even without kerosene while mine always lagged and went out and finally I gave up as well. She built a fire the way someone else might build a house. The great architect of fire, I called her. I don't blame her; it was cold in my house.

SISTER. Will you eat something, my sweet?

ADA. I never wanted to eat anything. But she set the table anyway in that careful way she had of making everything beautiful no matter how poor we were. She would find linen napkins somewhere and put the plates on them. Maybe she took the napkins home and washed them and brought them back again. I never noticed except for a flare of color. Deep blue sometimes, wine red.

THE WITNESS. Ada spent hours in front of the empty fireplace or huddling on the porch. The entire year passed gray to beige. She bundled into a sweater in the winter and changed to a black cotton shirt when it became warmer. Then it was winter again. Old winter stretched out gray a long time. Sometimes she slept in her clothes, pulling the stone sheets up over her shoulders for warmth. When she went to the cemetery, she always wore her coat, in any season, because she didn't know how long she would stay.

ADA. I would have brought him something to eat, would have cooked some little meal he used to enjoy, leaving it to the side so he could reach up when I wasn't looking and pull it down if I had been another kind of woman. But I was not. If he was going to lie around underground, I wasn't going to do anything for him.

THE WOMAN. Did you love him?

ADA. Yes, I loved him.

THE WOMAN. I mean, did you still feel love for him after he died?

ADA. No. I didn't love him, I hated him. What difference does it make? I wanted something from him and I wasn't going to leave until I got it. He owed me something. He died too soon.

SISTER. Give it up, Ada. They all fight. It's how they are. Look at my sons, scrabbling in the dirt before they are three years old, tumbling and bumping against each other like dogs.

ADA. My sister had put me into a nightgown, turned down the blankets, banked the fire and locked the door behind her. Did she leave the light on thinking it might comfort me or was she unwilling to look back and think of me in the house dark as his grave? Whenever she came over, she turned on all the lights. Once she brought candles and seeing I didn't have any candlesticks, maybe someone took them or stored them, I don't keep track of anything, she turned over the egg cups and put the candles in those. Lit them all. And wouldn't let me blow them out. "Candles are for the dead," I told her. But she laughed and put another box of candles on the shelf, prominently displayed next to the little jar of olives she had brought—the artichokes, hot peppers, egg-plant, all the slippery, spicy things she knew I used to like. "You're kind to me," I managed to say.

SISTER. I wish you hated him.

ADA. In that moment she hated me as well for all the love she felt.

SISTER. They all make war. One starts and the other finishes. It's the only cooperation they know. Oh, yes, I hate the General, as well. He doesn't get any butter or milk from my cow. Yet, I wish you hated too, enough to let go of all this grief. One death's enough per family. We have fulfilled our quota. Until my sons are old enough. I hate to send them out to play. Every game rehearses death. If the General is still around, they'll try to kill him, won't they? Little heroes in their uncle's image. I'm glad their father didn't stay around too long. We might have had two deaths already. Better that he's dis-

appeared and drunk somewhere. Life was too difficult for
him. He couldn't work when the baby cried. He had delicate
ears, the musician. Where's your hate, Ada? Do you think
my husband's dead as well?

ADA. You think love can be put out like a candle with the pinch
of the thumb and forefinger. So. Pfft. Or with a bullet. Pfft.

THE WOMAN. But I thought you said . . . ?

ADA. I said I would tell this story in my way and in my own voice.
Nothing much changed in the year after my husband died.
The women said it was hard to live in the village without
men. Almost all the men were dead except for the very old
or the very young and the very few who had gone over to
the other side. The old one whose job it was to bring the milk
muttered:

MAN. What kind of man am I? I can no longer fight; all I can do
is refuse.

ADA. One village man watches me climb the General's gray stairs
thinking perhaps my body will come to him when the General tires of of me. He can not take his eyes off my red shoes.

THE WITNESS. Some system had been set up to care for Ada, but she
was oblivious to it. Maria brought her cheese, and her sister
left pots of cooked foods on the stove.

ADA. I don't remember what I ate that year. Once, I said I could
manage by myself, but my sister knew I wouldn't eat. She
murmured softly:

SISTER. I always wanted a girl child.

THE WOMAN. It's a long winter. In this early evening light I can still
see that the voices do not leave footprints in the snow. Once
again no one can come uninvited down the Ladies' road.
Is Ada a friend? I am afraid to ask that aloud. In the morning
when it is still dark, the roosters seem to call her name in
a long anguished crow.

ADA. In January it had been a year since he had died. Nothing had
changed except there had been grass on the grave for some
months and now it was bare again. Around me everything
seemed the same. My dead husband never spoke. Sometimes
he came into the house, and while he sat silently in a corner
our eyes never met. Once out of habit or pity, I made him a
cup of tea that turned cold, and I spilled it out.

A woman who kept cows was dead, shot in the mouth,
interrupted in the middle of a scream. Maybe the soldier had
asked her for the breast, but I think it was simply that she
refused him a pail of milk. And a young boy was beaten for
dangerous thoughts till his skin dissolved, and his mother,
Marina, was called "the Widow" from then on. If we hung
the dead like banners there would have been a flag for every
house. I kept a light on in the house at night so my sister
would not be afraid for me.

Once I walked to my sister's house to try to repay her the
care she had given me. She had asked me to come so many
times. But in the end I sat outside her door in the old chair
watching the flies buzz around the geraniums. She still had
flowers. I think it was defiance.

Even I couldn't avoid hearing the story of little Sophia.
She was playing outside by herself throwing pebbles into the
sand and then sweeping them up quickly in one little hand
while she bounced a rubber ball with the other. You know
the game: throw-two, throw-three, throw-four. The secret's
in the wrist and how quick the fingers are.

MAN. I want a glass of water—

ADA. —the soldier said, stooping down. Not looking up, Sophia said
her mother wasn't home. What's a soldier to a little girl who's
playing ball?

And so he took her by the hand, led her into the house and
lifted her up onto the sink so she could reach a glass in the
cupboard, and when she squatted down to get the water,
his fingers slipped between her legs, her belly to his mouth,
and so he held her. And since she was only five, he lifted her
like a doll, a sweet licking candy on his fingerstick, and lay
her on the bed and opened her wide, only the finger to ease
the way.

And that's how her mother found them. He jumped up angry to be interrupted but without a gun, he could only hit the woman with his fist and ran out pulling the little one with him, but her mother grabbed the other hand and somehow kept the child. She locked the door behind her, screaming, begging someone to burn the house down so they could both die.

THE WOMAN. I met a girl who was attacked when she could not refuse a man a drink of water. Rebecca at the well. She said she had the right to offer someone a glass of water. She said she had that right.

ADA. I went and sat on my husband's grave for a long time. In daylight this time so he could see me. And I said I had never betrayed him before. Anger stirred in me. I could feel it melting the ice, and winter dissolved just when, in fact, outside winter was coming. When I went home I began to sew a dress using the little bit of fabric left from before the war. Then I washed my hair and rubbed my body with oil, removed the hair from my legs and looked in a mirror again.

I didn't know where to begin or what to say. The dress was very pretty when I finished it, black and white, resembling my robe which is black with splashes of white bamboo making me think of spring and other countries where I imagine there is also a war or had been or will be.

THE WOMAN. Ada, is it too cold in your house to sleep?

THE WITNESS. Every night Ada gets up impatiently from the bed where she has learned to cling to one side. The cold of his absent body seeps into her bones. Nightgowns aren't made to keep out the ice and she feels the chill in the feathers of the dead geese.

THE WOMAN. What do you dream, Ada? What presses against your body in the early hours of the night?

THE WITNESS. The dreams escape her, lost dreams like a dead husband, something almost grasped, the entire body and mind engaged and the sensation remaining while the images fade until nothing is left except loss.

In the middle of every night she sets out in one of two

directions. One leads to the cemetery, and the other to the General's house.

And you talk to yourself, just as I do.

ADA. Of course. Who is around to mind? If I thought he were calling me I wouldn't resent getting up in the middle of the night and straggling out to the cemetery in this damned cold when he sleeps so comfortably and without interruption. Poor man, without a care in the world. The dead don't suffer insomnia.

THE WITNESS. As she walks, the curtains move slightly in all the houses she passes, so she is not surprised at the light in the last house. In an occupied village, everyone is always alert to movement and women are not ashamed to peek out into the street. They expect danger and surprise, but it is only Ada, and this agitated walk is familiar to them.

As she passes the last house, the door suddenly opens and Tina emerges without a sweater thrusting a bundle of wild winter flowers into her hand. "Take them with you," she says.

"Are they for Mikos? Or for Dimitri?" Ada asks. She has twice as many dead as she needs.

"It doesn't matter. Put them on your husband's grave, the one where you finally sleep."

ADA. How tired she looks from the struggle to stay alive. I've long since given it up. Don't I wish the grave will open tonight and pull me inside, don't I long for that bony white hand to reach up and offer a calcium shoulder to pull me down finally into a cold communal bed?

What do I do with these flowers so awkward in my hand? I've never brought him any of my own.

THE WITNESS. "I don't have time," Tina whispers. "I've hardly been to the cemetery. Once for Mikos and once for Dimitri and who has time even to cry. When the women came they cried for me because they're my friends. Now you do it. Mikos will hear you and know I have good intentions. If you like, though it's not necessary, go to his grave and tell him the concealed hens are laying, tell him the rooster is still strong and crows every morning. Tell him the sun comes up like it used to and there are eggs every morning just when it's light and the General won't ever find them."

\*     \*     \*

THE WITNESS. When Ada goes to the General's house, she brings him eggs. The villagers reluctantly supply most of his needs, only in the area of eggs they resist. "There aren't enough," one of the women says. "There is one for each child and no more. Your soldiers killed too many hens. Do you hear roosters in the morning? How many roosters do you hear? Not enough. And the remaining hens don't always lay." She rubs her fat baker's hands on her thighs. She is a woman who was raised on bread.

The General insists that eggs, after all, are not gold. He is not asking for horses. She shrugs, offers him a roll. She says he's lucky to have bread.

Ada goes to the hen house and sits with her hands under the body of the fat hen. It knows her now as the woman who throws grain when she leaves, but first sits there, feather on skin. Ada's hands are warm and softer than the roost. She does not move for long time. She thinks she can feel the chicken heart pulsing through her own fingers.

ADA. Let me be cold. Let me be dry. Let me be barren.

THE WITNESS. The egg is warm, falls into her hand from the chicken's soft underfeathers. Sometimes she sings a little song under her breath just for the sake of the little creature.

ADA. Little hen, little hen
May I take your egg?
You will have another
You will have another.

THE WITNESS. If I had a child, she thinks, I would like it to be born like this, in such a shell.

ADA. I imagine it is as easy for you to lay an egg as it was for me to hold a man. After my husband and I made love, I didn't move. Yet sometimes he slipped out of my body, so. I always waited for him to stir himself, holding him, letting sleep flow from him into me, taking his tired body on to my own. I didn't want to rouse him, to remind him there was a world outside his dreams but then he always slid away, like an egg falling into straw.

*             *             *

HER FRIEND. What is the name of the enemy?

THE WOMAN. I don't know. They always have different names. I can't remember.

HER FRIEND. What is the name of the village?

THE WOMAN. I don't know. They keep changing the name. The borders are rearranged.

HER FRIEND. What is the name of the country?

THE WOMAN. Don't you know?

HER FRIEND. If you won't tell me the name of the country, tell me the name of the enemy.

THE WOMAN. The enemy? I don't know.
     Oh, the enemy? That's easy. He always has the same name. He is always the General.

HER FRIEND. No. That's not true.

THE WOMAN. Well then, the General is not always the enemy.

HER FRIEND. Are you sure?

THE WITNESS. The General wishes to accompany her home, but she insists on walking alone.

THE GENERAL. You must let me walk you home. A woman who wishes to learn your trade has to learn to be more accommodating. You need my protection, anything might happen to you.

ADA. No. I am perfectly safe. No one will touch me now. You have a long shadow and there is no more harm that can come to me than has already come.

THE GENERAL. Your tongue is not a shadow and you do not curb it. Have I done you so much harm then?

ADA. Only what was in your power. Maybe it is the ultimate harm. But maybe even you are limited in your evil.

THE GENERAL. Is that what you wish to know?

ADA. Yes, that is what I hope to know.

THE GENERAL. Will it redeem me in your eyes?

ADA. No, but it provides some relief.

THE WITNESS. The road curves up the hill. She looks back and down to see the sun slipping into the sea. She moves so slowly and precisely you would think she could reach out to hold back the sun, could keep the red sphere hovering on the water only with her hands. But it slips through her outstretched fingers and goes out. The rays explode up and out of the water, the sky crimsons, a red dye spreads over it, saturates the blue and then the clouds move in gray, absorb the red in their feet and stamp it out. In a moment the sky is so blue and gray that someone without memory would not be able to re-invent the sun. There is no trace of fire anywhere on the horizon. And Ada turns back toward her dark house.

*                    *                    *

HER LOVER. You were going to tell me about the mermaid.

THE WOMAN. I was. But why are you so interested?

HER LOVER. I saw one once and didn't follow her.

THE WOMAN. And why should I tell you the story, if you are unwilling to discover it yourself?

HER LOVER. Because I am interested in enchantment.

THE WOMAN. I thought as much. Legend has it that there is no way we can conquer you but by turning you to stone.

HER LOVER. Are you thinking of Medusa?

THE WOMAN. Perhaps. One enchantment or another. No man will follow the woman's path by choice. It must be against his will.

HER LOVER. Many have given their entire soul to it.

THE WOMAN. Eventually they become resentful and belligerent. They pout and declare, "I have lost my will and my freedom."

HER LOVER. And what do you think they mean by freedom?

THE WOMAN. The right to go to war.

                    *                    *                    *

THE GENERAL. I don't understand why you've come.

ADA. Why do you let me in?

THE GENERAL. Perhaps I will seduce you some day.

THE WITNESS. She shrugs her shoulders, a bank of earth moving into place against the river. She does not move with ease. She is rather more like the table, like the chair where she sits. She will go no further with him than the kitchen. She always arrives in the afternoon, before it is dark, the dark belongs to someone else. She has not given up that allegiance. Each day she gathers herself together, pulling her body out of the terrible mid-day sleep which is like death without cause, and trudges to the General's house. Juggling delicately in her pocket are the little white eggs wrapped in worn paper so they will not break. Arriving at his house, she no longer knocks but enters and sits at the table, silent, morose, indifferent.

THE GENERAL. You move so slowly,

THE WITNESS. Neither knows how much time has transpired, how many times she has come.

ADA. I scarcely know I move. Why move? Do trees move?

THE GENERAL. They say the continents are drifting.

ADA. Toward each other or away?

THE GENERAL. I can't remember. Away probably.

ADA. Then some must be attracted to each other.

THE GENERAL. Yes. But I don't think so. Perhaps the earth, like the universe, is expanding.

ADA. They say there is a fire in the center. Perhaps it is because of that.

THE GENERAL. What shall I call you?

ADA. Ada.

> And I will call you "General." Your name is too common. It reminds me of myself. And "General" reminds me of who you are.

THE WITNESS. On the way home, she stoops to fill her pockets with pebbles picked up at his doorstep. In time she has a small collection of stones.

> When she is home, she empties her pockets and sits down to a little meal. She will not eat with the General. First a bit of bread, some cold soup, some cheese and finally the sweet plum. No one to say a word. Now in her world, it's only the General who speaks.

&ast; &ast; &ast;

VOICE. No one asks me my name.

THE WOMAN. Sometimes you know the names of voices and sometimes they have no name. Voices do not knock at the door, do not ask permission to be let in.

> I walk through the house, laughing aloud, thinking of offering an evening sherry to a ghost.

THE NARRATOR. Because La Malinche is given, the twenty women are given also. They are the gift which accompanies the gift. Perhaps they are as beautiful as La Malinche, but their job is to grind corn, to prepare yerba buena, to make the needle and thread and rope from the maguey. The rope as well which will bind them.

> They are the twenty given to Cortez who distributes these gifts among his men. He can be generous with this gold. The more men killed, the more women remain. There is an endless supply. For a time at least they are the ones who carry the blood for these white gods who have no blood in them. Yet when they cry they say:

VOICE. No one remembers my name, not even as a curse.

THE WOMAN. We have been given like you have. At our wedding, our fathers give us away.

\*                    \*                    \*

THE LOVER.  You were telling me a story . . .

THE WOMAN.  About the mermaid.

She smooths his skin running her hands down his hips onto his thighs, avoiding the center of his belly and his groin, smoothing down the skin turning opalescent under her fingers, the scales forming where she strokes him—thin, delicate armor, sharp, transparent petals, layered one on the other. The water follows her unimpeded, the scales directing the rivulets toward deepening pools. His feet join at the ankles, the toes thin and spread. The bones dissolve. Fins or seaweed emerge where his feet were. The bed is water. They absorb the common motion of the currents. Wherever she touches him, he alters. "I have always dreamed you this way," she says.

And at the waist, her flesh midriff against his chest, still flesh, her breasts against his nipples, their mouths make the fish, her hair carried damply across his face, the sweat is cool as sea water, they thrash about each other. Her skin glistens and his hands follow the light but that her tail slashes and the spray covers them. He enters where he can enter. Her mouth like the whale opens for what small fish will winnow through her teeth. When the jaw clenches behind, the probing finger can open it, and he jumps into the cavernous body across the pink ribs and into the salt-reeking dark among the smooth creatures, the odor of surf, shells pounded to sand by the thunderous ocean tail, the open bones, plankton, sea horses, jelly fish, all the transparent wonders are there. He holds her fingers up to the light to see the blood in her. Kelp winding itself about her body is the snake which holds her, the smooth rope which ties her, the live girdle encircling her, which turns her to the creatures which move in the dark. Ink to close her eyes and more hands than she can count.

Now he bridles her. The little pods of kelp break in her mouth. The cold tails beat in the water and the white foam passes the seeds through their water bodies. "I dream you this way," she whispers, her eyes opening from under the tide.

"I would be a moray eel," he answers. "I am so voracious."

"And your colors, what colors are you?"

He puts his fingers on her eyes and closes them. "Can you see," he strokes her, "the colors only the dark knows?" He slides into her, one fishing opening its mouth and the other entering, this constant devouring; he is whole within her and yet he holds her. The beating tails keep them afloat; she extends to the shape he assumes, the tails flutter, and the spindrift catches them, tossing them whitely.

"You are more ravenous than I." Still he emerges unmarred. The tide pools are gentle. The anemones close or open to the sun.

*       *       *

THE WITNESS. She who is as weary when she returns as when she leaves sits down on the bed to remove the red shoes and then aligns them perfectly in the closet, hangs up the silk dress, smoothing the wrinkles which come from sitting wooden on a straight-backed chair. But even as she appears to sit in mahogany silence, she is moving. The water is no longer still, is in internal motion. Slow deliberate and absolute, it insists on its path and is edged forward as a delta is constructed imperceptively over the years; the earth moving down from the mountains where it is created by trees which offer themselves every winter to their roots, turning green in summer, extending in needles and falling, rotting back into themselves over the long winter creating under the snow the imperceptible heat of transformation. They are taken back up again with the aid of water. But sometimes the water escapes from the trunk, flows down rather than up, heads toward some river pushing the earth in front of it until the burden is too great and is dropped on a dark plateau. The water moves on by itself toward the salt sea and another cycle: leaves left behind and fish entered.

THE WOMAN. I wanted to tell you about the mermaid. But it is all a dream. When she walks, she is hobbled but in the sea, she is the dance itself. It is told that the mermaid carries song in her hair, the sound the wind makes strumming.

HER LOVER.  Let me comb your hair now as you sit here on the bed. Don't speak, just give me the comb and let me pass it through your hair, watching how it falls down over your shoulders. Sssh. Don't say a word. Only listen. Do you hear anything?

THE WOMAN.  On occasion I have been able to create enough silence to hear my own heart beating.

HER LOVER.  Yes, perhaps that is it.

THE WOMAN.  The hair of the mermaid is not kelp, but longing, and is the thread which she throws in a long line to the shore. She is the fisherwoman and he who is wandering on the sand is sometimes caught and pulled into the water. If he is alert, he may see the thin cord but even then he does not always recognize it, mistakes it for a fish, the flash of a fin, the leap of the porpoise, a spume of water, the sexual longing of water for water, the . . .

                    *                    *                    *

THE WITNESS.  Ada lifts her hand and knocks on the door. One piece of wood tapping against another. When the door opens, she enters without saying a word.

Ada lifts her hand and opens the door, without knocking. One door opening onto another. She enters without saying a word. For a year, the only man she has spoken to is her dead husband. Despite the rainfall, she performs a vigil at the foot of his stone. With a cold finger, she pokes at him, demanding to know,

ADA.  What is the point of this? How long will you play dead? Oh, it was easy for you. You didn't like the war so you just walked out on it. And you, the one who said you couldn't turn your back on your comrades. "The war must be faced and fought!" you said so self-assured and moral. "I have no choice." Well now, dear one, have you left me, a woman, to fight your battles for you?

Well, I've buried your gun; you know that. I'm not a private taking orders from you. What are you going to do about all this?

THE WITNESS.  Even if the grave had hurled up the pistol, she would not have taken it, if the earthquake which often came to that part of the county had, as it is often said, opened the graves and thrust the pistol into her hand, she would not have taken it. But she was not worried about such events; there was no sound from the dead man who burrowed deeper into the wormy ground despite all her belligerent entreaties.

ADA. Then the rain entered her and she no longer minded the cold because she was the same temperature as the water. She became the water. Where her blood had beat, the rain passed through her and into the ground and so her feet were mud and she couldn't tell the difference between one life and another. She had become a cold-blooded creature who blended into the elements about her. If she had been at the sea rather than at his grave, she would have thought she had been changed into a . . .

THE WOMAN. Mermaid?

ADA. Perhaps. I must learn to use this body.

THE WITNESS. Then Ada goes home and sits in her house in the dark for a long time without a single light. And she thinks about . . .

THE WOMAN. The General?

ADA. Sophia, the little girl.

When I first saw the dark shape of the General in the doorway, I thought for a moment how much he resembled a man. Yet he was quite like a bird, broad and black-winged, the kind which casts shadows when it flies. I wondered, what do I say to such a thing?

No words came. On my way to his house, I had robbed the chicken's nest to use the egg as a pretext. The theft prepared me for other crimes.

*　　　　　*　　　　　*

GRACE. I don't know why you always liked to walk in the woods, Pearl. If you were here now in this dainty little cage they've fixed up for . . . who'd ever think I would have ended up on such display? The Dodo bird that can not fly. I bet you'd

try to sneak out to the woods. If you could sneak out. If I
could fly. If I cackle enough, will they think I'm a chicken
and let me out to roost. Never knew where you were. And I
wasn't about to go get you. Not going to look for you now.
You're just a big worm. Well now's your chance to sleep
outdoors. We wouldn't let you in those days. Sorry. Lots of
things they won't let me do now. It's not sleeping outside or
alone I care about. Where's Alf? He's the sheriff. He could
flash his badge and come nest down in this little bed. Know
what frightened me in the woods? I always thought I'd meet
a man. Ha! The trouble with me is they always want something for free and then have no respect. Alf always liked to
show me his guns; I thought it was pretty safe as long as we
were indoors. Wouldn't trust him with a putty knife if I met
him in the woods. Wouldn't turn his rod down now. I'm an
endangered species, Pearl. The last of our kind. God damn it,
nurse, I'm a free woman, a national monument. Nurse!
Where's the damned bitch? Can't tell the difference between
a dying swan and a cockatoo.

THE WOMAN.  Damn it! How naive I am. I watch Ada go down the
street toward the General's house and then return home and
I hope no one will know where she's been, though it's afternoon when she goes out without even the cover of dark. The
curtains are moving. Everyone watches the street. Where are
you going, Ada, in your red shoes?

CHORUS.  Ada.

THE WOMAN.  Ada, who has not worn anything but mourning for
the year, Ada, you sleep on the hard ground in the cemetery
every goddamned night. Ada, why do you think they've
brought you milk and cheese? Ada, are you the only one
whose husband has died? There are hardly any men left in
the village. You are not the only one to have suffered loss.
Why, then? Isn't it because of your grief?

CHORUS.  ADA.
    Where are you going?

ADA.  I go where I please.

CHORUS.  Are you going to the General's?

ADA.  I go where I please . . .

CHORUS.  Will you kill the General for us? Why not go to him at
      night. Your husband is dead. What good does he do you in the
      dark? Go to the General's bed. Plunge in the knife.
          We will wash you. We will take you back. We will wash
      you. It will rain. Kill the General for us while he sleeps in
      his bed. These are the promises we can make.

ADA.  I do what I please.

THE NARRATOR. War city shack. Little flowered curtain, thin lily girl, reed body, soft breeze shakes her, rice breasts. "Lie down. One dollar a half hour." Takes off her silk robe. Unbuttons your shirt. Just a little English. Your buddies taught her. "How nice you are." Unbuttoning. Smooth as plum wine. "How strong you are. Like to touch your skin. You give me good feeling." Opens shirt. "Did you kill my brother? Did you kill my mother? Only one dollar. You give me good feelings. I like to lick your ear. Did you teach me fucking? Sleep on my breast. You're a good man. It feels good. What do you like?" Hand down his back. "In the delta there are little animals. The sweet taste of rice. Water buffalo. My sister laughs. Her name is . . . I don't remember. Tomorrow you go to delta. Don't shoot the little birds."

HER FRIEND. Who would you go to?

THE WOMAN. I don't know.

HER FRIEND. Could you?

THE WOMAN. If I lived with guns, had always seen guns, if the general were close by, if my village were occupied, if I had known this occupation from the time I was a young girl, if someone was breathing the air that was given to us and there was less of it, if my mother bent over for lack of breath, if my father or brother or I had secretly trained to carry a gun, if at fifteen, let us say, I had to say goodbye to someone I loved, if I had children in hiding or knew children in hiding, if I had learned how to start barn fires, how to meet friends in stealth because houses were closed to us, how to creep through the forest at night without being seen, if I had to learn how to carry messages, if I hated wounds and war because I had seen them, if I had to listen to the wisdom of chickens, if I could hear oracles in the scatter of corn and the scratch of their feet, then I can imagine, if I had seen the enemy face to face and had smiled, then I can imagine, if he were so familiar to me, that I would give him my body to distract him; if I knew in that moment whose lives I was protecting, if you were trying to escape, and when I gave him my body all that time you were breathing, another breath, another breath for each thrust of his body, even if I only bought you five minutes, if I knew who was the enemy and who was able to keep breathing in and out, in and out, in and out; Live! Live! Live!

Wouldn't I use my body? It is such a small thing.

HER FRIEND. Where did you learn that?

THE WOMAN. I hear all the voices.

ADA. One afternoon, my sister comes to my house empty-handed and sits stiffly on one of the white kitchen chairs.

SISTER. I would have brought you something but I hear you suddenly have all you want.

THE WITNESS. Ada sits across from her sister, her hands in her lap, waiting. The afternoon passes. As children they sat this way watching clouds move across a hot sky, silent, unmoving except to edge the porch swing in a slow hypnotic circle.

SISTER. You might offer me coffee. Don't you have any? Chocolate, then.

ADA. You sound so bitter.

Why don't you look in the cupboards? You stocked them yourself.

SISTER. The village women see you walk down the road every evening. You disappear into a house, they say, and later you come home again. The little straw bag you carry is not empty in either direction.

ADA. And what else?

SISTER. You wear a silk dress and red shoes. They must be the ones we bought when we went to the city together before the war. "Where are you going to wear them?" I asked you then. "You can't walk on them on these roads and we hardly ever go dancing."

And the house at the end of the road where you go . . . ?

ADA. Is the General's house.
Do you watch me as well?

SISTER. I am not interested in such sights.
Why are you so lonely? All the women are alone now.

ADA. I am not lonely. It is not for that.

SISTER. That is not what they say.
Do you have coffee?

ADA. No.

SISTER. Tea, then.

ADA. No. Nothing like that.

SISTER. What's in the bag, then?

ADA. What I can find. No one sells to me and nothing is left at my door. There's milk coming to me, but . . .

SISTER. The woman who kept our cows is dead.

ADA. I know. Whoever milks them now can keep the milk.

SISTER. Have you no supplies?

ADA. Less than before.

SISTER. So you are not even compensated for your labor.

ADA. I have turned down every possible gift.

SISTER. How do you live, then?

ADA. On what remains from what you gave me.

THE WITNESS. It is evening. Her sister lights a fire. Habits of loving are difficult to break. Ada offers her a shawl, for nothing ever completely warms this room. Except for the firelight, the room is dark.

SISTER. I am not trying to protect myself from being seen with you.

ADA. You may have to.

SISTER. And you?

ADA. For me everything is too late.
    I have to leave soon.

SISTER. Does he wait for you?

ADA. I don't know.

SISTER. Did he ask you to come?

ADA. He has never asked anything of me.

SISTER. And you come home every night?

ADA. It's my choice.

SISTER. Don't you wish they had left you the gun?

ADA. I scarcely think about it.

SISTER. What occupies you?

ADA. Sophia, the little girl. I might have had one so little.

SISTER. Will you come back to my house?

ADA. I can not tell her that I still need to live alone. Maybe I shrug
    my shoulders. She understands my gestures. I can sit on her
    porch but only in the dark when she is sleeping. I can crouch
    on her stairs or squat in her barn with my hand under her
    chicken. I can steal into her storage cellar knowing she will
    share anything, even now, without my having to ask. I can
    not bring myself to open her door and go into her house. I
    am glad my mother is dead and doesn't have to see any of
    this.

THE WOMAN. What's in your little basket, Ada?

ADA. Eggs.

THE WOMAN. Who are the eggs for, Ada?

ADA. Generals who claim they can not live on air.

THE GENERAL. I'm hungry, Ada.

ADA. Generals are always hungry. You expect us to feed you. I
    know about hunger, but of a different kind. I can't eat; some-
    thing eats at me. I've brought a gift . . .

GENERAL. I'm hungry,

ADA. . . . a gift which you can not eat.

Take this egg, General, which you must not eat. Line your pocket with silk, open your pillow, extract the warm white feathers, make a nest in your handkerchief, General, and put this egg in it.

Take this egg, General, which you must never eat. Keep it warm, put in your armpit, fold it in the elbow, hide it in your groin, General. Hold it warm there between your legs by the little sack of eggs you carry. You have neglected to think of yourself as a hen, so hold the egg there by the little wrinkled pouch, the delicate brown bag, the leathery wine skin filled with other eggs, thousands of eggs, little swimming eggs, tiny tadpole eggs, devil-tailed eggs. It's not the hunger that matters, General, it's the chick.

THE GENERAL. And my hunger?

ADA. That's easy. Do what I do, what the village women do; think tomorrow you're going to eat . . . tomorrow will be a magnificent feast. Think when the war is over there will still be hundreds of chicks. That is what you must think. You think your husband will come home, you think he will learn to bear the shame of this war and will get up out of the grave, you think he will stop lying down in front of bullets, you think he will stop dying just because there wasn't time to milk the cows, you think he will stop burrowing down into the corn roots just because the General got the ears, you think tomorrow he will come home and you will make a decent meal with all the things he loves, but until then you don't eat by yourself, and you must hold the little egg in your body pocket until the two of you lie down, egg to egg. Until then, you keep it warm.

HER FRIEND. That isn't the way it happened.

THE WOMAN. Ask Ada.

HER FRIEND. I can't. It's your book. You are making this up.

It's not possible. You don't know what an occupied country is, you don't know what a general is. This is all in your mind; you don't know the enemy.

THE WOMAN. I can imagine.

HER FRIEND. You can, but you haven't.

THE WOMAN. You know what I know; you know what I have seen;
you know what has been acted out against me.

HER FRIEND. How do you account, then, for your innocence? After
what you have seen and what has been enacted against you,
even without a declared war, even without a holy cause.

THE WOMAN. What happened then?

HER FRIEND. You tell me. You know.

THE WOMAN. A story: A woman who lived in an occupied village
went to the General's house one morning disguised as a
whore with the pretext of bringing him eggs. When he opened
the door, she told him she saw no point in her life and had
decided to become a prostitute. "Naturally," she said, "I was
attracted to you."

"Are you a virgin?" he asked.

"No," she admitted.

"Then what good are you? I have the pick of the village,
why would I choose you?"

"I'm the one who came," and she leaned against the door-
jamb. Since she was a beautiful woman, she could afford
that ease.

"What do you charge?" he inquired in order to remain
amused.

"Oh, a good fee, so you will not feel ashamed."

"I am the General," he informed her. "I can have you for
nothing. I could have you for nothing even if I were a common soldier because you are a woman alone in a man's
house. But as the General, I can have you brought to me—my
soldiers do such things. I could have you savored, to see what
quality you are. I can have anything I want."

She turned to go, saying, "I'm sorry, I came only to know
what a general is like. But he is like any other man, only
better fed, perhaps, and his clothes are pressed. He has the
look of someone who sleeps in a room by himself and is not
used to being disturbed."

"No one knocks by chance at my door. No one enters

unless I say, 'come in.' No one speaks to me unless I speak first. No one leaves without my leave.''

''Then, good morning, General, because I must go.''

But he only lets her turn her face to the door and then puts his hand on her shoulder and pulls her around to throw her on the bed. ''No one enters or leaves without permission,'' he says, ''Let us see what kind of a whore you are.'' If she is a gate, he opens her; if she is a door, he breaks her; if she is the arch, he goes through her.

She lies there wondering, ''How did I come to this?''

Afterwards he throws the money on the floor. ''When you come tomorrow,'' he says, ''be sure to bring me eggs.''

HER FRIEND. A failure of imagination.

THE WOMAN. Is it?

HER FRIEND. A failure to imagine how bad things really are.

THE WOMAN. What do you think happened then?

HER FRIEND. Shall I tell it?

A story: A woman who lived in an occupied country went to the General one morning to deliver eggs.

He opened the door.

He pulled her in.

He threw her on the bed.

He entered her with a passion both orderly and contained.

She lay passive as a wrinkled sheet.

He saw that she was stained.

She served no purpose for him.

He shot her with his gun.

—Do you recognize that story?

THE WOMAN. It's historic . . . and I don't want it to be true.

ADA. That's not how it happened.

THE WITNESS. A story: When she walks up to his door, it is with a
motion which has no hesitation to it. All in a rhythm as if
she were a dancer and the music continuous and, therefore,
the motion itself continuous, insistent, uninterruptable as
long as the notes continue, the motion continuing and nothing
can stop her. The plants which grow according to the music
played in their vicinity must take into them the tones, the
irreversible, irrepressible impetus which is outside of argu-
ment and concern, and becomes the vegetative dance. Un-
thinking but thoughtful, uncalculating but shrewd, alert,
wary, cognizant of the dangers but unheeding, she proceeds
as in a trance, not the way we imagine trance, but how it is,
in a state of heightened awareness, focused, resolute, insu-
lated from all distractions. There is the woman. There is the
General. And the road between them which she must cross.

He opens the door, without knowing to what he opens the
door. Perhaps he thought it was his aide-de-camp, but when
he opens it, it is as if he finds a tree knocking, or the rising
river pressing against his house.

It has been a year that she has been preparing. You can say
she has the power of the dead within her, that she has sucked
it up from the grave where she has lain now an entire year,
night after night. If you wish you can say that. But she claims
the opposite. She says the dead turned their back on her and
this is her action alone to the extent that this act belongs to
anyone, that it can be claimed in the way one can, if you
will, claim a gun.

And the wide smile, the back easing up against the door-
jamb, the lolling posture, so studied, careful and humorous,

where did she learn it? Surely, he sees the ruse as she enacts a few stock gestures; their code is clear: the red mouth; the plunging neckline; the skirt just a deliberate quarter-inch too short; the legs without hose, despite the cold, thrust into the red shoes, just a shade too high to be polite; the small of her back arching against the door; the mouth open, laughing, and the face, intense, provocative, and triumphantly innocent.

"I want to learn how to be a prostitute," she says. "And I am certain you are the most experienced teacher."

The ploy. Accepted. And behind it, an irresistible determination to which the General must respond.

THE GENERAL. Come in.

THE WITNESS. Even animals do not move the way she moves. Perhaps the movement in her not of the single animal but of the herd leaving for other feeding grounds and the opaque shadow of birds going south and the heavy bear trampling through the forest toward the encounter with sleep and the lope of the gathering caribou. It is the inner psyche of the glacier gliding indefatigably and undemoralized, a foot or two at a time down the continental fall. Distance and time are of no concern to that icy consciousness which is driven forward by the insistence of its own weight and which presses before it the foot of its own snow, avalanche on avalanche, those drifts are sacrificed, bodies falling into the sea.

The General attempts to regain some power in this situation, and so not to be outdone, leans back also and slowly unbuttons his shirt.

THE WITNESS. She scrutinizes him and he understands that his body alone will not give him any leverage in this situation. She leans against the door and all the weight is with her; he is up on the ledge, on a teeter-totter compared with her. Suddenly he is a mere child dangling in the air where all he can hope for is her sense of play and to pretend he enjoys the game. Otherwise he must slide ignobly to the ground admitting his fear. She leans heavily against the bottom of the see-saw, asserting her resolute mass. Impervious to his discomfort, she laughs.

He knows that it will not be his body which will aid him

though he has kept it in good repair. It is damaged. How could it be otherwise? The spirit reveals itself in the flesh.

It is not his beauty; he may have had it once, but it does not exist for her, nor could it, since he is a general.

He is not the kind of mettle she admires.

THE GENERAL. I can teach you to be a whore.

ADA. Oh no. Not a whore—a prostitute, a wage earner.

THE WITNESS. She answers laughing, exhibiting her enormous smile, the wide brazen teeth, the affrontry of her eyes. Eyes which do not invite any challenge, do not elicit response, there is nowhere to hold on to her, to spar with her, that is the difficulty of this. If there were a battle, he might have a chance. He is skilled in battle. She does not offer him the option of engaging in a confrontation. Being a woman has educated her to subversion. He recognizes her mask, but what lies beneath it, he has never encountered before.

ADA. I intend to be well paid. According to my needs. And in a variety of ways. I expect you to prepare me for the payment that is due me. No, indeed, a whore has no power. But a prostitute is a businesswoman who sees and protects the value of the commodity which is offered for sale.

THE NARRATOR. When she laughs, that broad devouring smile encompasses her face. Her full mouth is wide open and her face is a demon mask with broadly carved wooden lips curving like taut stretched bows toward each other, the arrow tongue ready to kill.

ADA. And, you see, I am fortunate to have something to sell which exists in a limited but not finite quantity. I will not run out of it as one might run out of gold or diamonds or oil, or as a general might, you will forgive me for mentioning it, but as a general might even run out of death.

THE WITNESS. A woman who lives in an occupied village, whose husband has been killed by the enemy, goes one afternoon to the General's house.

Afterwards, she turns quickly and exits from the house, down the three steps onto the gravel path. Her back is straight and she can not admit into her consciousness the thought which her husband would have had to consider, that it is of the utmost danger to turn one's back on anyone especially a general, so inclined to use a gun, one so skilled and haphazard in its use. She has to maneuver perfectly across the pebbles without stumbling, or faltering, or scraping her shoes, and then on the road she must assume a comfortable steady pace, without increasing her speed, resisting the instinct to peer back over her shoulder. Her only caution must be to take no precautions at all.

This first straightforward and simple return is perfectly executed. She could be a woman returning from the market, from visiting her sister, from inspecting the milking cows. Is she not a woman returning from a quiet afternoon in the church? The red shoes? Unfortunate. She may not have others. As she walks she carried the coolness of the dark nave with her, thoughts sweet and spiritual floating disembodied through her internal air.

At home she rids herself of her clothes and lies down on her cold bed. How tired she is. Even a river flowing downhill tires of the boulders it pushes with its long watery arms and is exhausted by the roots which drag at it, sucking up at it, and the heaviness of the earth sluggishly moving along under its swift flow.

And tomorrow, if she is to pursue this course, she must be prepared to return, even as water leaps over a jammed log and falls down again. She will have to walk back as carefully as she walked away and then again she will return home. At the end of the evening she will no longer be safe from the General or the villagers, but she will not take the back way running through the trees and brush sneaking from shadow to shadow. In her mind there is one way to proceed and that is directly down the road from her house to his. When she goes in the opposite direction, she comes to the cemetery. There is a direct line from the cemetery to the General's house. And she intends to walk that entire road before dawn without being shot in the back.

THE NARRATOR. A story: From the newspapers—or how the Woman
remembers it.

    Let's say it is very hot. It's summertime in the south and
the electricity naturally goes out in such a heat. The man has
been making rounds and now he gropes toward the ice box
in the hall. Occasions like this are not unique and some
things must be kept cold, some perishables, insulin, and beer,
of course. Opening the door for a drink, he notices the cake
of ice and hacks at it with an ice pick until he has enough
chips to cool his mouth. Then he goes out again; it's dark,
the electricity is still out, there's only a dim bulb working
off an emergency generator. He forgets that he still has the
ice pick in his hand. He comes to his cell to check on her.
It is his job to see that she never escapes. There is no one
else in the corridor, but even if there were . . . it is so dark.
He stands a long time outside her cell. Is it that she is so difficult to see? Squinting, pick in hand, he selects a key from the
large ring attached to a chain attached to his belt and extends
it toward the lock. She says:

THE PRISONER. You can not open the cell until morning. I can see
you; you can see me. Lockup was at nine o'clock and even
if I were ill and called to you for help, you would not be
allowed to open the cell unless you called a doctor and then
only when he came.

THE NARRATOR. She pauses. She continues. She repeats. She looks
at him with studied derision.

THE PRISONER. It's the law. Those are the prison rules. You may
not open this cell door. I can see you; you can see me. You
can hear me. I am here. You can not open the door.

THE NARRATOR. There is a warning in her voice and in her body which is motionless. He hesitates, but there is something so confident about her, so immoderate yet calm in her anger, that he can not turn away. He is drawn to her. She does not move. He wants her to move. He wants to see her in his own way. He listens to the tumblers falling, the bolt retracting, the clean sound of metal moving against metal. These are sounds he understands. The cell door opens. There is some clanging but also a clarity to it. The sound doesn't linger in the air like bells do; it is sharp and final. He likes to open doors.

He throws her down on the cot and himself upon her. It is easy to do. She is a small woman, wearing only a light dress because it is hot. She is barefoot. Her shoes are in a corner out of reach. And he has the ice pick in one hand, the chain with the keys in the other. He grabs her with the right hand and throws her on the bed, holding her down with his left hand and the ice pick pressing against her shoulders. He has mastered the gestures of violence. He is used to metal in his fist. So he can open his pants and enter her while still holding the keys.

But.

In the moment, the moment when he abandons himself, in that split second when he can hold on to nothing, she who appeared inert, lunges up. She who is wary is alert and fast. He loses both his balance and his grip on the ice pick which now becomes her pick. She swings. She pulls back, both hands on the pick. She stabs him directly in the heart.

\*      \*      \*

THE WOMAN. Am I ready, I wonder, to save her from that act, to take her place?

HER FRIEND. It would be a fine exchange, wouldn't it? One body for another. And what is gained, except his life?—which isn't worth a fig. Or is that what you're after? His life? Saving it?

THE WOMAN. No, hers. If, like Ada, I had gone to him, earlier that evening, he would have only brought his prisoner some cool water with ice because it was hot.

HER FRIEND.  A likely story.

THE WOMAN.  It doesn't matter. I can't do it. I can not even imagine it.

ADA.  And what was I thinking? I do not think I thought.

THE NARRATOR.  In the distance a man is chopping wood. How does she know it's a man?

THE WOMAN.  By the rhythm. By the song of the axe. By the love of the blade.

THE NARRATOR.  The Woman doesn't lock the door of her cabin, not even at night though she sleeps alone. When she walks in the woods, she does not take anything with her, not even a knife to notch her path on the trees. Once when she found a gray hunting jacket carefully folded under a tree, she was more afraid than if she had seen him stomping through the woods.

The last lodge guest taught her about elk. He sharpened the knife for her which she does not carry. When he was visiting, she could see the three rifles in his truck displayed in full view according to the law.

He said to her:

MAN.  Those of us who have taken up guns are tied to them. We can never trust ourselves absolutely to put them down. In a world without guns I will have to stay behind. What goes on in your house, I will never know.

                    *                    *

THE NARRATOR.  Grace, the last of the Green Dragon Ladies, covers herself with a sheet pretending it is a kimono. The flesh which was kneaded and pummeled has softened so much it can barely remain on the bones. Brown spots on her arms everywhere she was touched. What's in the doorway? Is it the door ajar? A shadow? Her eyes are failing but she will not admit it to herself. When they go, what is left to her?

Is it a customer or the orderly in his foolish green clothes? No self-respecting man would dress in that fashion in her day. In the past she could have refused everyone who looked so foolish. Yet, she is professional and would not turn anyone down today.

HER FRIEND.  What is war?

THE WOMAN.  War is taking what has not been offered.

HER FRIEND.  What is the opposite of war?

THE WOMAN.  Gifts.

*          *          *

THE WOMAN.  Let me attempt it again.
>     She is alone in her cell. It is inevitable that someone will
> try to enter. It is a hot night, the electricity fails. I know what
> is coming.
>     Do I get up then, one morning, and comb my hair with a
> purpose? Do I drink coffee that night and plot? When I get
> to the jail house, do I scan the bulletin boards to learn when
> the shifts change? And when he is the only one on duty and
> alone with her, is that when I return?

HER FRIEND.  How well you fit into his scheme. He gets what he
>     wants or he takes what he wants.

CHORUS.  There is a name for women like you.

THE WOMAN.  What is it?

CHORUS.  Collaborator.

THE WOMAN.  What do you suggest?

CHORUS.  You have to have something other than your body which
>     he wants and can't get and that he's willing to bargain for.

THE WOMAN.  Like what?

CHORUS.  Oil. Gold. Uranium. Land. Atom bomb secrets.

THE WOMAN.  How do I get them?

CHORUS.  Like he does—steal and kill.

THE WOMAN.  I think I've heard this story before.

CHORUS.  You have. It's the only story.

THE WOMAN.  Again, I must imagine it. How can I enact it in my
>     life if I can not see it even in my own mind.
>     You wake up in the morning with the smell of your sister's

fear on your hands. It is an ordinary day. The visiting hours
at the jail are in the afternoon. You dreamed he looked at her
through the bars and you go into the jail looking for those
predatory eyes.

THE NARRATOR. Malintzi knew the jaguar, but not how to hunt. She
had not been educated to the jungle.

THE WOMAN. It is dawn. You have the taste of your sister's fear
in your mouth. Your tongue mixes the thick sleep with the
remains of your dream. You've never done this before. An
empty paper shopping bag from an elegant store on your arm,
but you don't know why. What matters is how to insure that
the jailer will keep his word. He can come to you but he must
not approach his prisoner. He may not even ask. She has
nothing. What she has is danger. She has no protection. The
bars open only for him, but not for her. She can not lock
herself in at night. You must not fail.

He is not handsome and he is not young. And there's the
smell of uniforms and urinals on his thighs, the stench of
unwashed testicles, nicotine and shit under his shin.

Do you find a cot? Did you bring a sheet? There has to be
some loving in this. You must pluck his two fruits—greed
and rage. You must do this with your clothes off.

He watches you from across the room. He locks you into
a cell. He removes your brassiere. Does he take off his gun?

You know the taste of fear in your mouth. You must move
your hips; also there must be some loving in this. You do not
speak. Perhaps you think of her. If there's no pleasure here,
how can you find love? You try to remember that he was once
a young boy. You ask him to send a gift to your friend. You
ask him to take nothing from her. What she has is danger.

His sperm shoots into your body. You practice "glad, glad,
glad" against your involuntary hate. You say, "Now you
must give my sister a gift."

THE WITNESS. Ada pulls the coat over her shoulders and in her
sleep, if it is sleep, she strokes her black skirt and blankets
herself in it. This wool is her only embrace. The night is cold
enough, but this grave is even colder. And though she presses

her head down firmly so as to rest on his shoulder, she can not hear his heart beating and that comfort, that regular rhythm would ease her more than if she heard her own heart. Only the regular creaking of a branch. And sometimes the alarm of the insomniac mocking birds. The General sleeps well in his own house where the faint regular ticking of the clock serves him as well as any heart.

When she arrives at his house she looks pale. White cold seeping into her skin as the grave grit settles down into the pores. Earth too deeply engrained to be removed rouges her cheeks.

CHORUS. At least she's getting her loving. Should be roses in her cheeks.

THE GENERAL. I had a dream.

ADA. How fortunate you are. I don't sleep enough for dreams.

THE GENERAL. Am I keeping you awake?

ADA. Death keeps me awake with his long nails.

THE GENERAL. I'll tell you my dream.

ADA. It will pass the time.

THE GENERAL. There's a stage. I can't see the audience. The light from the stage reflects off their white hands.
I come out on the stage. A voice says, "Kneel down." There's a stock so I put my head into it. The voice says, "Have you forgotten your lines?" I have a script in my pocket. I repeat each line three times.
Ada, are you listening?

ADA. What else is there to do?

THE GENERAL. I speak and speak. I expect applause but there isn't a single sound. Maybe they're dead, I think. But even if they're dead, I believe they can hear. Has that thought ever occurred to you?

ADA. No.

THE GENERAL. It only came to me in the dream. In the morning, I remembered the lines. Do you want to hear them?

ADA. I never want anything.

THE GENERAL. Nothing?

ADA. Nothing.

THE GENERAL. Then why . . . ?

ADA. Necessity.

THE WITNESS. It's in her shoulders. A triangle of fear or resignation. Her shoulders pull forward and the spine is exposed. When she puts her hair up even those who watch from behind the windows turn aside as she goes by. The General sits across from her and hesitates to stand at her back. With her hair up, her neck is absolutely naked except for the few curled dark hairs framing the neck bones.

THE GENERAL. The lines I said were: "When I was in the war, I killed a man. What do you expect? What do you expect? When I was in the war, I killed a man. What do you expect? I was a young kid. It was my duty. It was my duty.

"I only did it once. I only did it once. I only did it once."

That's not my voice, I think. And yet it is. I recognize the body. I think I must still be a young kid.

"I knew better. Okay. I did. I knew better, but I did it. It was my duty. Why aren't you pleased?"

I say the lines well. The audience doesn't stir. Must I go on? I put my hands in the stocks as well. I can only see the gleam of white.

"When we went out the shots came and I shot back. The shots came and I shot back. The shots came and I shot back. I tell you it was to protect my buddies. But I didn't give a fuck about them. I never have. It's always been my skin, not yours, baby. My skin, not yours, baby. Save my skin, not yours baby. There wasn't one of us who wasn't lying when he said 'I'll die for you boys.' I'll die for you boys. Maybe we had to live in this grim place, but we weren't going to die here. I was not going to lie in that mud for eternity. Not me. Not me. Not me.

"Okay, so I killed a man. And then I went a little bit berserk. A little mad. 'I've killed a man,' I say. 'I've killed a man.' And then I went a little mad. But no one's there. I don't know where the others are. Maybe they're dead. Maybe they're dead. Maybe they're dead.

"I'm shouting and I'm running. I think I'm calm but then I know I'm not because I'm shouting and I'm running. And maybe I'm crying. It is hard to know because I don't know where I am. I don't know where I am.

"When I get back to the hut, I'm not surprised. When I get to the hut I'm not surprised. Maybe I ran a week, or two, or two. It was the hut, I passed before. A week before, or two, or two. I recognize the little house. It looks like all the others. And there she was, she was, there she is. The woman I had taken the week before. The woman I had had the week before. The woman I had had. You know you just go in and take the spoils of war. The spoils of war.

" 'Where where where's your husband?' I asked her. I knew enough words to ask for the essentials: Information, Food. Sex. Money. Sex and money. Sex and money. She was silent but I could see she was used to plunder. She lay under me like a worn mat. She went cold under me. It was like fucking ice. It was like fucking ice. I needed a woman. Listen. I needed a woman. Listen. Give a guy a break.

" 'Where's your husband?' I ask barely getting the words out because I'm out of breath. I'm out of breath. She says, 'You killed him last week.' She says, 'You killed him last week.' She says 'You killed him last week.' 'Me?' I say. 'Me?' I say. 'I've never killed anyone. I wouldn't hurt a fly, baby. I believed it then. I wouldn't hurt a fly.

"Do you know what I did? I didn't do anything. There was nothing to do. I did nothing. Outside her house. I sat there. Doing nothing. Only outside her house. I didn't want to intrude. Then I saw an axe and wood that wasn't cut. I put myself in bondage. I build the fires. I build the fires. I chop the wood. I turn the soil. It's a bitch. It's filled with rocks. It's a bitch.

"We do not speak. We do not speak. I intend to stay here. I don't go in the house even when it rains. We do not speak. I intend to stay here. I watch over her. It's the least I can do. It's the least I can do. It's the least I can do."

Those are my lines. I wait. There's no applause. The house-lights do not come on. That's where the dream ends.

ADA. The Widow won't have you.

THE GENERAL. Why don't you call yourself a widow?

ADA. I didn't lose a son.

\*          \*          \*

THE WOMAN. Do you hear that voice? It's Malintzi. Do you want to know what she says?

LA MALINCHE. I am the one who was given. I am the gift. And the man who gave me made a war upon me in that act, but nevertheless I was open. My legs were open and my mouth was open and I gave what was asked of me. I am the one they call the whore. *La Chingada. Chingar. Chingar. Chingar. La Chingada.*

THE WOMAN. I draw close to her. I feel her little bird body nestling into mine. She is a thin bird, a febrile bird, a brilliant turquoise bird. She is the endangered quetzal.

   The jungle hisses around her. She is condemned in the market place. The crowd gathers outside her door. *Puta. Sangre de la madre. Chingada.* She shouts:

LA MALINCHE. What do you want of me? You who also managed to survive and to remember me, you who condemn me as your mother, you who call me the gate, the door, what do you want of me?

CHORUS. They say his name was Cortez. That he lay with you. That he slept. He who no offering satisfied, he lay with you. And he slept. Why didn't you in one gesture—you had seen the ceremony at the pyramids, you had been a witness—why didn't you steal a flint knife and in one motion—it only takes a moment and not as much strength as you imagine—why didn't you plunge the knife into his chest and pull out his beating heart?

LA MALINCHE. And to what purpose?

   Yes, I could have founded an order of priestesses who practiced the cutting out of hearts. But he did not offer his heart to me. The warrior always gave his heart to the sun. I couldn't take what had not been offered. I couldn't take it. Even as I was taken, I couldn't do it.

\*                    \*                    \*

THE WOMAN. Listen. The axe continues, the tree is unsteady, soon
it will be burning in my fireplace. My own life, especially
here, is so tame. Last week I wrote the following in my journal: "Today the man tried to teach me how to shoot elk.
Elk and venison, he insisted, were the best meats. Lean and
hardy. He said to eat only that which fed itself on the range,
that which grazed and nibbled on trees. He said to avoid
everything which is corn-fed. And as he prepared to leave,
I saw him standing beside the cab of his truck in which the
three rifles were displayed according to the law, inspecting
a leather case, two feet in length, narrow and flat, and to my
surprise, lined with blue velvet. And in it? A flute."

THE NARRATOR. The woman writes—

THE WOMAN. A story: Once upon a time there lived a man who
worked with guns and also learned to play the flute. From a
distance, the woman he befriended in the woods, could not
discern which instrument was pointed toward her. He himself found the shapes similar and did not always know which
he intended to use. One morning the woman drilled holes in
the barrel of the rifle. But though she was quite careful in the
placement and size of the holes, the man could not play the
gun the way he played a flute. It did have the same song no
matter how he put his heart to it. And the rifle was ruined.
It wouldn't sing and it wouldn't kill deer.

HER FRIEND. And we know it won't lay eggs.

THE WOMAN. I spent all morning chopping wood in return for rent.
I sharpened the axe and then lifted it above my head, brought
it down with two hands and split the log. Hour after hour.
Last week the flutist sharpened my knife for me. He said:

THE WOODSMAN. This will cut anything now. Test it on that paper,
on a hair. It's a good knife, I know because it has taken me
so long to hone it. A sharp knife is a beautiful thing.

THE WOMAN. Does Ada go to the General of her own free will?
Or have I put her up to it?

THE NARRATOR.  A story:

THE WOMAN.  Quiet. I'm tired of it. And of you. And of all the
others. If you can't tell me what we make happen, I don't
want to hear it. A story is not what happens to us. It is what
we do.

*                    *                    *

THE NARRATOR.  She is the descendent of the first priestess who is
La Malinche. She rises without her official robes having forgotten the prayers and stands still in the center of the little
cell where she has been isolated. She looks out the window
at the noon sun. She is without any distraction. She paces
back and forth, back and forth. No one knows who she is
and she herself does not know that she is waiting for this
moment.

The old blood has been passed on through the generations;
La Malinche had a daughter and the daughter of La Malinche
had a daughter. And the daughter of the daughter had a
daughter and so on. And even in the generations where there
were only sons, the blood rage was passed on as well through
the son to his daughter.

The first priestess had been a witness and she had seen
the offered hearts cut out of the warriors and given to the
sun and she had seen the sun hot as her own belly rise in the
dawn and hover hungry over the land pulling the corn and
fruit out of it with its own ravenous force. And she had
known that hunger herself and had kept it alive without her
and then had passed it on, a heat as hot and wriggling as the
hearts offered to the sun until it leaped by itself, a wild animal in the kill.

And she had seen the other deaths, the deaths without
offerings. The deaths demanded by the white god who was
not a god but a ghost. And she had seen the spirit of her
improperly killed brother hover frightened in the air and
burrow finally for warmth in the ashes that came from the
houses which the white ghosts had set on fire. These were
not the sun gods returning, these were not the walking stalks
of corn, this was not Quetzalcoatl, this was not the Morning

Star. These ghosts had no fire in them. Pale spirits desperate
for gold and blood to light a fire in them. And she had seen
the terrible emptied plaza where once the sun had reigned
and now had set. And on her belly every night the little
twisted ghost squirmed and sweated to raise a child.

And the blood slept for years. And would have died but that
she had a daughter. But it was not the daughter of the squat
ghost, but the daughter of some Aztec warrior that she had
found in the jungle and who had in him some of the old heat
from the sun which had burned now fifty-two years and was
about to go out. She passed the blood to her daughter without
awakening it and the little girl, when she was grown, passed
it on as well. And all in silence so as not to disturb the sleep.

In the cell the new priestess paces back and forth and stops
momentarily to look at the noon sun. She measures time.
She measures space. She has been waiting more than four
hundred years.

An animal paces in its cage. It does not know what it is
required to do. The jaguar is a summer beast.

There is the familiar heat. And silence. She knows in detail
what is outside her window but there is another scene which
she will never see with her own eyes teaching her as well.
She doesn't eat. The food, it's said, is rotten, and down the
hall the inmates clank tin plates against the iron bars. She
hears another drum. A ceremony is beginning. The food is
rotten because she must not eat. How will the test come after
all these years? In what shape and in what form? She has
forgotten everything. Indeed she does not know she is a
priestess. And a new age beginning and a fire to be lit.

Instinct will teach her and instinct is this blood memory,
is this blade of sun which cuts into her cell and does not leave
despite the movement of the sun across the sky. That is the
sign.

It's very hot. The lights go out. Electricity fails. The dark
is fierce after the sharp sun fades.

The man gropes his way down the hall, sweaty and sucking
ice. He's absentminded, carries the ice pick while he proceeds about his rounds. Routine is his habit and he does not
know this is a sacred day.

Before she came to the temple, the white ghost had found her in the jungle. He thought he could pluck her out. She was only a jaguar to be caged. He built a zoo for her. The deputy passes her cell and sees the priestess lithe as an animal. Pacing. Something of the jungle in her. Or the savannahs. The tall grasses and the lianas which can hide any manner of things. The jaguar is in her legs, the way she moves, in the yellow eyes. He catches her leathery heat. He thinks he is required to hunt.

What animal cry which no one else can hear engages his attention so that he is drawn to her cell? He extends the chain of keys attached to his belt and fits one into the lock.

She is not certain who he is. She is not clear about what she must do. After all, she does not remember the prayers, the rites; she has forgotten every ceremony. She says:

THE PRIESTESS. You can not open this cell until morning. I can see you; you can see me. Lockup was at nine o'clock and even if I were ill and called to you for help, you couldn't open the cell unless you called a doctor and then only when he came.

I am in solitary and I have the right to be alone.

THE NARRATOR. Instinct silences her. She can not reveal who she is. She does not know what is coming but it may be that action will be required of her now. She has spent a long time preparing, trying to remember the prayers. This blood has aged in her over four hundred years.

She bites her tongue and pushes up against the wall the way a cat backs up against a tree in order to leap.

He sees the woman but he smells the cat. Prey calls to him. He has never been challenged in this way. His grandfather showed him how to take a fox but that is small game compared to this big cat, to jaguars which he has never seen, not even in books.

Some pyramids are cool and high and open to the sky and eagles come. Some pyramids are hot and high and open to the sun and jaguars roam among the lianas.

He puts the key in the lock. A smile spreads across his face, whatever smile he is capable of, it resembles the slash of a knife which has ripped his gums apart. He hears the rattle of the tumblers, the clear sound of metal falling upon metal and the erotic slide of the bolt back into the door. It is all enacted in this moment. Metal excites him like gold.

She moves toward the window where once the sun slit the dark like a knife. She pads on bare feet. Nothing is there to help her now. How is this to be done? Or is this only another preparation, the test of her endurance, her suffering, the refinement of the will? She is ready for anything. She is pure. She has been alone in this cell for months. She is worthy to perform the necessary act.

She waits. He moves toward her. Her thin dress is striped as a pelt. Remember how hot it is. So hot he chipped at ice and took the ice pick with him without thinking. And it is very dark. Because the electricity failed, they say, but it is simply the disappearance of the sun for a moment. The universe has come to a stop and everything depends on her.

He grabs her in his sweaty awkward grip and with his left hand still holding the ice pick and the right hand clenched with keys, he throws her down in one motion and with his right hand opens his pants. Her dress tears. The keys help him. They are heavy and work to open her. She does not flinch. She is all attention. Surely this is not only a test. Surely there is more to this than her endurance, more than humiliation and degradation which is so commonplace. Surely something else is required of her.

The jaguar does not close her eyes even when her death is certain. The jaguar always contains the leap within her. To the last moment the jaguar keeps her teeth bared.

He does what he wants. She does not stop him. And he is very careful, but in that moment when he must abandon himself, she who is fully alert, leaps and in one gesture grabs the ice pick from his hands and as he staggers off her, half pleasuring and half shocked, she with her two yellow hands pulls the pick back over her head and plunges the flint blade into his chest and then extracts his beating heart.

It is not night. The sun has not set. The light blazes blood red on the horizon.

LA MALINCHE. Is that what you wanted? Is that the rite? Are we avenged? Or am I still the wound?

THE NARRATOR. The smells of the compound. The smells of the old
woman. The smells of an old age home. Mold. Where the
rain comes in, blue mold spreads on the white baseboard.
Blue veins up her arms. The red network across the nose.
Liquor trails. Ant trails. The old lady turns in her bed. The
house creaks. The wind. She passes wind. In the old days
she crowed.

GRACE. "Whores! Make any sound you want. We're not ladies you
know." Do you think I'm a lady, Joe? Of course, you wouldn't
leave your big lumber company for just a common whore.
Come for lunch, Joe? Well, lickety split. Damned white belly
and pink face you're just like a strawberry ice cream cone
except for those black hairs. White sideburns. Acid breath.
You wouldn't dare fart, Joe. You are too refined. If you do,
I'll know it's an accident and get a match. If only they'd let
me keep a candle burning. A green one. We always had
green candles burning in the compound. Scented. Winter-
green. Jake. Pine. Ten men in a single night fouls the air,
and you can't open the damned windows because it's so cold.

THE NARRATOR. She turns in her bed. Her own body doesn't smell
like it used to. She puts a finger into her vagina and brings
it up to her nose.
   Familiar but dry and urine scented. Oh yes, she did pee,
but just to spite the nurse.

GRACE. Where's the waterfall? Remember, Pearl?—no one knew
about it but us. We found it that Sunday we managed to get
away and follow the river bed down until we heard the sound
of it dropping off the cliff. We were above it in the dark

undergrowth, crowded with the trees that had been falling there for hundreds of years. Thousands, I bet. They grow too close and then they have to lean against each other and then they fall. Just like us, Pearl, flat on their asses. Oh, old Joe, he wanted to get his hands on that acreage and all those trees. Keep your hands where they belong, I'd say. Could you rub here? He'd bristle. Listen, I came to be taken care of myself. Ssh, ssh, I'd soothe him, right here, at the base of the spine, slower, now come around the base of the trunk, right between the legs, there. Aah.

THE NARRATOR. The woman imagines the old kimono she found in a corner of her cabin is one of their old rags.

Maybe it belonged to Grace. She paces up and down. Is Grace that woman in the old age home, the one they say used to be a whore? She wants to meet her. It's late. Why did she tell that man she'd spend the night with him?

THE WOMAN. Don't ask me why I told him, "If you cook me an an elegant dinner, I'll let you seduce me."

HER FRIEND. Trying to learn the trade?

THE NARRATOR. It's 9:00 p.m. The small man, his arms filled with the ordinary brown bags steps into the cabin and doesn't ask, not even with his eyes where to set down the packages. Then he insists she sit down in the chair he carefully has positioned so that she can observe each of his motions as he prepares the meal. It's her domain, but he knows where the kitchen knives are. He has chosen a delicate wine and proceeds with the ritual extraction of the cork. Careful. Careful. The ice. The fragrance.

He will not let her help, not even move. She is seated as if for a portrait but he is the one who displays himself. Each gesture precise, the knife sharpened against the whetstone until, as he demonstrates, it cuts paper. He pares the vegetables so thin the light passes through them, cucumber folding over mushrooms.

He spreads crackers with careful mounds of caviar sprinkled with chopped onion, with mashed yellow and white eggs. She dips her finger into the jar. He looks away with obvious distaste. She sucks on the roe, bursting the little eggs one by one against the roof of her mouth.

A man she once lived with had a fantasy of delicately sculpted bound feet and collected life-size triangular china replicas, soft infant toes folded down onto the instep, each porcelain foot encased in gold embroidered slippers, rare brocade. He kept them in the bookcase behind glass. "A foot like a phallus," he said, "perfect and white to slip into the mouth." And the women, his china dolls, so precise and still. Water arrested in its fall. Unmoving. Crystal feet.

THE WOMAN. I burned them. In the hottest fire I could manage. Porcelain exploding, the toes opening out, finally stretching free.

THE MAN. Please, don't get up. Let me help you. I'll do anything you ask. Your wish is my command. Command me. Don't move, please. Let me, on my knees. I'll wait on you hand and foot.

THE WOMAN. What do I do, Grace? I see you in the corner stretched out across the couch, your kimono bound tightly just like mine about your waist and your feet delicately held by those high-heeled slippers.

GRACE. It's only a fuck he wants, dearie, but in his own style. Do what he asks. Tie him to the bed and let him grovel about. What's it to you?

THE WOMAN. And later?

GRACE. You take a bath.

THE WOMAN. And then?

GRACE. You read a book. You are a free woman.

THE WOMAN. He says he wants to be the prostitute. Play the general, he begs. Command me. Let me serve. Let me wash your feet.

GRACE. He's never the prostitute, no matter what he says; he's always in charge.

THE WOMAN. I need to leave now. There's an old woman I must see.

THE NARRATOR. They say the Green Dragon Ladies formed a cooperative long after they were brought up the river from another country and planted here like the eucalyptus or Chinese elms.

THE WOMAN.  Did they ever learn to speak the language?

THE NARRATOR.  Grace turns in her bed, pushes the call button in irritated sequence for the day nurse to come and help her into her kimono and wheel her into the day room.

GRACE.  The parlor, if you don't mind.

THE NARRATOR.  Everything is out of order. She can't ask the orderly in the doorway to help her into her dress. Yet on the other hand . . . might it not amuse him? She raises her hair onto the top of her head, turns her white back to him and waits for him to fasten her brassiere. Now her stockings, she stretches out her white shapely leg pulling the hose up to the thigh herself and then slipping the pink embroidered garter up over it. And her shoes? Yes, those in the corner. The red ones with the very thin heels. She turns her toes down as a dancer might and waits for him to slip them on. Later it will all come off, she must remember the order, the magic is in the reversal, he will hold her ankle as he slips the shoe off, rolls the garter down, his fingers just pressing into her thigh as the stocking floats onto his hand, her leg extended, no underpants, the lips opening just slightly to his eyes.

GRACE.  Damn the hospital gown.

THE NARRATOR.  The orderly never seems to move. At odd moments during the day she looks up out of her memories and sees him staring, his body filling the doorway, his hospital mask limp about his neck. Slightly unshaven, patches of stubble, his arms dangling at his sides, rather too long, she thinks, for his body.

GRACE.  Oh, if only he would raise me up in his great white arms, oh! Where did the other girls put my comb? The ivory one I liked so much because my sister gave it to me before I left. The boat going up the river. Why was the water green, not blue? Water snakes and fish and the lingering warm mud smell of river water in my nose. One of the girls fell in and pretended she couldn't swim and so that odd gentleman went

in after her with all his clothes on and almost sank. And how
we laughed knowing she had been born near the ocean and
was trained at fourteen to dive for pearls. Off the cliff in a
straight line like a pelican. We called you Pearl always after
that.

He's there every time I look up. Have I been sleeping?
Where's the nurse? Why won't anyone dress me? I want to
be wheeled into the day room. Where's the deep blue kimono?
Pearl, perhaps you will help me with my corset and later this
man in the doorway, after it is on, he can pull on the laces
and we'll see how my waist comes in and my breasts plump
over the stays. He never moves. He is always there. You
might find my mirror for me. I've lost it.

GRACE. Where's my robe? Get it for me, and rouge also. I forgot
to put on lipstick today.

THE NARRATOR. She reaches to the night stand and finds a can of
of talcum powder.

GRACE. Shiny can, sweet smell. Do they think I'm a baby?

NARRATOR. She plays with the can, turning the lid, the little holes
open, one, two, three. She shuts it again and opens it, turning
it upside down, the powder falls out, little white mounds.
She dips a finger into it and rubs it under her arms and in
the folds where her belly meets her groin. He never moves.

GRACE. Do you remember, Pearl, how it used to snow and snow
and snow? I thought the men would never get through that
half mile down the dirt road through the trees, but they came.
Time to put in extra wood for the winter. "Cut us a few logs,
Joe," I'd say to test him. He always said, "Not on your life,
cutting logs is what I do all day." Pearl, you swung an axe
better than any man I knew. Could split a log in your sleep.

THE NARRATOR. The old woman lifts her shaky hands, her fingers
meeting in a V and brings them down hard between her legs.
And again.

Old smells of the compound lingering under the new
smells.

The floor buckling over the earth. Irises coming up wild
in the spring, bulbs used and reused. Off the porch is a pine

tree gashed where a clothesline had been tied and the young tree grew over the knot, a circle of rope caught deep in the trunk and the sap dripping down. The rest of the rope long gone. The woman hangs her jeans to dry on the back of a metal chair.

THE WOMAN. Do you know what a general is?

HER FRIEND. What?

THE WOMAN. A pink face and white belly covered with black hairs. A stomach which protrudes over a belt. The genitals unwashed. The smell of shit, faint but unmistakable from the ass. A cruel and limited desire. Detached erection. The mind in another country, the buttocks pumping. Sweat dripping down from the hairline. The face shaved clean. The hair short. The neck sunburned and lined. A callous on the second finger of the right hand.

HER FRIEND. How would you know?

THE WOMAN. From experiences I never had.

HER FRIEND. Your father called you a whore, remember?

THE WOMAN. I wasn't even fifteen.

HER FRIEND. You weren't even willing to fuck for a meal tonight.

THE WOMAN. The price wasn't high enough.

HER FRIEND. Liar.

THE WOMAN. Think of it; Maybe it is the only profession open to females.

HER FRIEND. There are others.

THE WOMAN. What are they?

HER FRIEND. Fire eaters and sword swallowers.

CHORUS. We admit only one thing: a prostitute is always a desperate woman.

THE NARRATOR. And the last time they made love when he'd driven her up to this cabin so she could feel safe, she left the curtains open to see out into the trees toward the green net which held them. She slipped down his body as into a river, grasping at the roots of the trees on the bank, her mouth in his groin, wetness to wetness, his hands entangled in her damp hair.

THE LOVER.  You should have been a courtesan.

THE WOMAN.  Perhaps I was in another life . . . or will be in the next one.


GRACE.  The ankles are still good. Don't you think? Where's that orderly? Didn't want to impose on him here in my boudoir and the nurse won't take me into the parlor. My skin is softer than it ever was. And I'm still small here in the waist, but you can't see it because of this damned gown. When Hank came to see me, all he wanted really was a hot bath. The day we found the waterfall, I wanted to wash my hair in it, but we were too far to even feel the spray. And we had to get back before the guys came. Always used to say those men would have torn the entire town apart on Saturday night if not for us. I thought we should have gotten a commendation from the marshall's office. Told that to Alf straight out. We were the best investment in law and order they ever made.

Green gown. So faded. Not like those green ferns. Rough. Where's the damned nurse? Who's coming tonight? Look at that lovely leg. I don't have to shave it anymore, hairs are so sparse and light, just like when I was a girl. And look at that bare cunt. I must be getting younger. Only a hint of hair. There's one. I always thought a bare cunt looked like a featherless bird, or one of those wet things coming out of the egg. When that guy complained about my screwing, I told him to get himself a cold hen and stick his dick in that. Little fingers still feet sweet. Nurse better not come. I ought to keep my hands above the sheets. If the orderly comes back, I'll have to ask him if he'd like some tea. Start slow and easy. How will I serve him? They never let me out of this damned bed. No one ever comes any more. No one comes.

THE NARRATOR.  Afternoon shadows fall into the room. Stripe of bedrails cut across the white linens. A tray of food seems to have arrived and been removed mysteriously. The old woman sits up on the bed abstractly twisting the few remaining pubic hairs as someone might worry a cowlick. Everything is thinning. Age is a pruning process. The branches diminish. The leaves fall. Everything turns brown and brittle and then, snip, it's gone.

THE WOMAN. Perhaps it is only a rumor that she is alive. Or that that she ever existed. Is she just another old woman out of work and without a pension? Who would acknowledge that she had been working for the state?

THE NARRATOR. The Woman paces up and down, thinking about Grace, and then returns to her chair to write, pressing her hands up against her inner thighs. "Grace is comfortable with her genitals," the Woman writes, "like an old dog burrowing with her nose into the piquant places between her hind legs, licking and licking." The Woman envies Grace. The smell of her own cunt confuses her. The smell of her lover's skin. The smell of sex in the morning, carried deliberately on her body, refusing to shower, the bit of private life carried through the day. Washing at night, before lovemaking, coming fresh to the sweet cycle.

THE WOMAN. Do you know what pudenda means?

THE NARRATOR. The Woman speaks to the empty room.

THE WOMAN. Pudenda means shame.

This is a book about eggs. Nothing more. And nothing less.

\*             \*             \*

ADA. I want to begin raising chickens. My sister has promised me a few hens. Even a rooster.

THE GENERAL. I thought there were no hens in the entire village.

ADA. True. There are none.

THE GENERAL. Then?

ADA. Nevertheless.

THE GENERAL. It is against the law to raise chickens. You know that. When they said there were no eggs because there were no hens, I said, "Let it be that way from now on." So why would you raise hens?

ADA. To roost in front of your house.

THE WITNESS. Usually, when she comes into his house, she sits down at the table and stays there for the entire evening. She can sit as still as anyone he has ever seen. Now she gets up and walks about. She is completely indifferent to him. Her foot scrapes idly against the old rug and she circles the table again. Her movements are slow. Finally she squats before the fireplace. The sound which emerges from her mouth is a bird sound, a chicken sound, a hen sound. The egg drops out of the ovary, is pressed down the tubes toward the uterus. The sound is pruck pruck pruck pruck. Her mouth is yellow and stiff. Her eyes dart about the room. Her arms tremble in an imperceptible flutter of feathers.

The cloth of her dress hides her legs in its folds. Soon her hand reaches between her legs for the egg which she places in her lap. Then she rolls it across her palm. She extends her hand to him. He reaches for the egg but she withdraws and places the egg gently into the pocket of her old sweater.

ADA. It is for the Widow Marina. Since her husband and son are dead, she can not protect the chicken coop from your soldiers. Sometimes there is not enough to eat.

THE NARRATOR. Before coming to the compound, the Woman had been looking for traces of Malintzi. In Cuernavaca, she was finally directed toward La Malinche's Villa which is not far from the Palace of Cortez. But in the end, the Woman did not go there.

THE WOMAN. Do you have any secrets, Grace?

GRACE. Secrets? What would I want to hide?

THE WOMAN. Let me tell you one of my secrets:
I was among the pyramids. The sun had run across the twilight sky as if a humming bird had punctured it with its incandescent beak. A man found me alone and spread my legs against the edge of his knife. He was a son of Malintzi and the General. But whom does he favor, the blood is so well mixed in him?
Is he also part of your revenge, Malintzi?

LA MALINCHE. I know nothing of any of this.

THE WOMAN. The pyramid is a hard bed. The old stones do not soften over the years. The man with the knife says he is taking revenge for an old wound. He says, "Give me your love." I force myself to smile, as a ruse in order to escape. Inside, a voice advises me: Why not take your pleasure since you are likely to be killed?

HER FRIEND. Had I known, I would have held you in my arms.

THE WOMAN. The question remains. If I were a true warrior, would I have used his knife to excise my heart for the sun?

THE NARRATOR. The Woman does not seek out Grace. It is almost midnight, even if she could find the home, there is no way she would be admitted. The friendship with this old woman will come slowly. The old woman tosses in the hospital bed. When the bedsores spread and deepen, she will be lying on pure bone.

GRACE. Don't you think I deserve a last good fuck before I die? Rude. Rude. Little girls get in trouble that way. The boogie man is going to get you. If only he would. I'll lie down and wait for him. He's the last man.

THE NARRATOR. She settles into the sheets lifting her aching legs, knees up, into a pyramid. All secrets are buried here. Perhaps this is how she dies.

THE WOMAN. Was it at the pyramid or in the jail? Shall I tell you about this or do you already know? Was it at the pyramid, or the jail that I met him? Was it the jailer, a general, the rapist, or was it my lover, I was meeting?

In the heat. In the stench of a thousand flowers. In the rot of centuries. Where the white flower grew like a vine covering everything which had occurred before. In the heat. Walking. Alone. Assuming a woman could not walk alone. I met him. In the pyramid street. Without introductions. In the hot south. Like a streetwalker. A prostitute. But I had not yet decided to be any of these.

CHORUS. Can't you rise out of the body? They will always call you flesh, when you offer yourself.

THE WOMAN. And you are like the rest of them. You are like he is.

You do not admire the body. You love only that which flies and has no substance. When I use my body to change him, don't call me a whore.

CHORUS. Do you want, then, to increase your weight? We will accommodate you with stones.

*          *          *

THE NARRATOR. When she leaves her own house, she is surrounded by a circle of women.

CHORUS. ADA!

THE WITNESS. When she emerges from the General's house, the circle of women guards the door.

CHORUS. ADA!

CHORUS. We are twelve women and she entering the circle, is she the thirteenth?

THE WITNESS. The moon is a white hole in the sky. They know the right time. Even her sister is among them.
  The circle is complete. No one can intervene on her behalf. Each one carries a stone. Those with allegiance to hell may kill by fire, those who occupy the earth have many means, but those who belong to the moon have only stones.

CHORUS. Ada! Beware. We carry:

Hearthstone
Altar stone
River stone
Field stone
Sandstone
Limestone
Lodestone
Pumice stone
Whetstone
Millstone
Gallstone
Grindstone

ADA. Gravestone

THE WITNESS.  The shadow of her as if the trees moved. The pointed
    darkness stretching behind her. Walking toward the sun
    which moves away from her. The trudge west. The sun
    always moving toward setting. The shadow now falling on
    the grave. The point of her head marking the hour. The chat-
    ter of the winter squirrels. Pebbles under her feet. The dark
    of her blunt steps.

    She doesn't wonder if he waits for her. In such a small
    village even a general can be bored and grateful for the
    distraction, such as it is, of a village woman. For the moment
    his position is not strategic. It is temporary. Nevertheless
    there are the jeeps, the cars, the telegraphs, telephones,
    ammunition, weapons. The military presence is everywhere.

    She pays no attention to any of this. She doesn't expect any
    sound or light to travel up the shadow she casts behind. She
    doesn't know where the shadow falls.

    Every night she returns to her own house, pulls the covers
    down at an angle leaving the right side of the bed covered
    and untouched and crawls in under the icy sheets. And every
    night after some hours, she gets up reluctantly, as if it were a
    new idea, and pulls the covers up to make the bed where
    the pillowcase is barely wrinkled from the pressure of her
    head, dresses and drags herself to that other cemetery bed
    where she tries to sleep.

    The General says:

THE GENERAL.  I want you to stay the night.

THE WITNESS.  She shakes her head.

    She is peeling an orange which he has given her, pulling
    the skin back from the pulp in four carefully slit crescents

and then dividing the bare fruit between them, though he suggests she eat it all. This is the first fruit she has taken from him. He does not know whether she hears any of what he says. She speaks rarely and then only when it pleases her. She appears deliberate and yet without thought. As if her body thought. As if the mind had so advanced, it had managed to permeate every body cell and she has become sentient intellect. The mind no longer abstracted, focused, purposive, but diffused, de-fused and enacted osmotically in each muscle, bone, nerve, cell.

THE GENERAL.  Will you spend the night?

THE WITNESS.  Standing behind her, he massages her shoulder and neck; this is the first time he has dared to press into her flesh. She shakes her head. She is satisfied with things as they are. Eating half an orange. Crossing and uncrossing her legs.

He doesn't say, "Listen, what are you doing here? I don't have all day."

She doesn't try to engage him in talk.

When he bends down and lifts her by the arms, pulling her to the bed, she simply sits at the edge, fingering the feather quilt.

ADA.  I recognize this quilt. My mother made it for the Widow Marina when she married. I don't remember if it was a commission or a gift. This square in particular, I recognize. It's very old. Out of the remainder, my mother made a dress for my doll. It was years ago. You can see by the frayed edges. The feathers will come through soon. You'll have to have it redone. But no one will do it for you. We won't work on stolen goods. What do you think she uses to keep warm at night, now that her husband is dead as well?

THE WITNESS.  He unbuttons his shirt and begins to open his belt, then pauses. Planning a strategy, he sits down, his back to her on the other edge of the bed. A man only removing his shoes. surely there is no harm in that. He urges her—

THE GENERAL.  Come to bed.

THE WITNESS.  She puts the pillows up against the wall and without removing her dress slides onto the bed pulling the comforter about her as she smooths her dress down across her knees.

He says:

THE GENERAL. You could remove your shoes.

THE WITNESS. She extends her feet from the bed and he goes to her and takes off her shoes but when he reaches for her, she pulls away.

ADA. I will return this quilt to her. The winter is too long for her to be deprived.

THE GENERAL. I need it as well.

ADA. Sleep in your clothes.

THE WOMAN. I have come to love Ada so. Don't let any harm come to her.

THE NARRATOR. There is nothing we can do. Her life is beyond our control.

THE WOMAN. And beyond our protection.

HER FRIEND. Do you think we are incapable of inventing guns?

ADA. What shall I do with this man? He presses against me through his clothes and twitches as men do in the moments before they fall deeply asleep. Whenever I slept with my sister, this didn't happen. Women don't have these night terrors.

THE WITNESS. She slips out of the bed, successful in not waking him. She does not have to dress, only to put on the red shoes and wrap a shawl over her head and shoulders against the winter air. She has never left his house at so late an hour. She knows that those who monitor the movements in the village will note the time she leaves as well as the new wrinkles in her dress. She doesn't need to see the curtains moving to know that even the dark stains under her arms are observed. The dress has become progressively more disheveled. Just this morning she mended a seam which had opened, but there is no time to wash the dress in this climate where nothing dries quickly. What would she wear in the meantime? This is the only garment she has which is appropriate to her task. And who, passing the dress drying on the limb of the tree, would not hesitate to tear it to ribbons and hang the triumphant flag in the street?

The two dangers: The contraband gun in the village; the General himself. His training is worthless to him if it can not be utilized. He is interested in limited dilemmas, in those which only appear to confound the mind. He has been educated, ultimately, to act.

THE WOMAN.  A love letter to Ada:

Dear Ada,

You lie on the earth among the cold stones. And afterwards you lie by the cold body of the General. Another stone. You get up. You go home. You get up. You go out. You lie down. You get up. You go home. These are the motions, the getting up, the lying down. The getting up, the lying down. The bed. The grave. And the bed. Your bed where your dead man sleeps. His grave where you sleep. The General's bed where the dead sleep. The General is also dead; his heart does not deceive you. Your husband is dead; his heart does not deceive you. And you? If only you were dead. But your own heart does not deceive you.

Hello, Ada. You pull your skirts smooth as you rise. The soil and leaves cling to you. Before you go to the General, you will wash. You bring nothing alive with you by accident. You do not wish to disturb the General too violently. You bring him one leaf at a time. If life were to enter him too quickly . . . then you would surely have to die.

Who, then, will bring warmth to your lover? Who will lie down on the grave? All the light is under the ground. The glow worm is the only creature you can rely on.

THE WITNESS.  At the grave, he stands over her holding a pistol in his hand. She says:

ADA.  You wouldn't shoot me here on my husband's grave.

THE GENERAL.  Why not? Do you think his ghost will protect you or haunt me when I leave? His spirit has done you no good up to now. Nor has he managed to do me any harm.

THE WITNESS.  She doesn't move. It occurs to her that her death here might be a convenience. They can open the grave and put her next to him. She will share his ignoble defeat. Dying can't be more uncomfortable than these cold and sleepless nights.

ADA. For a moment it crossed my mind to run, but I refused to be shot in the back. And if I am to die, let it be here to offend that silent husband of mine who doesn't even heave. A jerk at the knees or a kick would unbalance the General. Not much force is needed. Is his silence desire? Does he want me with him now? Or have his feet dissolved? Is he crippled? Are his bones soft? Have his limbs melted back lazily into the earth? Is he even more powerless than he was?

The gun, I thought, the gun, love, is by your right hand. I buried it myself knowing a man without a gun was useless to anyone including himself. Now's the time. Reach for it if you have fingers. I can't pull the trigger, but you can. You know how.

THE WITNESS. But the dead don't move and the gun has rusted and the barrel is filled with sand and little pebbles which root into it as the earth worms move about.

Even with a gun in your hand, it is possible to fall on a woman and if she doesn't run, then it is a question of strength and weight. Everything is in your favor. General.

The assault is unexpected. Her naivete astonishes her. A voice says she should have known and yet not this. Now there is no quilt and the dress pulls up under his hand. Nothing accommodates to her. The bed her body has made on the grave holds her tight. Everything conspires. She can not breathe.

ADA. Not here. Not on his grave.

THE GENERAL. Nowhere else.

THE WITNESS. Then all she wants is time. Time to prepare. Time. Time to prepare. He does not allow her too much breath before he presses into her. It is so familiar, the entrance of a man. The horror is that she knows the act.

THE GENERAL. You'll come to me tomorrow.

THE WITNESS. Ada doesn't answer. Her face says "never."

THE GENERAL. You'll come tomorrow. Now you know who I am.
Now your work begins. Before you were playing a game.
But now we are true enemies in our own styles. When you
arrive, you'll be paid. But nothing for tonight.

THE WITNESS. He doesn't look at her as he zips up his pants and
returns the gun to the holster, walking safely into the night
with only a slight mud stain about his knees. He does not
fear anyone will shoot him in the back. Even the cemetery
is a safe place for him since he has been its patron these last
months.

   And Ada? Her thighs fall together. Her dress is truly soiled.
She drags herself up, seems erect. She manages to return to
her own house where for the first time in over a year, she
sleeps, exhausted in her own empty bed.


CHORUS. ADA!

THE NARRATOR. But it is not Ada who is walking so boldly from the
cemetery. It is a man.

CHORUS. Ada!

THE WOMAN. ADA!
   You call out. You want her to turn around. You want to
step into her path. You hope she is a shadow. You jump out
of the bushes because you want to startle the dark. You want
to put your hands on her dark hair. You hope you will pass
through her hair, that she is only a ghost, that it is not a
woman who is dragging herself muddied toward the white
bed which has not been opened fully in over a year. You
believe in flesh and blood, but you wish it didn't exist.

THE WITNESS. The General walks matter-of-factly back to his house,
sidestepping the barking dog without so much as a glance
in its direction. No one will harm him. Nothing will bite him
tonight. He is not always so safe. He can not unwrap himself
from her.


THE WITNESS. The General paces in the small room which seems
smaller without Ada. His hands are muddy. The knees of his
uniform bear a dark stain.

As he got up from Ada, he must have noticed the bruise forming so quickly on her upper arm and the scratch across her cheek. It had been a long time since he has seen a woman weep soundlessly as if there were nothing he could do to alter her pain. And her mouth, open and stiff, curving as it did above her white teeth in that miraculous and diabolical curve, was sensual, pitiful, and bitter. There were tears, but the mouth did not cry. The eyes may not be restrained, but the mouth is wise. And silent.

After he entered her, she never spoke again. The eyes open wet and staring, reflected him. The lips fixed. In an instant, she turned cold, stiffened, as if she had died beneath him. And when he left her, the same wet staring eyes and the same triumphant mouth. And her body niched in the indentation upon the grave as if the earth had been her lover.

ADA!

THE WITNESS. Ada throws herself across the bed with the covers torn back, face down, the white sheets soil from her touch, one pillow tossed to the floor, her feet dangling off the sides. It appears she sleeps. The breathing eventually becomes fine and slow.

In the morning, she decides she must make another dress. This one is beyond repair.

THE WITNESS. Do not be surprised if Ada rises from bed and tramps to the General's house. The dead did not awaken. There's a life underground, but it ignores us in its own heated buzz. Anyone who has embarked on such an undertaking is not put off by worms.

CHORUS. Do you want more then? Didn't you have enough? Whore!

ADA. Now that you know my name, you may prepare a gravestone.

CHORUS. What will you wear, whore, since you've torn your sleazy silk dress and ruined your red shoes?

ADA. The sweater I've slept in every night for a year. The old skirt, shapeless as a shroud. The stink of the dead in my nose.

THE NARRATOR. And Malintzi in her summer palace carried the first boy child through the year it took to clear the Aztec dead. The alliance in her body—the terrible hope and shame. The bruise of the blue eyes. The mother is a virgin; the mother is a whore. The cock is engorged with blood. Why doesn't *it* bleed?

ADA. I've come to kill the General.

THE GENERAL. Really? Do you have a gun?

ADA. Men are killed with guns, but that does not kill generals. A bullet can not stop generals, no more than your fist can stop me.

HER FRIEND. This does not make sense at all.

THE WOMAN. Ssh. You, like the General, may also learn from this.

THE WITNESS. Ada doesn't knock. She enters his house and without a word to the General, she removes her coat and folds it carefully over the back of the chair, sitting down at the kitchen table. Her wool skirt, her sweater are both stretched out of shape. The hem is down; the seam is open.

THE GENERAL. Take off your clothes.

THE WITNESS. She refuses silently. After a time, she rises from her chair and goes to the General's bed. She removes the quilt and folds it with care, stroking each square.

ADA. Tomorrow you will take this to the Widow Marina. After that, you will lift the villager's prohibition against keeping hens. Tonight, you will cover me with your coat. The lining, they say, is made of silk.

THE GENERAL. Take off your clothes, then.

ADA. No.

THE GENERAL. Then why did you return? What do you imagine I want from you? Haven't you learned that I take what I want?

ADA. I know.

THE GENERAL. Did you like it then? I assume that is what they are saying in the village now that they have seen you come back for more. Was your icy body a fraud? How fortunate for you. So you will feel no guilt. How clever is your virtuous stand. And again the same ploy. How many times a night do you want to be forced? Take off your clothes.

ADA. No.

THE GENERAL. So. You are to remain the virgin and I am to remain the General. You say the General is always a General and does everything with a gun. Or shall I pick up a knife? Do your lily white hands remain lily white? Did you take your bruises to the mayor yet? Too bad he's dead. Or to the widow, or to your sister, or even to the cows? Did you weep pitifully at the hen house and all the time wanting to be forced? What do you want from me next?

ADA. Make me a cup of tea.

LA MALINCHE. And when I gave myself to Cortez, I didn't think he'd turn against his own son.

CHORUS. But he did. They do.

THE WITNESS. The cup steaming between them. The steam on the windows. Everything hidden in steam.

ADA. And now if you have some oil. We haven't any, you know, anymore. No one operates the presses. Everything which was stored has been requisitioned. The women don't bring me anything any more. A little oil, not rancid, if you don't mind. Fresh. And heated but not too hot, only until you don't feel any drops when you test it on your wrist. Then there are a few places on my body which must be oiled. The bruises will heal more quickly. It is not the sight of them, it is the pain of it. Where there were rocks and where the gun rubbed against me and the holster buckle and your fist.

HER FRIEND. I don't believe any of it.

THE WOMAN. Don't think about the General. It only matters what she does.

THE GENERAL. Would you like to shower?

THE WITNESS. Mud still on her feet and face. She rises to her feet, looking around, finds his robe and goes to the shower. The water is hot and she bends each of the bruises under the stream to take the cold out of her. The cold is deep and white in the bones.

THE GENERAL. I could learn to love your body.

ADA. Love or want?

THE GENERAL. I don't have to learn want.

ADA. No, you were born with it.

THE GENERAL. And you?

ADA. I had it pressed out of me in the same way that wine is pressed, with the feet.

THE GENERAL. Don't you ever feel desire?

ADA. Oh yes, desire is familiar. It comes up with the sun and then it sets.

THE GENERAL. We made a bargain once and I can teach you well.

ADA. I have had all your lessons.

THE GENERAL. Why are you here?

ADA. My house is cold. Your shower is hot. You have a winter coat which serves as a blanket. You have clean sheets. I do not have the strength anymore to wash sheets and hang them in the wind. I don't want the white to be interpreted as surrender.

THE GENERAL. Maybe you came to die.

ADA. I came for a cup of tea and here, to rub some oil on my bruises. Is it still warm?
I've brought you this.

THE WITNESS. The object she gives him is small and warm and round and white.

ADA. And now I'll go to bed. And you can sleep in the chair.

THE GENERAL. And in the morning?

ADA. I'll go home.

THE GENERAL. And in the evening?

ADA. I'll return.

THE GENERAL. Just so?

ADA. Just so.

THE GENERAL. I can take you again. One rape doesn't prevent another.

ADA. It's true.

THE GENERAL. Is that what you want?

THE WITNESS. Ada is silent.

THE GENERAL. In time you would have come to my bed.

ADA. Perhaps.

THE GENERAL. Then you may come to it again.

ADA. You will sleep on the chair tonight and in the morning . . .

THE GENERAL. Yes?

ADA. I will teach you to bring me a cup of tea and an egg.

THE NARRATOR. He turns his back and she sits on the edge of the bed. Weary. Determined. Her entire body hanging heavy, the flesh pulling down off the bones toward sheets as if she were sheets, as if she were winding sheets, as if the blood had left her but the body was heavy with death. The chemise she wears under his robe is not unlike a shroud. What pushes her, what force presses out through her when she rises unsure of the possibility of movement, but moving nevertheless, as the water moves against the boulder without asking if anything is in its path, as the water presses against a dam without hesitating upstream, as the water plunges over the precipice without halting fearfully at the edge before dashing itself down against the rocks?

She takes a pillow from the bed and the top sheet—she can spare that—and the table cloth, her sweater and skirt, and spreads the fabric on the two chairs she pushes together, then studying his height, thinks better of it and makes a bed on the floor by the stove where it may be warmer. His back is to her. Wrapped in the iron dark robe, the belt retied with a double knot, covered with the bitter-green coat, her eyes shut tight, she falls across the white bed. And closes as a gate.

HER FRIEND. And the General?

THE WITNESS. Sleeps alone.

THE WOMAN. Malintzi, I promised you this.

THE WITNESS. THE NARRATOR. THE WOMAN. The gate shuts. The doors are locked. Only light penetrates between the legs which are bars. The white sheets. The dark hair. The gates swing shut. The bars shut. The jailer is pushed out of the cell. The General sleeps on the floor.

THE WITNESS. When he was a little boy he slept thus before the fire. He entwines his fingers in the tablecloth and presses it against his cheek. Here, unwillingly, he dreams her. The fire burns low. Now chilled, he stirs, opens his eyes and sees her in the fire light. How warm she seems. Even on the grave with his knees in the cold mud and the dead sucking the heat out of him, he was warmed by her rosy belly. Sleeping in his clothes confirms the cold in the room. His knees, the icy tumulus, the cold barrel of the gun in his right hand, the cold belt against his calves, his head pressed into the marble stone. She's a flame. She turns cold, but she's a flame. The clothes transmit the icy frost. From her open frozen mouth, her reluctant breath is hot, a small furnace. She is comfort. Her cunt is the bellows sending the heat up his spine. If she loved him, he would ask her to blow on his frozen hands. In the snow when he had no gloves, taking his hand toward his mouth. Blow.

Standing over her. From an airplane, instruments can detect heat, cooking fires, animals, men, the pyramid of sexual energy. Bombs could fall on her from the sky. Guerilla warfare. Napalm. Fight fire with fire. The flush of her cheeks. Her hands out of sight. The angle of the arms seen beneath the greatcoat disappearing between her thighs. The fingers warming between the steaming folds of the delta. The heat rising from the swamps. Old oil, tar, bubbling up from the sulphur pits.

His hands extended over her sleeping body. Not too close to the flames. Turning them. Palms up. They are so empty. Waiting. Looks up to the ceiling. Everything is gray and cold. Turning them for the heat. And what if she died? Cold. He puts his hands to her mouth, she is breathing. His cold hands. Rub them together and blow. Palm on her head. Blessing.

Shivers. Pulls the edge of the greatcoat down to cover her naked feet which extend out of his coat. When the collar folds down, her neck is exposed. The dark hairs slightly damp. Where the robe parts, her hands angling down, the arrow of skin between the breasts. She stirs, turning into the bed, burrowing under the hump of the greatcoat, burying herself within the dark green barrow. He finds a rough military blanket and covers her.

THE NARRATOR.   THE WITNESS.   THE WOMAN. He walks backwards. Something pulling from behind. The gate swings shut at the cemetery. The clang of the cell door shoving the jailer into the corridor. The refrigerator door closes. The ice pick returns to the shelf. He lies down on the floor in the makeshift bed, winding himself about with the cloth and sheet, his hands swaddling into the white tablecloth against his cheek. Was in her hands. He dreams the feather bed. The beat of the old goose heart. Winding and winding into the white tablecloth. Stiff and cold. The hens ruffle their feathers and the cocks crow before dawn. The eggs drop fearlessly into the nest. The General will do no harm.

Cortez stiffens and withdraws from her body. La Malinche is young again. The blood gate is intact. There is no entrance into the city. The pyramids are sealed. Cortez stumbles backwards toward the brink of the world. The eastern edge of the continent trembles and the ocean snatches him down with shark's teeth. The little Indian girl has dreams dark as her skin. The sun is exaltant in the sky again. The trees circle her hut. Their child is brown as the sun. Her lover takes the first blood and marks her lips and his. She comes to the hut of her own will and lies down.

The General tosses restlessly on the cold floor.

THE NARRATOR. Seated on the edge of the bed, the Woman takes the hand of her Lover and places it on her heart, saying:

THE WOMAN. The mermaid . . .

HER LOVER. Oh, yes, I remember.

THE WOMAN. . . . plunged down under the sea . . .

HER LOVER. . . . and the man followed her.

THE WOMAN. And there for the heat of each other, she coiled about him and pressed her mouth against his so he could breathe, her breath passing into his blood and back and with one hand about her waist so that they floated together under the waves, he held her and with the other, his hands a gentle knife, parted the fin up to the delta and she spread the fin as if she had legs and there under the water while she gave him breath, he returned what was given, entering her.

WITNESS. In his half-dream, Ada whispers into the General's ear.

THE NARRATOR. La Malinche turns speaking in her dark sleep.

LA MALINCHE. I am the gift.

HER FRIEND. And Ada?

THE WOMAN. Ada claims the gift.

HER FRIEND. And the General?

THE WOMAN. He begins . . .

HER FRIEND. And you?

THE WOMAN. I call my lover and tell him I am coming home.

THE NARRATOR. Grace is laughing, her body heaving, the corset open and her full breasts plunging out of the black and white kimono. When the wine spills down her chest, Pearl splatters her further, the wine from her own glass flicked with thin fast fingers, purple drops across Grace's face. The man kneels to lick them. Grace rises, her stays undone, the laces open, the kimono bulging agape. She pulls him toward the bedroom. They fall onto the bed. The door is left open. "You'll stay the night, Alf," she shouts, "the snow has closed the road."

   "No, no. I'll be happy to shovel it clear, but later." He rolls with her into the snow drifts.

   "No. No." She laughs. "You will have to stay the night, Sheriff, here in the heat under the snow bank wrapped in these white feathers. In the morning, Pearl and I will shovel the road clear. Even if he owns a platoon of snowplows, no man will ever open or close that road."

ADA!

Will spring ever come?

As they sleep, the house is encircled by women. Each holds a stone in her hand. Hanging from their shoulders, are bags woven from hemp, filled also with stones. The women wait. They are still as gravestones. The sun rising between them marks the day.

Do you think she will be stoned?

The stones are to repair the road.

But . . .
    If the General does her harm . . .

# Healing Circles (1985)

*This piece is dedicated to two people. In the Winter of 1984, I began working with actor and director Warren Johnston, who had AIDS. Before Warren died in March, he had transformed his life and his community in significant ways. In January 1986, anthropologist Barbara Myerhoff died of lung cancer but not before she was the catalyst for the formation of a healing community.*

In the Eighties, there developed the phenomenon of people spontaneously gathering in small groups to take care of their ill and dying. The original impetus was the need to provide for those physical needs which the patient and immediate family could no longer maintain independently; friends shared responsibility for physical care, child care, transportation, and meals. When health necessitated a change of habits and patterns, the network researched, developed, and participated in diets, exercise programs, and meditations, as well as researching, scrutinizing, and coordinating medical information. As awareness grew of the necessity to maintain a positive emotional atmosphere about the patient, friends accompanied the patient to all doctor visits and lived with the patient in the hospital. This was essential because high technology dominated medicine to the extent that even diagnostic procedures had become aggressive, debilitating; in themselves, life-threatening. With some exceptions, medical practice was becoming increasingly erudite and authoritarian while medical personnel lost a concern of human needs. Medicine sometimes cured, but rarely healed. Interactions with physicians and medical personnel were often combative and a partner was needed to ask questions, supervise treatment and maintain the patient's well

227

being; in effect to insist that the ancient medical code, "Do no harm," was respected. As these needs became clear, the network, the extended family which had formed to provide physical care, diversified to satisfy medical, then emotional, and finally spiritual needs. Soon maintenance was transformed into a significant and effective healing process.

After awhile it became clear that a new social form was rapidly developing in response to the critical rise in the disease rate, the fact of extreme social alienation and dissolution, and the perception that healing necessitated social cohesion. This activity, though specific and highly ritualized, went unnoticed for a long time, though an interest in the humanization of dying had developed into the hospice movement. This new phenomenon was related but distinct; the new emphasis was on living, not dying. It gradually came to be understood that appropriate care, attention, the proper combination of science and prayer, of medicine and meditation, reversed illness, and miracles arose out of the joint efforts and purification of the individual and the community psyches.

Even in its primitive beginnings, this ritual activity was characterized by the dim perception that the caretakers were suffering as extremely as the patient, and that somehow they were also carrying the disease within them, if not [yet?] in its physical form. Sometimes the participants were affected by the healing activities even before the patient to whom they were directed, as in the case of Marjorie Reimar, whose neck snapped into place while she was meditating (for the first time in her life) for the health and well being of Barbara Myerhoff. This event (such events later came to be rather commonplace) occurred during the first meeting of Barbara Myerhoff's extended family. Fifteen people, not connected to each other except through friendship with Barbara, gathered to help in her healing process. They divided the domestic, medical, and emotional tasks among them. A different coordinator for each week organized the caretaking logistics. Different people took responsibility for different tasks, so as to provide Barbara with the maximum time and peace of mind to relax, meditate, exercise, heal herself. When it became clear to all that healing required nothing less than a complete change of life style and basic attitude, the network acted to create a clear space within which change was not only possible but inevitable. While one person meditated with Barbara regularly, another accompanied her on walks and encouraged gentle exercise, a third helped her complete a film which had been initiated before the illness, a fourth communicated regularly with perhaps hundreds of well wishers to all of whom Barbara could not possibly respond, a fifth organized her financial affairs, a sixth guided her through chemotherapy sessions, a seventh took over the car pool, an eighth established contacts with medical and spiritual counselors, a ninth established a dietary regimen and shopped and cooked, a tenth ran errands and did household repairs, others undertook childcare, even parented the two children, others provided transportation, engaged in research, accompanied Barbara on medical visits, read to her, and so on.

Unusual in the beginning, common if not ordinary in later years, these spontaneous caring networks formed for utilitarian reasons soon served more important spiritual purposes. Later research confirmed that the patient's quality of life changed significantly and that the patient began to thrive not because his or her life was eased, but because the love and care directed at the patient had a specific, verifiable healing effect. Of course it was many decades later that research and researchers were sophisticated enough to be able to isolate the elusive energy that was transmitted during these interactions. In the beginning personal healing was a hope and an intuition, while a very few perceived that social forms were being rejuvenated as well. For years apathy and selfishness had characterized most social interactions and whenever possible caring activities were delegated to the state, the institution least capable of assuming responsibility. During the Eighties, this tendency was reversed as individuals wrested control from the state over their bodies, families, health, and lives.

The spiritual, healing aspects of these activities were unacknowledged to begin with and the spiritual skills were rudimentary at best. People had not yet learned to communicate with the gods; as technology had absorbed and fascinated them for centuries, they were too concerned, initially, with the mechanics of ritual and not sufficiently with the essence of prayer. (Prayer of this type was not a simplistic appeal to a "higher power" but rather nothing more—but nothing less!—than emotional, intellectual, moral realignment with what in fact has deepest value and accords with eros, the life force.) Another way of understanding prayer was through the perception that this alignment allowed for the specific transmission of healing energy (which came into existence despite

science's inability or disinterest in identifying it). Perhaps the im-
plication of the innate interdependence of people, species, and environment was too challenging to the highly competitive and
aggressive social system.

Prayer of this kind was, by necessity, compassionate, ecological
and socially inclusive—political in its deepest sense. Most of those
who participated in these rites were not aware of the implications.
They simply wanted to create a healing pattern which could be
replicated. In some instances it was as if they were plumbers,who
having discovered water, had fallen in love with pipes. The people
were so far from communication, that is, alignment, that some
Eastern masters developed elaborate rituals requiring a lifetime to
master in order to facilitate communication, or should we say connection. These practices, however, were not appropriate for everyone, nor necessary; some learned them and some did not. Still,
some knowledge from these practices filtered into these rituals and
unlike most other activities on the planet, these did no harm.

In an odd way, the phenomenon resembled similar re-vitalizing
activities which had occurred in history (a subject which Barbara
herself had written about some twenty-five years before the event
of her illness in regard to the Shakers, who provided a positive example, and the Puritans, a negative example). Pagan druids, early
and Renaissance Christians, eighteenth century Hassids, Sikhs, and
so on, in response to one disaster or another, had each come to an
understanding of a sacred universe. Inevitably scholars ridiculed
these tendencies in communities to create heaven on earth as impractical, imaginary devices to compensate for intolerable conditions, but the ridicule of the scholars or realists seemed just as
foolish to the visionaries as the visions seemed to the realists. The
realists wanted empirical evidence and statistics; the visionaries
were too absorbed in trying to reach God and heal their con-
stituents, communities, and, in this case, the entire planet, to interrupt their work. (In fact it was the total dedication to the ritual,
avoiding the seductive return to the old forms, which accomplished the healing process.) It seems that disaster was sometimes
the occasion for authentic vision, and became an opportunity to
see and understand what was commonly rendered invisible by the
desire for comfort, prestige, renown, power, and material acqui-
sition. And though the possibility of the total destruction of the
planet may not have induced a spiritual vision, the possible

destruction of a beloved through a few "chosen" diseases, cancer (and AIDS) in particular, accomplished it. This was as it should be.

In early 1984 the idea first surfaced that AIDS, like cancer, might be healed through meditation and psychological and spiritual transformation. AIDS inspired the same terror and desperation as did cancer, perhaps because it was equally emblematic of the political and social diseases of the society; the AIDS patients, like the cancer patients, were the stages on which the most deadly extant social dramas were enacted. Through these two illnesses, disease came to be profoundly understood as holograms. When the society healed, individuals were healed accordingly—not only because the environment improved. And when individuals healed, the society was healed as well.

The early vision of feminism—"the personal is political"—was rendered even more profound when people turned their attention to disease as a political event. It was necessary for the people to return to the small and to the personal. They could not value a species, except abstractly, and therefore falsely, if they could not value an individual. They had lost the ability to guard the life trust that they were given when they had been given their own bodies, their own selves, but sometimes they could rise to guard the life of a friend, child or lover.

So in this situation, as in most situations on earth, irony was the prevailing mood. Cancer, like AIDS, bore extreme resemblance to the predominant political modes on the planet; AIDS patients, like all other human beings and species on the planet, became totally incapable of defending themselves against aggression. At the time when there was the greatest investment in defense, these systems were simultaneously rendered impossible; at a time when defense was escalated, the victims were most vulnerable to invasion by now one and then another aggression. Even as science and the military proved that there could be no inviolate boundaries, so the disease victims were unable to defend themselves against invasions. Cancer, which had begun to affect as many as one in four, was a disease whereby an essentially weak, immature, dysfunctional cell invaded and occupied surrounding territories, dislocating the inhabitants, destroying the territory, devouring the resources, providing no exchange whatsoever until the entire territory was devastated and the inhabitants died of starvation, suffocation or toxicity. This dread disease became endemic to the second half of

the twentieth century as tuberculosis had been in Europe in the
nineteenth, and the plague earlier. Ironically, cancer, which perfectly mirrored imperialism, became through its proliferation the
agency of spiritual and social—and therefore political—conversion.

In summation, these diseases were mirrors of the prevailing political moods and activities. They were microcosms enacted in the
human body of larger events being enacted on the social and political body. Odd as it may have seemed to those who believed that
every action had meaning, those who suffered the diseases were
not those who perpetuated them. The victims of the diseases were
exactly those who were also the victims of the political, militaristic
mayhem which dominated the twentieth century. The victims of
the diseases were exactly those who could not tolerate the prevailing aggression, the gentle caring ones who were neither imperialis-
tic nor overly defended by nature nor action. For as the century
developed there were those who could not tolerate the culture and
they succumbed, psychologically, spiritually and then physically.
But as time passed, fewer and fewer people could tolerate the conditions they had created; even the most stalwart were unable to
live in the nest they had fouled. So more and more succumbed, requiring vast numbers to organize themselves in opposition in healing networks. Soon even those who were responsible for the
original mess were being healed by procedures diametrically opposite to their psychology and their spirits were inevitably healed as
well. And so it was at the time of greatest peril that the most unlikely and relatively insignificant of activities changed the entire direction of world culture, re-established a healthy environment at a
time when doom was inevitable.

At the beginning of the twenty-first century when these events
were first chronicled, a historian was heard to remark, "The gods
are not gods if they don't have humor." He had just unearthed an
antique bumper sticker from the state of California which read,
"Cancer is the Answer." It had early on been suspected that cancer
might be the answer for individuals as it was a disease which almost always stimulated deep personal transformation, but it had
never been thought that cancer and AIDS might lead to political
transformation as well. Nevertheless that is what occurred. And so
the planet was saved by exactly what seemed to be one of the
modes of its destruction.

# Re-Vamping The World:
# On The Return Of The Holy Prostitute

Once upon a time in Sumeria, in Mesopotamia, in Egypt, in Greece, there were no whorehouses, no brothels. In that time, in those countries, there were the Temples of the Sacred Prostitutes. In these temples, men were cleansed, not sullied, morality was restored, not desecrated, sexuality was not perverted, but divine.

The original whore was a priestess, the conduit to the divine, the one through whose body one entered the sacred arena and was restored. Warriors, soldiers, soiled by combat within the world of men, came to the Holy Prostitute, the Quedishtu, literally meaning "the undefiled one," in order to be cleansed and reunited with the gods. The Quedishtu or Quadesh is associated with a variety of goddesses including Hathor, Ishtar, Anath, Astarte, Asherah, etc. According to Patricia Monaghan in *The Book of Goddesses and Heroines,* Astarte originally meant "She of the Womb," but appears in the Old Testament as Ashtoreth, meaning "Shameful thing." It was understood that war, holy as it might be, still separated men from the gods, and those who had blood on their hands had to engage in a ceremony of purification in order to participate in civil society. As the body, the sexual act, was the means for this re-entry, and pleasure, inevitably, its accompaniment, still the essential attribute of sexuality in this context, was prayer.

In Pergamon, Turkey, we can still find the remains of the Temple of the Holy Prostitutes alongside other temples, palaces, public buildings on the Sacred Way. Whatever rites we imagine took place in those other buildings, it is a Western habit of mind to associate the Holy Prositutes with orgies and debauchery, to emphasize the sexual and ignore the spiritual component. But originally, these women had been one doorway to God.

The first patriarchs, the priests of Judea and Israel, the prophets of Jehovah, had condemned the holy prostitutes and the worship of Asherah, Astarte, Anath and the other goddesses. Morality was the pretext behind which ecclesiastic power was consolidated as priests systematically replaced women as intermediaries between men and God.

Women had been the essential link to the three worlds. Through the mother one came into this world; through the Mysteries, the rites of Demeter or Isis, one entered the underworld; and through the Holy Prostitute one came to God. Access was personal and unconditional. In the days of the Quedishtu every woman served the gods as Holy Prostitute, often for as long as a year. This was contradictory to the hegemony that a priesthood required.

For the sake of power, it is often necessary to set the world upside down. Therefore the priests asserted that what had been considered sacred was depraved, that what had been a way to God was, in deed a way to perdition. Reversals such as this are not uncommon. Incoming religions often co-opt, then reverse, existing spiritual beliefs and practices. So Hades, the spiritual center of Greek paganism, became Hell. The descent into Hades, the core of the Eleusinian Mysteries, and a spiritually required initiation for anyone concerned with soul, was prohibited. By the middle of the fourth century, the Christians had suppressed the Mysteries and installed hell as a place of punishment from which people had to be saved. Where once Pindar had written, "Thrice Blessed are those who have seen these Mysteries for they know the end of life and the beginning," later Dante was to inscribe, "Abandon all hope, ye who enter here." Similarly, Dionysus, the life god, became Satan, as Adonis, the consort of Aphrodite, was co-opted into Christ. Mary Magdalene the Holy Prostitute was converted and transformed, Aphrodite became Eve became the Virgin Mary. The reversals were absolute. Psyche's journey toward soul was altered when the ordeals of Aphrodite, the mother of Eros, no longer beckoned the Self.

Three of the essential roads to the three worlds were blocked or debased. Maybe the gods did not die in Nietzsche's time but centuries earlier with the subversion of the priestesses and the secularization and degradation of the holy body.

This article is about seduction, about vamping. About eros. An attempt to restore a tradition, to reinstitute a way of seeing the world. It is not about literally restoring practices, it is about recovering the consciousness from which those practices derived.

What was the impact of the suppression of the Holy Prostitute? Many of the the practices that honored the way of the woman ceased. The Eleusinian mysteries, which had provided immortality, were suppressed; the male mysteries of the Cabeiri, designed specifically to redeem those with blood on their hands, were suppressed; procreation was infused with anxiety and guilt; fertility festivals which had provided a link between earth and spirit were condemned. When the priests separated the body from the gods, they separated God from nature, and thereby created the mind/body split. The world was secularized. We can only speculate as to the consequences, though we must assume there were consequences when men returned from war without the ability to clean the blood from their hands, when the physical, quotidian community between the gods and the people was not reconvened. It was not woman per se that was attacked, but the gods who were exiled. Perhaps the world as we have come to know it, impersonal, abstract, detached, brutish, was engendered in that division.

In a sacred universe, the prostitute is a holy woman, a priestess. In a secular universe the prostitute is a whore. How do we relate to this today, as women, as feminists? Can we resanctify society, become priestesses again, put ourselves in the service of the gods and eros? As we re-vision, can we re-vamp as well?

Vamp: A woman who sets out to charm or captivate by the use of sexual attractiveness.

Re-vamp: To mend, repair, renovate, refurbish or restore.

What does it mean to revamp a society? It means that we vamp again, become sexual-spiritual beings, priestesses serving eros and in this way we resanctify the society. It means that we identify with eros though society forbids it or seriously disapproves, even if it seems foolish, inexpedient, even when such acts make us vulnerable. It means that we attempt to rededicate ourselves to the old gods of the body, the feminine and the earth.

It is, however, exactly this rededication to the principles of the feminine which is so problematic. The feminine has been so devalued and degraded, has so little power in the world, we have suffered so much loss of opportunity, have been so oppressed, it is difficult to enact the feminine in the world without feeling as if we are opening ourselves to further violation. So we are caught in a terrible paradox. To feel powerful, we learn the very masculine modes that are so oppressive. In either case we seem to participate in our own destruction. Nevertheless, there is a leap of faith to be made: that the reinstatement of the erotic power of feminine consciousness will help to sustain us individually and contribute to the survival of the species and the planet.

When contemporary feminism was established sufficiently to offer real hope and possibility, women who had formerly considered themselves atheists felt called to spiritual matters. The goddess and goddesses were reinvoked. There was an extraordinary interest in spirituality, myth, rite, ceremony. The spiritual instinct buried in a secular universe erupted.

This spiritual vision engages several heresies: the re-sanctification of the body while returning to the very early, neolithic, pagan, matriarchal perception of a sacred universe. As a consequence secular thought, itself, is deposed and the entire universe that we have so carefully fabricated in our own image is deconstructed with all the attendant psychic pain of living, at least for a time, in debris until we learn to negotiate in the new world.

Susan Griffin writes the following in the last chapter, entitled "Eros," of *Pornography and Silence*:

"The psyche is simply world. *And if I let myself love, let myself touch, enter my own pleasure and longing, enter the body of another, the darkness, let the dark parts of my body speak, tongue into mouth, in the body's language, as I enter, a part of me I believed was real begins to die, I descend into matter, I know I am at that heart of myself, I cry out in ecstasy.* For in love, we surrender our uniqueness and become world."

If we become world through love, then love is essentially a political act. If we become world reaching to the gods, then love is a spiritual act which redeems the world.

How then do we become Holy Prostitutes? How do we bring this essence into being? How do we restore the temple? How do we engage this consciousness without imitating old behaviors? How enact the erotic and the spiritual in ways appropriate to these times?

Inevitably the one who takes on the Holy Prostitute, in these times, becomes a heretic, enduring the agony of consciousness that occurs when one holds one world view and the majority holds another. One commits oneself to eros, bonding, connection, when the world values thantos, separation, detachment.

The Holy Prostitute was once Everywoman. In the service of the gods, she made herself available to those outside the province of the gods. How might the contemporary Holy Prostitute bring the sacred to the ones who have been defiled? How might she or he take in "the other"? What rituals and ceremonies might a contemporary sacred whore devise as a context for making love with "the other" or the outcast for the sake of the reintegration and revitalization of the society, especially when it is not sex we are after, but something far deeper?

These questions are old and familiar, easy to ask, so difficult to answer.

The first task is to allow oneself to believe that the body is a spiritual field, that sexuality and erotic love are spiritual disciplines, and that, as a consequence, eros is pragmatic. Then one can honor the feminine even where it is dishonored or disadvantaged. From this vantage point, we can begin to scrutinize ourselves to see when we violate or when live accordingly to these principles.

Here, then, are further questions we might ask ask ourselves:
Whom do I close myself against?
When do I not have time for love or eros?
When do I find eros inconvenient, burdensome, or inexpedient?
When do I find eros dangerous to me?
When do I indulge the erotic charge of guilt?
Where do I respond to, accept, provoke the idea of sin?
When do I use sexuality to distract rather than to commune?
When do I reject eros because I am rejected?
When do I abuse the body?
How do I reinforce the mind/body split?
When and how do I denigrate the feminine?
When do I refuse the gods? When do I pretend to believe in them?
When do I accept the gods only when they serve me?
How often do I acquiesce to the "real world?"

Recently, I was confronted by a large, luminous woman, approximately eight feet tall, clearly an image of a goddess, though I had never before encountered such a figure in any of my meditations. Her hair was light itself. As she came close to me, I was filled with awe at her beauty and terror at her presence. I knew my life would be altered if I were to take her into me; I would have to give up many of the masculine modes I had adopted in order to negotiate successfully in the world. The woman was powerful, but her power was of receptivity, resonance, magnetism, radiance. She had the power of eros; she drew me to her; I couldn't resist her; I was afraid.

Immediately, I was reminded of a statement by my friend, Dianna Linden: "When it comes to the bell, we all want to be the clapper. We don't want to be the body; but it is the body which sings."

Through this figure, I, myself, experienced the terror of the feminine so often referred to. I found myself afraid of my own nature, but even so, I refused to step away from myself. At that moment, I committed myself to eros and the heresy of the sacred, to the slow and excruciating process of trial and error, investigation and insight, through which the Holy Prostitute might enter the world again. She is the woman I aspire to be.

# Personal Disarmament:
# Negotiating with the Inner Government

*In a small, segregated country, called Zebra, the Sun minority has rele-*
*gated the Shade majority to reservations far from the cities and the cen-*
*ters of power. Some Shades work for the Suns or are exhibited in the*
*lavish national parks developed for the enjoyment of foreigners. The*
*government is a theocracy, with a dictator who has allegiance to the oli-*
*garchy and priests.*

*The dictator, as well as the majority, knows nothing of the culture,*
*mores, values, or spiritual inclinations of the Shades; nevertheless, fear*
*and control of the Shades is behind every governmental decision. It is*
*fully believed that if the Shades came near prominence or power, the en-*
*tire way of being of the country would be altered. The minority does not*
*fear for its lives; it fears for its way of life. To change this would be*
*worse than death.*

*One day there is a serious power outage. The power lines have been*
*cut. Up to this point, energy has been the major export of this country.*
*The country is paralyzed. The Shades do not deny they cut the lines, but*
*assert that the power has always belonged to them . . .*

This scenario could describe conditions in any one of numerous
countries. In fact, it is a description of my own inner state of being,
a political description of the nation-state of my own psyche. I have
come to understand that an individual is also a country, that one
contains multiple selves who are governed as nations are governed,
and that the problems and issues that afflict nations also afflict individuals. For most of my life, I have been completely unconscious
of the real mode of government and the status of the beings within
my territory.

239

A few years ago, confronted by an inner coup in the making, I realized that, despite my politics and activities, I was not identifying with the Shades, the oppressed and disenfranchised majority within, notwithstanding the rumors of their vitality, spiritual development, and artistic skills. To my horror, I was identifying completely with the dictator, the official church, and the empowered. Unthinkingly, I was supporting the status quo, order for its own sake, separatist minority tradition, efficiency, production, export, and growth, and I was acting in loyalty to priests who had long forgotten the true meaning of a spiritual life. Forced to consider negotiating with the Shades (not to mention having to contemplate a coalition government or the demand that the Sun minority abdicate power absolutely), I was overcome with terror and despair. I knew nothing of the Shades, whom I distrusted and denigrated. I co-opted their cultural resources while forcing them to work as slaves at cultural tasks or menial labors. I believed that the Shades were irrational, incompetent, irrelevant people, who were emotionally manacled, distracted by sentimentality, and bewitched by occult practices and so-called literary distractions, and who now wanted to impose their silliness upon Zebra. I ridiculed the preposterous assertion that they could govern themselves, let alone the entire country, and take their chances in the modern world.

Until then, Zebra had been developing into one of the largest, most valuable and respected energy exporters in the region. Now the lines were cut, the energy sources occupied, and the army and police without energy were totally immobilized. Against my will, I had to learn to negotiate with these "barbarian" and threatening forces.

Feeling the demand to arbitrate from this position of extreme fear and distrust, I learned invaluable political lessons as real politics—personal politics—became real life. There was no choice; my country—that is, my life—was at stake. Having once had a life-threatening disease whose underlying causes in the psyche I'd come to understand, I knew the gravity of the situation.

When I began to think about myself as a country, as well as an individual, I was struck by what seemed an overwhelming truth. While nations suffer the delusions that they can destroy one segment of their populations and remain intact or thrive, a nation-state such as I was, like a physical body, cannot hack off one limb or cut out one vital organ, and remain intact. I had managed to

suppress some selves up to this time, but I suspected, and even the
Suns and later the Shades came to know, that extermination of the
opposition meant death. Therefore, albeit unwillingly, slowly, and
painstakingly, I began to dismantle the minority supremacist government. I did this although the Suns insisted this meant the end of
progress and growth, that it meant disaster.

Attentive to the alien feelings and ideas of the Suns inside myself, it occurred to me that this new empathy could serve me later
in political activities in the world at large.

I found it most difficult to give priority to the needs and demands of the Shade people when these challenged the "national"
goals of production, export, and defense. But the Shade council
government was adamant and threatening. Inevitably, I couldn't
please everyone. Elements of both the Suns and Shades were dis-
satisfied, wanting to take things into their own hands. The internal
Sun police continued working out of habit and desperation, and,
although they no longer had authority, they remained eerily com-
petent. The deposed minister of culture continued to control the
thoughts and habits of the dominant Sun population he was serving so that the theocracy and oligarchy maintained, for a while, its
unofficial but tenacious way of being. The Shades, still being repressed, remained mysterious and frightening.

Terrorism existed on both sides. Time and again, I was deprived
of sufficient energy to do work. In response, books and other creative projects were burned. There were many other atrocities. Cen-
sorship and spying still flourished, if ex officio. I fell into the
pattern of punitive, relentless, even mindless work, followed by
periods of utter collapse. The work was insisted upon by the deposed Suns while the collapse was the retaliation of the not-yet-
enfranchised Shades.

But while this desperate cycle continued, something new was oc-
curring. There was someone in me watching it, some interim government or peacekeeping force that managed to hold another
vision and to continue the careful process of change. Somehow,
against inner public opinion, I made a decision to forego violent
revolution or a new military coup and was not drawn into either alternative, despite provocations against each side and against the interim regime itself. It was difficult not to panic during the cycles of
terrorism and hostilities.

I don't know what finally changed the balance of power and

led to the development of a new government and a new country. Perhaps it came from empowering a group of international advisors and observers, or from honoring the interim regime. Certainly it derived from the inner realization that all-out war was untenable—the equivalent of a global nuclear holocaust. (There were, of course, a few apocalyptic souls who advocated this suicide, but we managed to occupy them enough with other concerns.) Perhaps it was the occasion of declaring a national holiday period and allowing the Shades a limited opportunity to rule. For whatever reasons, slowly, very slowly, things began to shift.

The real crises of conscience occurred after I regained a more natural affiliation with the Shades. Within the reality of my own psyche, I learned that the former brutality and ethnocentricity of the Suns came from enormous trauma, grief, and pain in their ancient and forgotten history. Despite loathing, I was forced to a position of compassion. Sometime in the past, Zebra had suffered a series of crises that threatened the existence of the nation. At that point, the Suns came to power and made certain naive but necessary decisions. These became entrenched—both the cause and the motives vanishing. Later these emergency procedures were codified as holy law. The culture of the Suns followed from this, developing out of the real need to protect the country. This ancient grief did not mitigate the contemporary suffering of the Shades but it had to be acknowledged. Just as I was finally reunited with the Shades, I had to recognize the value of the Suns. It became clear that if the Suns were massacred, imprisoned, or brainwashed, the entire country would become demoralized and disoriented. Energies would be diverted endlessly and unproductively toward defense and armaments, and the cycle would begin again in the other direction. I had to find a way to allow the Shades to govern with the Suns, despite the Shades' history of persecution and the Suns' connection with power.

This was not metaphor. Each time something interfered with the process of change in government, I could feel it in my body. The reality of the necessary integrity of a self or a country became physically and emotionally manifest. I experienced on the inner plane the risks, dangers, violence, and terrorism that characterize contemporary political life.

Soon it became clear that a lost function of government was being restored: to nurture, sustain, and protect the entire

NEGOTIATING WITH THE INNER GOVERNMENT 243

population, to support distinction, and to provide dynamic communication between the disparate elements.

Protection took on an entirely different tone. It did not have to do with police, prisons, armies, walls, or armaments. It meant providing for diverse needs, even without petition. Fortunately, then, intelligence work took on a different emphasis, while some of the skills (though not all) developed in my inner FBI and CIA were of the greatest value. Sleuthing the inner needs, motivations, and practices that had long been disguised and hidden became an honorable and essential activity. This time, however, the intent was not to eradicate them but to support them adequately. Rather than being militaristic or aggressive, protection began to feel maternal or paternal in the sweetest way. It was characterized by tenderness.

There were many limitations and deprivations in the recovery period: foreign travel, for example, was curtailed; there had been so much of it. Emphasis was put upon domestic travel (inner exploration). All public transportation was free and encouraged. Bus lines, trains, and domestic airlines were highly subsidized, and free phones, computers, and modems were widely distributed. Publishing increased. But this emphasis upon communication was also potentially dangerous. How could this level of contact, these modern systems, be introduced without destroying the Shades? After all, their culture was based upon the occult; to expose this might have dire consequences. Also, the Shades needed time to solidify their own culture, find the means to protect their ways and oral traditions against corruption and co-option, for their own sake as well as the nation's. So, while access to the lands of the Shades was encouraged, there were to be no new hotels, highways, or tours. When Suns came to the Shades territory, they had to live exactly like Shades. The Shades did not support themselves through tourism nor could they be subsumed into the entertainment industry. The government had to provide without interfering in their way of life so the Shade culture once more became the living vibrant source of meaning in Zebra.

Also, technology could not determine development as it had in the past. It was only one of many tools. It had no meaning in itself.

Of course, while this transition was in progress, there were grave economic difficulties, and, accordingly, the country, by one of the first national agreements, isolated itself from the outside world. Ironically, it did not matter so much now when people strayed across the borders in one direction or another. When immigration and emigration restrictions were eased, when no one needed a visa or passport one way or another, it happened that interest in international affairs (in the outer, public world) momentarily diminished. The decrease in publications for export similarly diminished international interest in the country's domestic affairs. Zebra was aided by the fact that its energy resources were depleted, so there was little reason for a foreign takeover. There was nothing to gain. Also, in these times, harmonious reconstruction is not as fascinating as civil war, and so the international press looked elsewhere for its news. After a while, it became possible to make new and surprising alliances on different bases altogether.

Power was no longer the primary motivation even when a modified energy system was restored. There were no longer plans to build nuclear power plants. Those that existed—even those which had supplied the outer world with energy—were slowly being dismantled, although the problem of atomic wastes was serious and had to be solved. I was not a dreamer; I knew that traces, even huge pools of toxicity, might remain in my psyche for my lifetime. If they could not be neutralized, they needed to be contained. This was also a national priority. I hoped that I would no longer pass their effects on, that they would diminish in time.

Now I was ready to attempt the most difficult work of all. Having achieved some harmony within my own nation, having begun to dismantle the inner police force and the system and values upon which it depended, I turned to the outer world and foreign relations (friends, family, community, and career). I had come to the realization that the inner enemy had been the heroic substance of my domestic life for eons, and that I had been dependent upon it as a source of identity and control. The concept of enemy had been a false and dangerous premise, wasting my resources and diverting my nature, especially because I'd been unconscious of the extremity and implications of the inner conflict. I hadn't known how severely I'd been deprived by being alienated from half myself. Now I was ready to examine my system of defenses and armaments vis-à-vis the public world. Because I had some experience in re-viewing the enemy, if only within my own borders, I turned to the enemy without.

In this period, I'd learned that the enemy is the "beloved." The enemy can almost singlehandedly bolster and maintain a sense of who we are. It was in contrast to the enemy that the Suns, for example, falsely considered themselves good, strong, spiritually disciplined, intellectual, hard working, god fearing, moral, and courageous. It was in opposition to the Shades that they became holy warriors. I had to see how that operated within Zebra, and between myself and others in the world.

I began to identify my external so-called enemies and drop the distinction of self and other in this sphere. I had to learn how I could maintain my own diversity and sense of self while yielding to the value of others, even those who seemed so contrary to myself. I had to see how we could coexist. I had to examine the weapon arsenals I had created. Secret information, hidden even from myself, had to be exposed, so that I knew the number and nature of every weapon I had. Instead of declaring war, I wanted to write treaties to protect our differences.

Finally, I wanted to bring myself to a single, sincere act of unilateral, personal disarmament. I wanted to do this as a sign, primarily to myself, of sincere desire to trust, of sincere abdication of the notion of enemy, of a sincere interest in peace.

I began the process of disarmament. It is slow, difficult work.

I admit that I came to consider disarmament only after I knew what invasions had in fact occurred in my country. I came to this process not only with the knowledge of several violent invasions, but also with the knowledge of ancient invasions that had been suppressed. I could only give up the notion of the enemy once I knew how and when I had been harmed. Otherwise, it would have been a gratuitous act. Aided by the propaganda machine that thoroughly distracted me from knowing what I was doing, I might have instituted a draft and revived the munitions industry at the first sign of sabre rattling in my vicinity.

I began for my own sake to seek out each instance where I created or reinforced the idea of an enemy, in order to deconstruct it. I sought out the information on every munitions factory and storage center and began to dismantle them. I began to take down the unnecessary walls. I did this not because I thought it was safe outside, but because I lived better with the possibility of safety. I lived better—even if it were a temporary condition—believing I could be safe. I did it selfishly to satisfy my own attraction to inner peace.

When I scrutinized my sincerity, I trusted my decisions exactly because I had personally experienced public calumniation and persecution. I trusted my decision to live alone in an isolated house that could not be locked, without a gun, an attack-trained dog, or an alarm system, because a man had once threatened my life for a year and because I'd been raped at gun point. I realized that even psychic disarmament must be tested within the real context of violence. Perhaps I would never have initiated this psychic process of disarmament and de-enemization if I had not been raped, violated, invaded, colonized, and betrayed. I could only be sincere if I acknowledged the real dangers to Zebra from the world as well as the real dangers of defense.

First I had to remember and reexperience the violences enacted against me, acknowledging that these had happened and that I had spent my life unconsciously protecting myself from buried memories. In doing so, again unconsciously, I had created an enormous inner prison, a country with reservations, and a deprived population. I realized that becoming an international energy czar had been a consequence of a sincere desire to help other nations and a means of creating economic growth, but it was also a formidable defense.

So I began with baby steps to live another way in the face of possible scarcity, retaliation, and injury. I began to live as best as I could, looking for points of reconciliation, without creating the concept of an enemy, without the backup of a military system.

I would not have been able to believe that a country could eschew past occurrences, could actually turn selectively from modern ways (without abandoning the modern altogether), could return to less lethal, if less powerful, forms, if this were not my own personal experience. I would not have been able to believe that a country could turn away from weaponry and war if this were not my own personal experience. But I was and am learning it in the only place I can know it thoroughly: in my own psyche, my own body, and my own life.

I realized that I was beginning to experience a complete, and comparatively bloodless, revolution in the political, social, military, cultural, and spiritual spheres. There was a change in government, in every aspect of my way of life. This tentative success, while living "in this world," led me to hope that it may be possible to achieve democracy, disarmament, and peace in the world at large.

Without as much hubris as I might have indulged in in the past, it occurred to me that I was training myself to participate in these larger changes once my own new nation was safely established. I was gaining some important knowledge: the personal history of a dramatic change in government and the experience of trying to sustain the change and protect its organic development even in relationship to the world at large.

Slowly and painstakingly, I continued to face the myriad internal and external dangers, the periods of forgetting and recidivism, the periods of fatigue and despair. I was sometimes encouraged in these activities to find ways to alter inner conditions, integrate a country, and thoroughly revamp domestic and national policy by thinking I was gaining political understanding that no courses in political science and history could duplicate. At the same time, I was healing a serious emotional condition and saving my life.

Long before I could begin to enact these changes, I came to understand that the system of government that controlled me internally was similar to the systems of government in the world. It took a long while to admit that this was so—in part, because I was always projecting into the world the systems by which I was living. It was heartbreaking to realize that all the work I'd done in the world was undermined by the constant seepage of contrary values from my inner being. I could not be a democrat in the world or promote democracy while I was a tyrant within. I had tried it. I had devoted my life to it. It looked good in terms of paper and deeds, but I had to admit that my efforts were fundamentally ineffective. Each day of my life, I had unwittingly reinforced and reseeded the world with what threatened it, myself, and everyone I knew: tyranny, slavery, militarism. I couldn't hope to accomplish change in the outside world until I changed the inner one.

This filled me with despair at first. There was so much to be done. I asked how was it possible to make any change if almost everyone had to change themselves internally. Underneath that despair was another more hidden despair. I didn't think I could make such overwhelming changes myself. I didn't know how.

Gradually despair was replaced by hope and confidence. I began to make some changes. I saw it was possible. No small measure of success or possible success was due to working on this through the imagination. Once I began to envision Zebra, to live with the realities of the Suns and Shades as within a novel, once I began to understand their dynamics as highly distinct from my own, as having their own lives and motivations, change, ironically, occurred in Deena. The efficacy and reality of the imagination convinced me that others could do it as well.

I began to see that the despair so many of us feel when confronting world conditions might also be alleviated. Those who feel that there is nothing they can do to affect such a monster can come to see that there is something they can do, that only they can do, that can be effective, a real and substantial contribution. They can at the very least (which might turn out to be the very most) institute a government in their inner world that has integrity with their ideas and ideals. And in the very mundane living out of that system, they can project into the outer world some of the ways they hold dear—democracy, equality, equal access, respect for indigenous peoples, environmental protection, disarmament, and peaceful co-existence.

This new way of thinking was very humbling. I had to lay aside all glorious ambitions to save the world either by myself or in concert with a special cadre of beings. The task of change, the ant work of only one individual, was tedious, overwhelmingly absorbing, and took all my energy. Each individual had to do it for himself or herself. I could not be a hero though I must confess the difficulty of doing it even for myself did at times make me feel heroic. Still I persisted, humbled and doggedly devoted. Why? Because I discovered I really cared for this little nation and for the world, and I did not want to continue to do them harm.

This is the story of a journey from within the journey. I knew before I started that we all live in an armed camp. But I didn't know that I was also one of the architects. I didn't realize how thoroughly I had introjected the realities of the outside world, had unconsciously internalized the hostile systems that surround us, had absorbed so many variations on duality, division, repression, suppression, hierarchy, superiority, intolerance, and violence, until the world I constructed was a kaleidoscopic image of the horrors and devastations of planet earth in the twentieth century.

I didn't realize how thoroughly I was living the way women have been living in Western culture, thrice colonized, first, by living under actual foreign (patriarchal) rule in the world; second, by living under foreign rule within themselves; and third, by being given the task of socializing their children according to the dictates of this foreign domination. It had long seemed to me that the forms women create reveal cooperative, noncompetitive, nonhierarchical, and intimate patterns that incline toward trust, interrelationship, and peacemaking; but women are socialized and then socialize others into paranoia, conflict, and war. I didn't realize that I was living this way and that, in fact, it was the way of women, and of men. We are all living this way.

So even the distinctions between women and men fell away from me. Because the inner world is an unconscious introjection of the outer world, it cannot be selective about the forms that influence it; there is no filter to keep out one system while absorbing another. Each of us breathes in all the tyrannies and dictatorships, all the enslavements and tortures. China, Africa, Latin America, the United States, the Soviet Union, Europe, Asia, the Middle East—all come to us democratically in one breath. We are each other. Even as we run from each other, try to destroy each other, we are each other. The entire universal, global armed camp in all its manifestations, all the variations on militarism, terrorism, imperialism, and expansionism, are in each of us. Different uniforms, the same organism. In the construction of these armed camps, nationalism does not divide us; we are all citizens of the same government. All of us, all people, all men and all women are living in an armed camp, are similarly colonized, similarly socializing ourselves and others, no matter how unwittingly, and we are projecting these violent and totalitarian forms into the world.

Once again, this realization caused me despair and then hope. Because I was beginning to hope there was a way out for me, I thought it might be a way out for some others. It seemed to me these changes were in our collective self-interest.

I began to develop a series of questions that I continue to pose to myself as rigorously as I can. I return to them again and again. Posing the questions, trying to understand the answers, and keeping the dynamics of Zebra in my awareness has been a way of clawing my way toward change. I try to be aware of the constant need to accord the inner reality of Zebra with my principles. I don't believe that because I've started this process it is automatically maintained. I do try to be vigilant. These are some of the questions I ask:

What is the form of my internal government? It is tyrannical, a dictatorship, an oligarchy? Is it a military government? Is it a police state? It is a false theocracy?

Who are my "beloved enemies"? Whom do I identify as the enemies within? The enemies without?

What are my defense systems? What are the natures of my police force and armies?

What weapons are in my arsenal? Do I stockpile? Am I in an
arms race?

What is the equivalent of my nuclear bomb?

Will I sign a no-first-strike treaty?

Do I have slaves?

Whom do I imprison?

Do I torture?

Do I have an internal FBI an CIA, a secret police?

What is the nature of my own propaganda and disinformation
bureau?

What territories do I seal off? Do people need passports or visas?

Who are disadvantaged, exploited, oppressed, or disenfranchised
in my country?

Do I exploit, invade, colonize, or imperialize other countries?

Do I pollute?

Am I run by ideologues?

Am I racist?

Can I learn to tolerate and then praise diversity?

Am I willing to disarm? To sign disarmament treaties? Am I willing to allow inspection? Am I willing to trust and be trustworthy?

Do I really want peace? Can I teach peace to my inner population?

Perhaps I began to speak about and teach this work prematurely.
Much of what is written here didn't become clear until now. Perhaps the work is ongoing, and even these insights will appear naive
some years from now. Once, however, in a personal disarmament
workshop, a man who'd been a peace activist had to confront the
extremity of his distrust of others. Gently, I raised the analogy to
the disarmament table. I suggested that the officials who sat at that
table trying to reach agreements were as distrustful, suspicious,
and injured as he was. He was broken by this realization and con-
fessed that he couldn't in their place conscientiously advocate
weakening the defense system; yet he had advocated disarmament
all his life. Admittedly, if he were in their position, feeling the way
he did, he would have to say, "More bombs." For a while, he lived

with rage and humiliation. Then he began looking in himself for whatever was possible to allow him to trust. He found inner defenses that were not aggressive. He began to validate inner security so that he could come to the negotiating table in a wholehearted manner. He did not disregard potential dangers or fears, but he did develop confidence by reviewing his history and validating what sustained more than what undermined until he was willing to take a risk. When he returned to the ranks of peace activists, he had a new authority. He had found a way to test the sincerity of his political positions as well as a way to reconstruct his inner world so that it accorded with his principles. He was creating a dialogue between the two worlds.

In another personal disarmament class, a woman recounted that her house had just been broken into and her roommates raped at knife point. This woman had been raped and physically injured by a stranger on two other separate occasions and had herself been abused as a child. She was agonized about the effect of all this upon her adolescent daughter. Yet, as she spoke about her response to the incident, all of us were moved away from despair. As awful as the break-in had been, her courageous refusal to create an enemy and to live in fear gave us enormous hope.

At the peace tent at the Non-Governmental Organizations-United National Conference on Women in Nairobi in July 1985, I asked an audience of African, American, and European women who it was that ruled their inner countries. The majority painfully acknowledged that they were ruled by tyrants. They agreed that nothing could change in the world until they also altered their inner conditions. The women had been saying similar things about foreign policy, that nothing would change internationally until domestic changes were instituted. Perhaps through the talk we'd managed to move the definition of the domestic closer to the heart and hearth. It wasn't that we thought we needed to stop efforts in the public world, but that there was other urgent work, on the inner plane, which had to be pursued simultaneously. I didn't realize how much consensus we'd reached until I was approached later by the head of the Soviet women's delegation. There were tears in her eyes. She said, "We have been working so very hard, so very, very hard for peace, we didn't even begin to think how urgent it was to attend to ourselves. We didn't even consider that we have personal selves who need to be attended. Now the Soviet women have to begin this inner work." Yes, I thought, for all our sakes.

# Healing the Planet/Healing Ourselves

We are living in a time of great jeopardy. Medical science triumphs but new mysterious and intractable physical illnesses appear. Living standards and conditions improve, but those who seem the strongest and most fortunate succumb suddenly and without warning to life-threatening or debilitating diseases. The cells rebel, defense systems break down, ennui and exhaustion set in most unexpectedly, surprising many at the very peak of health and activity. Malnutrition, over consumption, over work, erosion of private time, overproduction, exploitation of resources, foreign invasion, failure of defense systems, despair, delusion, toxicity, pollution, affect us intra-psychically as well as politically. Willy-nilly, the borders we try to hard to sustain become permeable and distinctions disappear. Individuals begin to suffer the conditions of the nation states. Nation states develop their own equivalents of physical diseases. We take the afflictions of the planet into our bodies as the planet suffers our conditions.

The diseases we suffer are also metaphors. That is, diseases are presenting themselves in personal as well as political and social metaphors. While it has always been clear that physical illness can be the consequence of world conditions, it has not been so clear that physical illness is an *analogue* of planetary conditions. This being the case, preventing or healing physical disease becomes a political act. And, preventing or healing political, social and environmental conditions ameliorates physical illness.

Imagine then that disease is a language, an alarm, a desperate code, written on the body to alert us to the grim situation of our psyche, the polis and the planet.

253

I also would like to heal something on this planet, a bit of earth,
a lost soul, even myself.

Fifteen years ago, I had breast cancer and took a typewriter to
the hospital because I had learned through writing that the silence
in me contributed significantly to the onset of this disease. I was
determined to be silent no longer, to look for the hidden silences
which unbeknownst to me had become lethal.

Months before I discovered I had cancer, I was writing a novel
about cancer and women, *The Book of Hags.* There I postulated
that cancer was silence turned against itself:

*The women who had died of cancer, had all tried madness first and
their madness had been plastered up, sealed, glassed in, submerged.
Then they lived a few years and cancer erupted which could not be submerged, ignored, boxed in, cut out, irradiated or controlled in any way.
It was a fierce raging growth and it took their lives.*

While writing, I had had a dream about a woman torturer, working for the *DINA,* the Chilean secret police. [Dina is, of course, a
variant spelling of my name.] When I discovered I had breast cancer in 1977, one month after I finished that novel, I began to examine that dream anew. It had something to do with the disease, but
what? Something was torturing me, but what? Who? Why? To keep
me silent and acquiescent? Why was the image a woman? Was I,
myself, the torturer, the silencer, the one who did not want her victim to know, speak or live?

During the last twelve years of health, while always aware that
our destructive relationship to the environment is immediately
translated into a rash of physical illness, I still continue my relentless search for the places in my psyche which make me even more
vulnerable to the onslaught of disease, to the places of unconscious
collusion with the destructive forces, to the places where the potentially lethal torturers and silences within myself reside. No matter what answers I find, I continue to pose the questions: What is
lethal within me? What is festering? What is repressed? What must
be spoken?

Each year something astounding, even horrific, which has been
suppressed, emerges. Then I try to ease it—my form of psychic
surgery; I prefer it to the operating room.

When I first considered the incident of a dream, or the metaphor of disease as an essential and serious map for the healing
process, I stepped into the reality of the imagination. This became

a significant part of the healing process. To value the images, to speak out, to find what is lethal within, to come out of silence, to honor the creative and the imagination as real worlds—these have been my life and healing work.

Perhaps the surgeon cured me. I think he did. But I had to heal myself. Cure is a state, health is a process. Cure is finite, healing is ongoing. A cure is singular, healing is a practice. Healing requires that we change our lives. In the ways we find to live differently, we eliminate or neutralize some of the conditions which contribute to the creation or maintenance of the disease. And, not ironically, as we change our lives for our health's sake, we often begin to live lives which are far more compatible with the health and survival of the planet.

When I began working with cancer patients, I wanted to see if we could find ancillary ways to approach cancer in individuals. Now that I see inextricable relationships between the illnesses in our bodies and the illnesses affecting the planet, I realize that healing the individual patient is insufficient. In order to heal our bodies, we have to undertake the healing of the body politic. And as we suffer from the same illnesses, the same remedies apply to both. The very processes of preventing or healing personal illness extend themselves to healing the world. And vice-versa.

What was most surprising to me when I had cancer was coming upon an alien voice in me speaking against my own life. Some years later, I find it is not uncommon for others to be similarly confronted. Inner despair, rage against oneself, self hate, are the frequent hand maidens of physical illness. Many of my clients with Epstein-Barr, Chronic Fatigue Syndrome, or other immune system diseases, have experienced debilitating depression and the sudden or gradual erosion of the will to live as a biochemical consequence of the disease. This emotional consequence is sometimes experienced as the worst of the symptoms.

When I look about me at the dire planetary conditions, I find that many people no longer care whether life itself goes on. We are suffering from global fatigue and despair, from cultural self-loathing, from national suicides, all of which lead to serious increases in attacks against life itself. The parallels are unnerving. As we hold the world's pain in our own physical bodies so we are living out our physical illnesses in the body politic. We have created an awful fellowship in despair.

The core of the issue may be that the will to live, individually
and globally, is being replaced by the will to die: Thanatos tri-
umphing over eros. We can postulate the causes: alien viruses, al-
terations in the DNA, aberrations in the immune system
responses, as well as the brutality, futility, meaninglessness, alienation, exploitation and poverty of modern life on a global scale;
these are legion. These conditions are intensified by the subtle love
affair Western Civilization has always had with death: Death the
redeemer; Death the phantom lover; the dark God.

In 1945, the Atom Bomb was exploded in response to the Nazis'
murderous frenzy. J. Robert Oppenheimer, himself a Jew, watching
the first Bomb test at Trinity, quoted Vishnu in the *Bhagavad-Gita*:
"Behold, I am become Death, destroyer of worlds."

The cures we have found for our circumstances perpetuate the
illness.

Expectations of the Apocalypse begin to seem fitting: threats of
war, repeated incidents of genocide, torture, chemical warfare, nuclear disaster, radiation poisoning. Illness everywhere. Environmental diseases and environmental devastation. A variety of
plagues and scourges.

And now this dilemma: The plague comes home. Cancer, AIDS,
CFS, emotional and physical exhaustion become commonplace, affecting, among many others, many of those who have committed
themselves to confronting the dread koans of this century: genocide, nuclear destruction, environmental devastation. We do not
seem to know yet how to confront these without ourselves being
severely jeopardized. While the suffering in the world is extreme
and must be alleviated, we are not finding the strength and knowledge to confront it. The capacities of our psyches and bodies are
not increasing proportionally with the escalation of emotional,
moral, political, spiritual, and ecological crises.

We must ask ourselves: how can we to do the work we need to
do while maintaining a state of health at the same time? In learning
how to maintain our personal health, can we discover how to
maintain the health of the planet?

Recently, I was invited to speak at a conference on Women's
Spirituality. Three out of five of the speakers canceled their partic-
ipation because of extreme fatigue or illness. I, myself, had had serious doubts about attending—also for reasons of exhaustion. A
growing number of people who have undertaken healing work are,

themselves, being thrown into serious physical crises. Living in these times, we all suffer serious assaults, wounds and weaknesses. Each passing day precipitates further health crises and extreme conditions. Many of the more common illnesses are chronic and undermining so that it is often impossible to take care of oneself. The seriousness of this is compounded by the fact that many people now live alone.

"Perhaps," I said speaking to a friend, "your work is not only your research on the causes of war. Perhaps your work is larger than that. Perhaps our work is also to find how we can protect ourselves against the diseases which war against us, to find out how to do this work without being overwhelmed by illness." I suggested this, even though I was aware of adding another imperative to an already overwhelmed situation.

My friend was suffering from a breakdown of her immune system. The analogy with our political situation was unavoidable. Her immune system wasn't working. Militarily, our immune systems—defense systems—also do not work. These days, we are far more injured by them than protected. Clearly, it is in our personal as well as collective interest to address these synchronicities.

Individually, and nationally, we are discovering that we cannot isolate ourselves from outside forces, from 'the other.' We cannot keep ourselves from being invaded. Even if we keep large armies at bay, we cannot fully protect ourselves against the invasions of terrorists, against economic or cultural take-overs or infiltrations. Increasingly we live in a fractal universe that is complex and fluid. One thing flows into another. Sharp differentiations disappear. The concept of an inviolable boundary becomes as anachronistic as the Maginol Line. Yet, precious resources are consumed in the attempt to build up our defenses as our stockpiles of weapons threaten to turn on us before we use them. We cannot launch an attack to destroy the enemy without seriously injuring ourselves. Every time we think of launching an attack, we are ourselves jeopardized by that action. Every enemy we make endangers us. The myriad forms of 'friendly fire,' self attack, besiege us on all fronts: Chernobyl, Three Mile Island, T cell imbalance, auto immune diseases. Death hovers at the edges of our imagination.

When I first started working and consulting with people with cancer and other serious diseases—and afterwards when I discovered that I also had breast cancer—I found that it was possible to translate an understanding of the illness into personal metaphors. While for each person, the metaphor may be different, the impact or relevance of metaphor itself remained consistent. For one person, throat cancer represented her untenable silence. For another, thyroid cancer represented an inability or unwillingness to regulate energy, and for a third, stomach cancer translated into greed.

Cancer, in general, behaves much like a modern world power or nation state. An essentially weak, immature, uncooperative dysfunctional cell invades and occupies nearby or remote territories, dislocating the inhabitants, destroying the area, parasitically devouring the resources, providing no exchange whatsoever until the entire territory is devastated and the inhabitants die of starvation, suffocation or toxicity.

"This is imperialism," I said. Then I began to look for political approaches, for the causes, signs and manifestations of imperialism within myself which I might alter and, accordingly, heal. Admittedly, I could no more find an easy solution or instant cure with this approach than governments have been able to establish instant world peace or international economic equality, but the analogy provided new ways of approaching the illness. Ultimately I did find ways in which one part of myself improperly dominated others, in which inner resources were used up without regard, in which alienated economic and cultural plagues overwhelmed the more sustaining native traditions, in which my energy was depleted without regard for the body and spirit which sustained it. This approach caused me to change the way I was living and thinking and empowered me to participate in my own healing and use the imagination in pursuit of health.

When I began thinking about AIDS after working with several clients with that illness, I began to see it, metaphorically, as the demise of the defense system which had been undermined, even taken over from within, leaving the body unable to defend itself, a victim to any scourge. If a new defense system cannot be instituted, or as is frequently happening with the increase in auto-immune diseases, if the defense system itself turns against the host, it is necessary that we learn to live with the foreign body. Perhaps a change of definition—relinquishing the concept of enemy—will allow for healing through co-existence. Or perhaps, as we watch the invading cells recoding our own DNA until there is no difference between our cells and the invader, we will invent ways to coexist with virulent aggression without losing our own integrity.

We are not yet sophisticated enough to be able to heal ourselves completely by using such an approach, but we can make a difference in the length of time we stay healthy, in the severity and speed of disease. Very often, mediation, reconciliation, co-existence with what was formerly defined as the enemy—whether it is something within our psyche or whether it is someone or some condition external to us—can also alleviate or relieve some of the physical symptoms we are suffering. For example, dismantling the rage which generally consumed him and the consequent state of 'red alert' in which he lived, made a significant difference in the T cell count and state of health of one of my clients with AIDS. The reduction of enemies without seemed to translate into a reduction of enemy cells within. If we give up the idea of an enemy, or come into relationship with what we have predicated as "other," and resist setting up barriers against what we fear, perhaps we may be able to heal ourselves more fully. Equally important is the necessity to maintain oneself despite the virulence of the invasion. The Dalai Lama instructed one of his delegates to Mao's government that he would not be effective until he stopped hating the Chinese. The task, then, was to give up hate without in any way relinquishing Tibetan culture and practice.

Much of what we suffer socially and politically is because we accommodate to ways of life which are unhealthy in every sense, physically and morally. Not one of us is free of the stigma of collaboration with some of the worst aspects of industrial and post-industrial anti-culture, including the making of enemies, the relinquishment of ourselves and the acceptance of alienation from nature. It is no surprise to see how frequently health occurs as individuals free themselves from the life-style of these anti-cultures. The attempts we are witnessing among many people to return to a life style compatible and interactive with nature cannot be dismissed as romantic. The fact is that retreat from contemporary life is promoting healing in many people. Maintaining an alliance with nature can often mean the difference between health and illness.

Multiple sclerosis is like friendly fire, a disease in which the defense system attacks itself, a munitions or nuclear plant exploding in its own territory, or a unit being bombed by its own planes.

Essential communication is stymied because of a break in the line. The ability of one part of the system to receive a message from the other part of the system is impaired.

Asthma is an illness in which the air taken in can't be given out. The bronchial tubes which must open, close down. The essence of the life force is perverted, so that one suffocates in the very air that can't be released. It is a mirror of what happens in us when we resist the creative, take in but do not release, are inspired but fail to express. An action dramatized in the body which is a pattern in the society. It is also like the segment of the population which co-opts and hoards essential resources, water, for example; taking in without giving out, closing down to others, without realizing that vigor and balance are eking away, until the very life of the country is threatened.

Those suffering from Epstein-Barr who are physiologically afflicted by unrelenting terror and despair and extremely diminished vitality, re-experience in their own bodies the circumstances of the modern condition. Rest and diminishing activities do not necessarily relieve chronic fatigue. Often, recuperation results from one's willingness to engage in strenuous activities which are vitalizing and to suspend those "sensible" activities which actually sap the zest of the individual. Enthusiasm, passion and creative expression are often the unexpected medicines for this illness.

Similarly, we can see the political or social equivalents of a heart which is attacked, bruised and broken when access to it is impeded, when the highways to the heart are blocked, when the activity of the heart is limited.

Sometimes the dilemmas of our own personal lives are enacted in our bodies and sometimes the dilemmas of the body politic are enacted in our bodies, and sometimes both. In each case, internal imperialism kills, imbalance is lethal, terror is rampant, communication breaks down, paralysis occurs, our defense systems become obsolete, too expensive or turn against us. Diseases are mirrors of prevailing political, ecological conditions. They are microcosms enacted in the human body, in ourselves, of larger events being enacted on the social, political and earthly body.

To heal ourselves is as rigorous and difficult as healing our societies or healing the planet. Healing the body requires exactly what it takes to heal the planet: a major, serious reorganization, if not total change, of one's life. This is where we see the intractable hold which Thanatos has upon our individual and collective psyches. Those old but not wise ways, familiar and habitual, so-called safe, socially sanctioned, economically expedient, culturally proscribed ways which manifest clear and evident dangers, hold fast within us nevertheless. It sometimes takes an action as extreme and violent as the illness itself to wrest ourselves free from the very 'beloved' conditions which are killing us.

I want to say a few simple but urgent things here. These images and metaphors are not absolute; they must be shaped by the experience and understanding of each individual. My experience is that healing occurs or health is improved exactly when individuals commit themselves to finding the metaphors which are the perfect analogues for the nature of the illness which has afflicted them, their own psychological issues and the conditions in the world at large. The more particular and specific the analogue, the greater the opportunity to heal the condition.

Secondly, when I speak about disease as a metaphor, I do not mean that we are solely responsible for our illness. Genetics, environmental toxins, bacteria, viruses are real things to which we also fall victim. To blame the ill for their disease, to assume they did something wrong or did not prevent it from happening or did not respond appropriately, is as pernicious and naive as blaming the rape victim for the rape or the holocaust victim for the Death Camp. Nevertheless, it is infinitely useful as a healing procedure to ask why this person in particular might be suffering this illness in particular at this time.

Working within the metaphor of the disease, seeing how the symptoms resonate within, empowers us to act on our own behalf. Sometimes unbearably helpless against the already overwhelming disease-creating conditions of our society, we find ourselves capable of mobilizing heart, mind and spirit to participate in healing what might otherwise remain a grave condition. But individuals must determine what the metaphor of the disease is for them and work from that.

Disease is a desperate story which the body tells in the hope that we can act to change our life so not to lose it. On a personal level, if we can find the individual story the disease has enacted in us, we have a chance of changing the story, of finding the healing story which may save our lives.

These images are realities of the imagined world. They are

acting upon us in our daily lives. To give them credence—without
attributing full responsibility for the conditions—is one step toward giving voice to what has been stifled in us, and beginning on
the road to health.

There is another aspect to this, and it is also part of the healing.
First cancer, then AIDS, and now the rash of immune system diseases, have forced us to create healing communities. Families and
communities otherwise severely alienated and distracted from
each other often find that the imperative of cancer draws them together and that somehow the individuals who care for the person
are healed themselves, especially from their alienation. The kind
of camaraderie we have seen in this century in resistance movements, solidarity movements, civil rights and women's movement
etc., now occurs in the home. One sees this most vividly in the gay
community as it confronts AIDS. Person after person seems to become the recipient of a kindly communal care involving everyone.
Many people who for one reason or another were forced to give up
children or family find themselves, not ironically, gaining their
lives, not in child-rearing, but in the equally momentous task of attending someone who is dying. These death watches have become
the means of soul making and community building.

In these times one factor after another forces us toward isolation, self-centeredness and self-absorption in our own lives. Ambition and the profit motive daily erode what we used to rely on as
fundamental human values. Caring, empathy, and interdependence are too often dismissed as the illness of co-dependence.
Those values which tied individuals, families and communities together have all but disappeared in the complete global demoraliza-
tion since Guernica and World War II.

To be challenged by the absolute necessity for community and
mutual caretaking is a dreadful blessing. The incontrovertible need
to take care of each other, to cherish what is precious, to tend what
we love, are joys to which extremis demands we return.

The core of this global issue is the will to *Life,* as distinct from
our own individual or species will to live, distinct from the unin-
formed individual and species reflex to persist or survive no matter
the way or the means or the consequences.

The will to Life and the values of Life. To live our lives devoted
to the life force, to this planet, to nature, to what is green, is a shift
of the most radical order.

Some years ago, I dreamed the earth had been devastated by nuclear war. In abject despair, I contemplated suicide, but a Voice demanded, "Have a child. New life! New life!"

Every day, I confront the tendencies inside myself to deny Gaia, to have other gods before Her, to diminish, trivialize and undermine zest, passion, play, solitude, idleness, contemplation, creativity, fertility, my love of the outdoors, the tenderness for the green things. Consciously and unconsciously, we need to come to the moment when we say, "We have become Life!"

Ethics, the oldest of philosophic concerns, long ignored in this half of the century, returns now as a constituent of the healing arts. How we live our lives, how we act toward ourselves and others, how we treat the environment, how we regulate our inner lives, has become of crucial relevance to our physical health. Finally, how we live as ethical beings directly affects how we live as physical beings. The health of the soul and the health of the body—and the health of the planet—have become as one.

# Afterword

It is twenty years since I had cancer. The occasion of gathering together in one volume these different but intrinsically related works on healing offers me the opportunity to review what I have learned in these twenty years.

I have been concerned with the nature of healing for my entire life, but everything I thought I knew was melted down and then reconstituted in the crucible of the experience of cancer, the rigor and ordeal of the healing path which is on-going, and the privilege and challenge of spending the same twenty years as a lay analyst working with so many individuals suffering life-threatening illness.

When I first wrote *Tree*, I did not know with certainty what I now know: these diseases which afflict us out of season, which are not the means for the natural, inevitable and necessary breaking down of the body during its timely sacrifice to the great gods of death and transformation, are sociological, political, psychological and spiritual events. Of course diseases also have internal and personal causes: genetics, one's own constitution, history, circumstances as well as external and impersonal causes: viruses, bacteria, environmental pollution, etc. But disease is also something else, very mysterious and powerful; disease is an image of the world within which we live. Illness, as it afflicts us and breaks us down, also enlightens us and presents the means to heal far more than it has undermined. Illness offers us the ability to heal our bodies, our lives and the world as well.

I have spent my entire lifetime thinking about disease, cancer and totalitarianism. When I was a child, I imagined myself a warrior against injustice, and found many causes to which I wanted to offer myself. Before I was ten, I wanted to fight the Nazis and when I was a young teenager, I imagined pursuing science so I might cure cancer. In both instances, I had the deep conviction that the Holocaust and its aftermath and the extent and circumstances of cancer were not, as the insurance companies say, "acts of God," but injustices that should and could be righted.

When I was young, I thought the enemy was outside. Then I came to understand the concept of an internal enemy. Now, at the close of the twentieth century, I am bitterly aware that we are our own worst enemy and the enemy to the world at large. Harsh and extreme as this may seem as a statement, it is a harsher and more extreme fate. However, it is also information which allows for healing ourselves and others.

Disease in the overdeveloped world is not what it once was or may still be elsewhere on the globe. I don't know if disease, like the King's Fool, always served to warn and balance individuals and nations of power but I believe this is its function now. Why is this so? Because we have come to the end of the line, our condition is critical. The global society and the planet are tormented by diseases which are our own creations and which are life-threatening because they spring from our impulse to set ourselves against life. In this sense there is a just ecology between what we have wrought and what we suffer. We haven't escaped disease, we've just made it our own.

It is not a matter of having aligned ourselves with death against life or inorganic against organic, it is more that we are pursuing a counter world—the artificial. We construct the artificial as a way of containing, eradicating, superseding the natural and circumscribing the sacred. Our lives have become an assault of the artificial upon the lively, the constructed upon the natural, the human upon the cosmos. The artificial is imposed willy-nilly on everyone, everywhere, and on the environment as well. Our diseases reflect this and, at the same time, carry within themselves warnings against our hubris.

But disavowed though they may be, the Gods are still generous and have found baffling ways to inhibit us. However much we try to alter and control the world, we cannot control the diseases we have created. C. G. Jung once said, "The Gods have become our diseases." Did he mean that the Gods are taking on new forms by burrowing into diseases? Though they appear to most of us as the 'spites' of human suffering released by Pandora or the 'furies' that punished Orestes for killing his mother, they are also messengers, or as they are Gods, both messenger and message at the same time. Disease in its elemental manifestation, as it radically threatens or alters our lives, is a particular metaphor for those forms of our own creation that are killing us. In other words, disease is a hieroglyph encoding the ways and means of our cultural and personal self-destruction, but also healing. Ironically, then, disease enables us to transform what is left of our individual lives so that our living, finally, and our dying undermine what is dangerous in us and reinstate the life force.

There are two characters in this book who are one: the General in *The Woman Who Slept with Men to Take the War Out of Them* and Cancer in *Tree*. They are the same entity which, like spirit, takes many different forms. The General did not spring fully formed into the world. This General comes out of our now global culture and philosophy that is ego driven, greed driven, determined to dominate and entirely separate from spiritual concerns. He comes out of imperialism and its ally, totalitarianism.

Cancer is that same ego, that same imperialist force interested only in itself, devouring and dominating everything, giving nothing, and participating in no system but its own.

It is these forces, in the form of the General, that Ada confronts and in the form of cancer, that Deena confronts. Furthermore, Ada and Deena must confront the General and cancer without taking up the means, the entire arsenal, methodology and thinking of the General and his other face, cancer; without becoming similarly totalitarian in the interest of victory and healing.

Yes, Deena does take up the sword—she is no saint, after all— but she is grateful that she can enter into one-to-one combat and avoid making full scale war on her body and the environment. She understands chemotherapy and radiation as cures invented from the mentality of a culture which thinks in terms of impersonal and global violence, winning, dominating, eradicating and exterminating, which does not consider the 'fallout' of its activities. Deena wants to act differently. She is also concerned—based on research, experience and intuition—that radiation and chemotherapy, like nuclear war and chemical warfare, may kill her. But she is also extremely fortunate. Surgery, it turns out, is sufficient.

The cancer is cut out and the rest of her healing is in her own hands.

Ada fought the General with her liveliness, as Deena fought cancer with hers. Even as she felt defeated at first, she found a spark, 'Toots,' and persevered. Why did she even imagine that such a ploy might be successful?

In each of a pair of opposites exists a God. Even life and death contain the Gods: Demeter and Persephone; Zeus and Hades; Isis, Osiris, Horus, Set. These opposites do not deny each other. Life and death emerge from and move into each other across a vital common border, a fractal edge of paradox where they co-exist and dance with each other. In contrast, the artificial is toxic because it establishes itself outside this natural order, outside the cycle of generation and regeneration. Liveliness, when it can hold its own, restores the world in which one can thrive.

Who is this Ada? I ask now as if I didn't write her. Who is this Deena? as if I weren't she. Who is this Deena who was writing a novel about women and cancer, then got cancer herself, was able to avoid chemotherapy and radiation, scheduled reconstruction at the insistence of a physician, which, fortunately, circumstances prevented—the electricity failed in one of the largest hospitals of the world—and survived all of it, out of her, it seems, liveliness. Years later I cannot believe that the failure of electricity was 'accidental.' The consequences of reconstruction have only just been recognized; another way in which the supposed cure—this time for the 'shame' of amputation—backfires. Reconstruction itself causes serious illness. The body does not co-exist well with silicone. And women's belief that they can be beautiful and desirable after a mastectomy is undermined by the medical urgency to hide the scar.

The photograph taken of me by Hella Hammid has become known as the Warrior. Our intention in turning it into a poster was to invite the world to look at a one-breasted woman and exult in the health and vitality she had not carried so powerfully before cancer. The illness I suffered was the means of profound spiritual transformation.

I come to these texts again awestruck that Ada and Deena are fighting the same battle. I wasn't aware of the relationship between the two women when I was writing the books, nor when I insisted that they be published together as one work in two voices. Creativity often knows what the intellect doesn't. I know that now and respect it. I return to these books as if they are lost manuscripts which have, fortuitously, fallen into my hands. Understanding these texts is a next step in elucidating the journey toward healing and transformation.

How did Ada fight the General without raising armies and inflicting more of the same on the world? She had already seen where battle had gotten her husband. Her grief that he died fighting the General, her anger that he sought out his death, her outrage that such wars are waged, overwhelmed and leveled her, then animated her. She mustered her own self, her life force from within the torpor and heaviness and unconsciousness of grief. She is not driven by anger, revenge or need, she is driven by a consciousness which is far outside the established and traditional ways and means of the society, she is far beyond even the wisest of her contemporaries. Consciousness that arises after she has been reduced virtually to dust, consciousness that emerges after everything that was once Ada has disintegrated, and something else that is more Ada than Ada has ever been emerges out of that wreckage. It is from this lonely place that she acts—not to subdue or overpower the general but to transform him, even at the risk of her own life. Can this be done without love which adheres in the recognition of the other? Apparently not. What a bitter and confusing koan this is for our century.

The General and the system to which he is beholden can not tolerate such liveliness; he was fundamentally challenged by its very presence. Similarly, cancers, like so many other diseases, are inhibited by boosting the immune system and by vitality in general. Cancer and zest, totalitarianism and authentic individuality, cannot co-exist within the same dimension. One or the other will be transformed.

Will Ada always win? Is Deena's healing inevitable? Can their ways be translated into exact protocols or methodologies? Let's not be naive.

I wrote a book about cancer and followed the insights of the book as well as I could. Within a short time of surgery, I did much of what people have begun to do when they learn they have cancer: I moved to a rural area, left a five-year relationship, changed my diet, and stopped teaching at a Community College which, like most colleges and universities nowadays, was no longer devoted to knowledge or wisdom, in favor of teaching privately where the intellectual or spiritual restrictions were of my own making. Soon, I was working as a lay analyst emphasizing creativity and life-threatening illness. Dramatic as these changes seem, I believe that what ultimately saved my life was entering the realm of psyche, searching out the silences, imperialism and totalitarianism within myself. Rigorously setting out to live an ethical life on newly-defined terms.

This is the way I proceeded on a path that was difficult but generous to me. Each individual must proceed in his or her own way when the messenger announces that something is terribly wrong. It is the afflicted person's task to discover both the injury and the healing. A diagnosis such as 'breast cancer,' combined with an analysis of the kind of cell, the exact site, and the history of this disease in others is, for the healer, very rudimentary information. Instead the healer seeks out what is encoded metaphorically in the nature of the disease. In the world of healing, unlike the world of medicine, there are no protocols, no prescribed regimens, no standard strategies; each person must find his or her healing path. In the world of healing one steps into the unknown, attempting to live according to one's nature despite the possibility that one may not survive: many have not.

If survival isn't certain, why engage the rigors of the healing journey? Why not capitulate entirely to the dominant mode which demands so little, lays out well traveled paths and promises so much? Why choose this time when one is already so weak and afflicted to examine one's soul? Because this is the gift of life-threatening illness. At the very instant when our life is slipping out of our hands, when we recognize how little of it is remaining to us, we are called to scrutinize our lives, to sacrifice comfort for truthfulness, to re-value everything. In these times of crisis we are called upon, finally, to be, what spiritual practitioners call, 'Awake.'

It is often only in such a crisis that we recognize that we have capitulated to personal and global systems that are intrinsically anti-systems and that death is flowing from them: death of body, spirit, heart, hope, mind and world. In this deciding moment, we often come to see that our life has value only as it is lived authentically, that it is measured not in years but in understanding. In the moment of dying, we can become models of how to live.

Sometimes, like Ada, we also recognize that individuals among the various generals will not be able to sustain themselves in the face of the life force that is mobilized within us under such critical circumstances. We understand then that the General is not only a military force but the ubiquitous presence of the totalitarian mind which is so profoundly controlling our possibilities in the modern world, the force which insists that its economic and political goals take precedence over the human and the natural worlds.

Still, after there seemed to be no hope whatsoever for eastern and central Europe, surge upon surge of life and vitality have been challenging, sometimes even overwhelming some faces of tyranny. When I was writing *Tree*, the forces of democracy which had organized around Salvador Allende would well have survived if other generals world wide—the general is a *total*itarian animal—hadn't panicked and joined forces against them. Twenty years later, in the case of Chile, some of the generals have been vanquished by the life forces which first appeared to have been decimated but had, in fact, gone underground, reorganized, reconstituted themselves and emerged in new and vigorous forms. But having gained some autonomy in relation to the military, we do not know if these countries—and the 'emerging' nations of Africa, Asia, Latin America— will be able to resist the economic invasions and more insidious rape and domination by the citizen-generals of the over-developed world.

In "Personal Disarmament" I regard my psyche as a nation state. In that country of Zebra, the minority voices, the Shades, were disrespected and degraded even though they carried the life force. The Shades, who were the artists, suffered among other indignities restriction to reservations and compounds—much like animals in a zoo—where their lives were regulated according to the whims of the tourist industry which sustained the majority, the Suns. An artist reduced from a seer, priest or prophet to a commercial entertainer is no longer an artist. From that moment on, that artist has become a commodity, a thing. Further, a commodity culture has no intrinsic energy—commodities are not alive—and when the original, innate dynamism is no longer available to the nation, organism, or individual because all the energy has been withdrawn or suppressed, the entity collapses. I wrote "Personal Disarmament" because I had collapsed. That vital aspect of myself (called the

Shades) which I had dishonored and imprisoned, cut, as it were, the power lines and immobilized me until I was willing to change my form of government.

In Zebra, the Shades were finally acting to protect their own liveliness and as a consequence my entire country, my self, was ultimately regenerated. For a time, the Shades insisted that the entire nation of Zebra isolate itself so that the structure of the society could be rectified. I withdrew, temporarily, from public life. A process of purification was necessary so that the non-life components would not continue to infect that which had been restored. When I returned to the world, it was after I had fully allied myself with the Shades and learned to govern myself, Zebra, according to their values and ways of knowing. First cancer, and then collapse, taught me how to live.

Since I had cancer, I have accompanied many people on their healing journeys, have sat at the bedside of many who were gravely ill or dying. It is not rhetorical to say that this has been a privilege. And it is not rhetorical to say that with almost no exceptions, the moments of wrestling with illness and of dying were identified by the individuals as the most profound and precious moments of their lives. Short of knowing what they had come to know earlier and by other means, they would not change their circumstances. The process of healing and, many times, also, of dying, was a process of enlightenment which they valued above all else.

When my student and friend Houlihan Burke died singing, her arms raised to the sky as she said, "I had never expected it to be like this," she was continuing to be the teacher she had become when the diagnosis of breast cancer led her to relentlessly examine the impact of spiritual fascism upon the feminine, her life and her community.

Spiritual practice and wisdom traditions teach us that the function of the life's journey is to shed the masks and demands of ego and social pressure so that the soul can emerge and live an authentic life. This is called transformation. Illness, loss, ordeal are classic means through which this process is entered or achieved. Illness breaks us down to do the inner work we are not willing or able to do otherwise. Then the rigor and difficulty of the healing journey cracks our armor further; one way or another, disease, mental anguish, loss are inextricably woven into the scenario.

What of society then? The analogy applies. Global society is breaking down. It is wracked by its own forms of illness, loss and ordeal, and is being devastated by forces run amuck. The system as a whole is disintegrating. Thus when we consider the individual process we are asked to undergo, we find we have a map for social transformation as well.

We have two choices. We can continue to respond to social and political disasters as if they are plagues and epidemics to be resisted or overcome. Or we can look at the disasters as divine messengers, allowing them to break down our ideas of ourselves, how things should be: what is good, right, important, urgent, absolute, using the afflictions as means to slough off ego-driven, violent, dominating, greedy modes within us individually and as a global culture, in order to release the soul of humankind to its authentic life.

Understanding all of this means that we avoid the classic anguished question associated with illness and disaster: "Why me? Why do the good guys suffer and not the bad guys? " Whatever the social and political factors in the creation of illness, it is important to recognize that we are all chosen to learn the ways and means of healing, to transform as individuals and thus contribute toward saving the life of the global community. Even as we agonize over the AIDS epidemic, we are becoming aware of how AIDS in the United States and the epidemics of breast and ovarian cancers are also serving to form, shape and deepen the gay community and the women's community. It would be foolish and naive to imagine that we will not all be positively affected and altered by the individuals who, like Ada, from their grief, despair and outrage, are re-inventing, in these times of alienation, the ways and means of community. We can not yet imagine who we will become by living alongside those who have taken on the healing journey as principal actor or companion, and among those who are attending each other so profoundly at the time of great physical suffering, dying and death.

Needless to say, the hope of this book is that we will learn what we must learn without suffering untimely illness or the horrors of combat which have now invaded the streets of almost all our cities. That we will come to change our lives without the desperate kick in the ass that serious illness and social ordeal have become. What might this new global culture be that we have the opportunity to co-create? Just as we cannot imagine how we might be transformed by disease, we can not imagine how the world might be transformed when we have freed ourselves from what has driven us so willfully and destructively all these thousands of years. To try to imagine it is to impose our most naive understanding on the future and, consequently, to continue to re-create the world in our own deformed images.

Still, my deepest longing is that the changes will be global, that they will benefit everyone on the planet including the animals, the plants and the land. As it is clear that we are suffering the diseases of a dominating global culture separated from the life force, we can imagine that healing and transformation will bring us back into the web of life.

> —Deena Metzger
> Blue Wolf Hill, Under the Mogollon Rim, Arizona
> 15 January, 1997

Grateful acknowledgement is made to the following for permission to reprint previously published material:

"Healing Circles," under the title "Cancer is The Answer," The Sun, Issue #110 January 1985, Chapel Hill, North Carolina.

"Revamping the World: On the Return of the Holy Prostitute"originally appeared in Utne Reader, No. 11, Aug/Sept 1985, Minneapolis, Minnesota.

"Personal Disarmament: Negotiating with the Inner Government,"originally appeared in ReVision, Vol. 12, Number 4, Spring 1990, Washington, D.C.

"Healing the Planet, Healing Ourselves," originally appeared in World Futures: The Journal of General Evolution, 1992, Gordon and Breach, Philadelphia, Pennsylvania.

Excerpt from The Three Marias: New Portuguese Letters by Maria Isable Bareno, Maria Teresa Horte, Maria Velho da Costa. Copyright © 1975 by Doubleday & Co. Reprinted by permission of the publisher.

Excerpt from "Things You May Not Have Known" and "One Word" by Robert Cohen © Robert Cohen. Reprinted by permission of the author.

Excerpt from Change of Skin by Carlos Fuentes, translated by Sam Hileman. Copyright © 1967, 1968 by Carlos Fuentes. Reprinted by permission of Farrar, Strauss and Giroux, Inc.

Excerpt from The Diary of Anaïs Nin, Volume Three. Copyright © 1969 by Anaïs Nin. Reprinted by permission of Harcourt Brace Jovanovich, Inc.

Excerpt from "Poems and Rhythms" by Wallace Stevens © by Wallace Stevens. From The Collected Poems of Wallace Stevens, reprinted by permission of Alfred A. Knopf, Inc.

This book was written with the assistance of the National Endowment for the Arts and Yaddoo, which the author gratefully acknowledges.

Poster of the cover image available from Donnelly/Colt, P.O. Box 188, Hampton, CT 06247, (860) 455-9621; fax (800) 553-0006.

Deena Metzger is a writer, healer and lay analyst who has taught and counseled for over thirty years, in the process of which she developed therapies (Healing Stories) which creatively address life-threatening diseases, spiritual and emotional crises, as well as community and political disintegration. She teaches writing in Los Angeles and at workshops around the country, leads retreats nationally and internationally and conducts training and supervision groups for medical and health professionals on the spiritual, creative and ethical aspects of healing. She has taught at the California Institute of the Arts, Los Angeles Valley College, and The Feminist Studio Workshop. She founded the Writing Program at the Women's Building in Los Angeles. She has two sons, is married to writer/healer Michael Ortiz Hill and lives at the end of the road with her wolves, Owl and Isis.